Chicken Soup for the Teenage Soul's
The Real Deal: SCHOOL

Chicken Soup for the Teenage Soul's

The Real Deal: SCHOOL

Cliques, Classes, Clubs and More

Jack Canfield
Mark Victor Hansen
Deborah Reber

Health Communications, Inc.
Deerfield Beach, Florida

www.hcibooks.com
www.chickensoup.com

Library of Congress Cataloging-in-Publication Data

Chicken soup for the teenage soul's the real deal : school : cliques, classes, clubs, and more / [compiled by] Jack Canfield, Mark Victor Hansen, Deborah Reber.
p. cm.
ISBN-13: 978-0-7573-0255-8 (tp)
ISBN-10: 0-7573-0255-6 (tp)
1. Teenagers—Conduct of life—Juvenile literature. I. Canfield, Jack, 1944- II. Hansen, Mark Victor. III. Reber, Deborah.

BJ1661.C297 2005
158'.083—dc22

2005046051

Publisher: Health Communications, Inc.
3201 S.W. 15th Street
Deerfield Beach, FL 33442-8190

Cover and inside book design by Lawna Patterson Oldfield

CONTENTS

INTRODUCTION

SCHOOL. Love it or hate it, it's where you spend most of your time (at least the hours you're *awake*). When we first set out to write a book about school life, especially one called *The Real Deal,* we wanted to get down to it and talk about the highs and lows of student life for today's teenagers. What we found out is that teens all over the world are dealing with the same things—peer pressure, bullying, cliques, sports, stress, gossip, changing schools, struggling to keep up the grades, getting a bad reputation, having no reputation at all. It's pretty clear that being a student these days is challenging stuff.

This first book in *The Real Deal* series has what you've come to expect and love from the *Chicken Soup* books—*real* stories and poems from real people. For *The Real Deal,* we wanted to go one step further so we only included stories that were written by teens just like you. I hope you'll find that the result is a collection of stories that speaks to where you are right now, written by people who are dealing with the same kinds of things you are.

The response to our call for submissions was overwhelming, and we want to thank all of you who took the time to submit your poems and stories for consideration. We know what an effort it is to get organized enough to submit, and we don't take that commitment lightly. Unfortunately, we couldn't publish all of the wonderful writing we received, but please know that we did read each and every submission, and their content helped us figure out what issues are really important so we could make sure *The Real Deal* was as true to your own experiences as it could be.

As you flip through this book, you'll see that *The Real Deal* is also different from the *Chicken Soup for the Teenage Soul* books in that it's full of quizzes, little side stories and tidbits on everything from movies to see and books to read to different ways to approach problems or things to write about in your journal. We changed up the design too, so the book would be as engaging and fun as it could be. *The Real Deal* is full of so much great info that you can flip to any page and in just a few seconds discover a new interesting fact or be challenged to think about a situation from a different point of view. We hope that this makes *The Real Deal* a book you'll go back to again and again, and that you'll take away something new each and every time.

There's one more new feature in *The Real Deal,* and that's the addition of my voice throughout the book. So who am I? Well, I'm a thirty-something woman living in Seattle who's worked for Nickelodeon and Cartoon Network, and I have been writing for as long as I can remember. I work with teens a lot, and what do you know . . . I used to be a teen myself too. My own life as a teen was rocky, full of so many emotional ups and downs that it resembled a ride on the Great American Scream Machine at Six Flags. In many ways, I've taken this opportunity to go back and write about the things I wish I knew when I was a teenager. You'll get to know me very well through the introductions to all of the teen stories in the book, especially since I tell it all—from my first real kiss to the disappointments of being a "late bloomer." My hope is that my stories will draw you in, make connections with the teen stories, and help you realize just how universal our experiences as teenagers are.

It's an honor for me to have you reading *The Real Deal* right now, and my hope is that you see yourself in the pages of this book, and that in some small way, you find comfort and inspiration inside.

Deborah Reber

ACKNOWLEDGMENTS

THE PATH TO *Chicken Soup for the Teenage Soul's The Real Deal: School* has been a challenging and rewarding one. Our heartfelt gratitude to:

Our families, who have been chicken soup for our souls!

Jack's family, Inga, Travis, Riley, Christopher, Oran and Kyle, for all their love and support.

Mark's family, Patty, Elisabeth and Melanie Hansen, for once again sharing and lovingly supporting us in creating yet another book.

Deborah's husband, Derin, and brand new son, Asher, for sharing their love, energy and encouragement with us every day, as well as Dale, MaryLou and Michele Reber, and David and Barbara Basden for their ongoing support.

Our publisher, Peter Vegso, for his vision and commitment to bringing *Chicken Soup for the Soul* to the world.

Patty Aubery and Russ Kalmaski, for being there on every step of the journey with love, laughter and endless creativity.

Barbara Lomonaco, for nourishing us with truly wonderful stories.

D'ette Corona, for her incredible powers of organization and securing all the permissions and bios for this book, as well as answering any questions along the way.

Patty Hansen, for her thorough and competent handling of the legal and licensing aspects of the *Chicken Soup for the Soul* books. You are magnificent at the challenge!

Laurie Hartman, for being a precious guardian of the *Chicken Soup* brand.

Veronica Romero, Teresa Esparza, Robin Yerian, Jesse Ianniello, Jamie Chicoine, Jody Emme, Debbie Lefever, Michelle Adams, Dee Dee Romanello, Shanna Vieyra, Lisa Williams, Gina Romanello, Brittany Shaw, Dena Jacobson, Tanya Jones and Mary McKay, who support Jack's and Mark's businesses with skill and love.

Bret Witter, for placing his trust in us to take a different approach in connecting with teens, and Elisabeth Rinaldi, Allison Janse and Kathy Grant, our editors at Health Communications, Inc., for their devotion to excellence.

Terry Burke, Tom Sand, Lori Golden, Kelly Johnson Maragni, Ariana Daner, Julie DeLa Cruz, Patricia McConnell, Kim Weiss, Paola Fernandez-Rana—the marketing, sales and PR departments at Health Communications, Inc., for doing such an incredible job supporting our books.

Tom Sand, Claude Choquette and Luc Jutras, who manage year after year to get our books translated into thirty-six languages around the world.

The art department at Health Communications, Inc., for their talent, creativity and unrelenting patience in producing book covers and inside designs that capture the essence of *Chicken Soup:* Larissa Hise Henoch, Lawna Patterson Oldfield, Andrea Perrine Brower, Anthony Clausi and Dawn Grove.

All of the *Chicken Soup for the Soul* coauthors, who make it so much of a joy to be part of this Chicken Soup family.

Our readers, who helped us make the final selections and made invaluable suggestions on how to improve the book, including Ed Adams, Tipton Blish, AnneMarie Kane, Jamie Koeln, Bridget Perry, Renee Zak and Alice Wilder.

WriteGirl (*www.writegirl.org*); PBS's Youth Media Network, Listen Up! (*www.listenup.org*); Kathy Kirtley's Resources for Teen Writers (*www.davidbarrkirtley.com/teen writer/TeenResources.html*); The Merrimack Valley Library Consortium, The Words Work Network (*wow-schools.net/*); Write On (*www.zest.net/writeon/*); and About Creative Writing for Teens (*teenwriting.about.com/*), for reaching out to teens everywhere in the search for submissions.

And, most of all, everyone who submitted their heartfelt stories and poems for possible inclusion in this book. While we were not able to use everything you sent in, we know that each word came from a magical place flourishing within your soul.

Because of the size of this project, we may have left out the names of some people who contributed along the way. If so, we are sorry, but please know that we really do appreciate you very much.

We are truly grateful and love you all!

CHAPTER 1

THE SOCIAL SCENE

Perhaps no aspect of school is more stressful than navigating and making sense of the social scene. We received more submissions about your social lives than any other theme in this book, and we did our best to make sure "The Social Scene" reflects the range of things you're dealing with. Maybe you've had to deal with peer pressure or have been the target of gossip. Maybe you've never quite found a group of friends, or worse, you had one but then had to move and start all over again. Whatever your experience, the following chapter is guaranteed to give you a fresh take on dealing with the social scene in your school.

DOES YOUR SCHOOL HAVE ANY "QUEEN BEES"? You know the type. They're the girls who are impressively pretty, impeccably dressed and impossible to be around—unless of course you're one of the swarm. In *Queen Bees and Wannabes* (the book behind the movie *Mean Girls*), author Rosalind Wiseman explains that these queen bees rule their circle of friends through charisma, force, money, looks and manipulation. Like a hurricane gaining strength as it moves across warm water, these girls become more and more powerful by getting others to follow them.

So where do these power mongers come from? Some bizarre island in the South Pacific where designer clothes grow on trees and perfect complexions are handed out for Christmas? And where does this sense of entitlement come from, anyway? My guess is that this entitlement, at least in part, comes from us.

I used to be guilty of "queen bee worshipping." I thought that perfect appearances meant perfect lives. And even though I didn't necessarily want to be like these girls, I still fell victim to their powerful sting. I fed their hunger by letting them run the school, by being too afraid to stand up to them, by acting honored when they noticed I existed.

THE WORD

Charisma is kind of like charm, but even more powerful. People who are charismatic can gain the adoration of everyone around them without much effort. Unfortunately, some people use their charisma for the wrong things.

For Real?

Some people say school uniforms would reduce stress over cliques and fashion, but **83%** of students think uniforms are a bad idea.

Now, looking back at those girls who were the queen bees at my high school, I can't believe that I ever thought they were "all that." They somehow seem so mediocre, so *normal*. I guess that without the constant worshipping of other girls, these bees really were no different than I was. Better dressed, *maybe,* but the same through and through.

Seen It?

Teen queens are nothing new. Remember Alicia Silverstone's unforgettable character Cher in *Clueless* (1995)? She and her best friend are the **ultimate queens** at her posh Beverly Hills high school.

Behind the Scenes of Two Teen Queens

Bored with my life, irritated at who I was, and aching for change, I decided that middle school was the perfect time to introduce the "new me" to the world. My goal wasn't to become "popular." I was simply yearning for a new life.

But as I began to morph from an awkward, frizzy-haired, acne-infested brace-face to a smiling, straight-haired, lip-glossed teenybopper, that was what happened. My peers flocked to my side, and I was swept up into a whirlwind of parties and gossip, friends and boys, makeup and drama. Life in the fast lane. I loved it. I loved life in the "in crowd."

For Real?

Freaks and **geeks**, **goths** and **jocks**, **preps** and **slackers**, **queens** and **populars**, **punks** and **ghettos** . . . most teens define themselves by **which social group** they belong to more than anything else.

Seen It?

Mean Girls (2004) gives a realistic glimpse of teen queens through the eyes of actress Lindsay Lohan, whose character unwittingly gets sucked into her high school's **"it clique"** with **disastrous results.**

Amid my radical transformation, I met Laurie. We became best friends—we were inseparable. We spent the days together, with the air conditioner buzzing, the TV blasting and brand-new glossy magazines strewn across her Winnie the Pooh bed sheets, sticking to our shaved, lotioned legs. We would point at the pictures of beauty: ladderlike stomachs, narrow calves, straight, blonde, highlighted hair. Inspired by these images of perfection, we'd spend hours in the drugstore, searching for the perfect eyeliner, cover-up or lipstick, then rush home to recreate the sultry looks on our own pale, youthful faces.

Three times a week we would go to the gym. Passing mothers and fathers, old people and teenage boys training for track, we'd run until we were the fastest, the most graceful, the most beautiful. We'd sit across from each other on the thigh machines, leaning forward, straining, counting breathlessly to 100. Or we'd be side-by-side on the ab machines, grunting in pain as we tried to rid ourselves of our "love handles" and baby fat. We would take breaks to sip at the water fountain and watch others work out. Envious of their dedication, we set weight goals for ourselves: 98 pounds, 95, 90.

After working out we would slip into our colorful, tiny, two-piece bathing suits and ease into the hot bubbling fizz of the Jacuzzi. Our eyes closed, we would sit in the water, beaded with wetness, listening to the jets and feeling our bodies pulsing in the heat.

Our friendship seemed simple. We were the "teen queens,"

the coolest in the grade. With our trendy clothes, hair ironed straight and faces painted, we strutted through the hallways, savoring the attention and basking in others' envy. We were smiling images of perfection, Polaroids of future prom queens. We looked so happy, confident, carefree.

But images often deceive. Sometimes, if you look close enough, you can see through goops of eyeliner and mascara and into the eyes. If you looked closely at either of us, you would see that we were simply living a façade. We knew it, and that was why we were best friends. Because together we could be insecure and imperfect, together it was okay to be ourselves.

HOW ABOUT YOU?

Do you **identify yourself** as being part of a **group** or **clique?**

Laurie and I no longer speak. It wasn't a devastating, heartbreaking fallout. Rather, it happened naturally, slowly, over time. Neither of us are the teen queens we once were. Without each other, the power was lost, the charisma gone, and each of us was left with only ourselves.

I thought that I needed Laurie. I thought I needed her and our status as the "most popular" to be happy. Being with her, being part of the "in crowd" made me feel visible, like I was seen, and there was no need to question anything. I felt alive. I thrived in the spotlight and reveled in the atten-

For Real?

29% of teens say they feel the most pressure about the need to fit in.

tion. But as I have grown, my dependence on others to blossom has dissipated . . . I have realized that the "it" girl I once was wasn't really me. It was me simply playing the part. It was me, going through the motions of who I thought I was supposed to be.

Jessica M. McCann, Age 17

I'VE NEVER BEEN "THE NEW KID" in school, and I'm glad. I'm not sure I could've handled the pressure. I always felt so bad for the new kids, forced to introduce themselves in each and every class, all eyes drilling into the very core of their being, analyzing their clothes, their shoes, their braces, their cell phone, their *pores*. Yikes.

Yet there were new students who survived and made it look easy . . . the ones who spoke their names with confidence, correcting the teacher's horrific mispronunciation. The ones who didn't back down when the tough kids at school gave them a hard time. The ones who had more friends by lunchtime than I'd acquired in my whole school existence.

For Real?

The **number one** reason **families move** is because someone gets a new job. Other reasons are moving into a better home or neighborhood, shortening commute time, and divorce.

Seen It?

The WB's *Everwood* tells the tale of teen siblings Ephram and Delia as **struggling new kids** after moving with their dad from posh Manhattan to a small town in Colorado.

Address Book

If you **move** around **a lot** because your parents are in the military, check out Military Teens on the Move (*www.dod.mil/mtom/*) for all kinds of **information** and **support** to **help** you get through it.

When a fresh face walked through the front door of my school it was like a "new kid alarm" went off. Everyone knew about it by the end of first period, the word spreading like wildfire. *He's so hot! I heard her dad is the new principal. Did you see what he was wearing? Check out that hair!* I can't imagine being put under that kind of microscope.

When kids are forced to go to a new school, they're essentially starting from scratch. It's hard to imagine until you step back and look at your own social circle. Think about it—how long did it take you to acquire your group of friends?

So maybe next time you see a new kid in school, do something unexpected . . . say "hi," or let him or her sit with you at lunch. Who knows? Someday you might find yourself in the petri dish of a new high school, and you'll be looking out for a friendly face to do the same for you.

Being New Is Tough

I walked out of the guidance counselor's office determined and ready to embark on a three-year journey that would impact the rest of my life. It was a completely new start for me. This time, I was going to be popular, the smartest kid in school, pretty. Everything was going to go right. And it did—until I walked into my first-period class.

I was never fond of wearing expensive clothes, putting on makeup and spending hours doing my hair. All of my past friends and I were simple girls from middle-class families. Being a "prep" just wasn't for me. So when I walked into my

Consider This . . .

Many cliques are formed based on factors like fashion and style. How important is fashion to you? If you're like most teens, it's a big deal. Teens spent an average of **$1,700** in 2004 **on clothes** for themselves, most of it going toward labels like Abercrombie & Fitch.

new high school, I was in for a shock. It seemed like every single girl was identical—long, blonde hair, high heels, short skirts or tight jeans, and tank tops that boldly declared "Abercrombie." The guys all had shaggy hair, pants that defied gravity and a certain cockiness in their step and attitude.

Bewildered, I wondered what I had in common with these teens. I walked to my classes, looking for a friendly face in the crowd, but not coming across any that would even look my way. I had changed schools many times before, and I usually made quite a number of friends before lunch. However, it wasn't so easy this time around. Nobody, that is, *nobody,* seemed interested in talking to me (or looking at me for that matter). I was utterly alone. Lunch rolled by and I didn't even have anybody to sit with.

Seen It?

Movies about teens moving from the big city to the middle of nowhere used to be all the rage. In *Footloose* (1984), Kevin Bacon uses the power of dance to go from outcast city slicker to cool small-town icon.

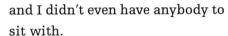

Up to now, I had maintained a calm and cool attitude, but walking aimlessly around this new campus among the voices and sights of happy kids reunited with their friends tortured me. I casually took out my cell phone, called my mom, and promptly broke down. Everything that I had done and been in the past fifteen years of my life seemed to dissipate before my very eyes. I would never go to school with my old friends whom I had grown extremely close to. One always hears adults talking about their high school years and how great they were. At night, I sit awake and wonder if I'll ever be able to say that.

Many weeks have passed, and the social aspect of my new school has been a hard reality I have had to face every day. I have to learn how to make the most of the high school years without the popularity I have always dreamed of. I am constantly being reminded that school is not necessarily a place to socialize and be a beauty queen. However, having friends is an extremely important factor in succeeding academically and personally. I yearn for a friend who I can trust and share my sense of humor with.

Although my hopes and dreams have been severely shaken, I'm sure somehow, someday, I'll take a step up this intriguing and complex social ladder. Until then, the only thing I can say is that it's tough being new!

Cori Oprescu, Age 15

Consider This . . .

More than any other mode of communication, teens say **IM**ing and **e-mail** are their top choices for maintaining their friendships. But be careful not to make any of these common e-mail bloopers:

- Send a heartfelt e-mail to the wrong person.
- Vent your frustration in an e-mail and hit send before you have a chance to cool off.
- Hit "reply all" instead of "reply" with personal opinions that were intended only for your friend.

For Real?

Believe it or not, the African desert locust spends half of its five-month life moving around. In 1988, a swarm of these locusts traveled 3,000 miles in 10 days!

OUTSIDE THE BOX

Maybe someday you'll find yourself faced with a tough move. If you do, here are some ideas for making it a little more bearable:

- Make a plan for staying in touch with your old friends, whether it's daily IMing, weekly cell phone calls, or visits over Christmas or summer break.
- Make a keepsakes album of all of your favorite things from your previous home so you can whip it out when you're feeling blue.
- Join a club or sport as soon as you start your new school so you can get to know people right off the bat.
- Instead of focusing on the negatives of being "the new kid," think about the positives, like getting a fresh start. Nicknames, stigmas and reputations from your old school don't exist anymore!

HAVE YOU EVER "SOLD OUT" A FRIEND? Not sure what I mean? Well, have you ever . . .

- not stood up for a friend who was getting picked on by someone more popular just because you wanted to save face?
- not wanted to be seen with a friend whose bad sense of style embarrassed you?
- heard a rumor going around about a friend and not done anything to clear it up, or worse, helped spread it around?
- put down or teased a friend just to make yourself look better?

Think long and hard. Most of us are guilty of selling out a friend at least once in our lives. It's part of human nature. I know I've done it. I had this friend who used to act kind of obnoxious around a group of seniors I was trying to impress, so behind her back I would roll my eyes at her right along with them. To this day, I can clearly remember the guilty feeling that went along with my betrayal and hoping my friend would never discover what I had done.

Now I realize that no matter what the circumstances, selling out a friend just doesn't end well. Either you're muddled with guilt, or your friend finds out what you did, or the people you're trying to impress decide they don't want you as a friend anyway, because, well, you obviously don't treat your friends very well! So I made a decision a long time ago: I would accept my friends for who they are, weird clothes, obnoxious behavior and all. So far, so good. Thank goodness they do the same for me every day.

Seen It?

In the teen movie *Can't Buy Me Love* (1987), Patrick Dempsey pays the **most popular chick** in school to be his girlfriend so he can go from **loser** to **BMOC.** Unfortunately he screws over his old friends and forgets who he is in the process.

Popular

I wished it had never happened. I wished I had never done what I did. I look back in time and think of how foolish I was. I remember what happened clear as day, replaying it over and over in my mind. In my mind I would change the events. Instead of going along with the scheme, I would say "no" and walk away. But that's not what really happened, and as I hard as I try, I can't change the past.

For Real?

Only **16%** of students say fitting in with a certain crowd would **raise** their self-esteem.

At the beginning of the school year I was a new transfer student. I dressed plainly and always tied my hair back. I had no extravagant clothes, wore no makeup. Let's face it—with my look no one was going to notice me.

Over the course of my first few months I gained a true friend. She introduced herself to me the first day I was in school, and we had eaten lunch together ever since. We talked about everything and trusted each other with our deepest, darkest secrets. In only two short months we were like sisters and did everything together. We often joked about what it would be like being the most popular girls in school and how it would be so cool to have everyone love us. I had seen the girls who were popular, and they were gorgeous. Perfect hair, teeth, skin, smiles, and most of all, perfect lives. From the outside, they had it all.

HOW ABOUT YOU?

Would you be happier if you were **more popular** at your school?

Then, a week before winter recess, the most popular girl in school, Rachel, came up to me in the hallway and pulled me into the empty locker room. At first, I wondered if she thought I was someone else. She had the usual girls and boys trailing behind her and they were all looking excited. I didn't know what was going on, but I just went along with it.

"Hi. You're Jenny's best friend, right?" she asked, obviously knowing the answer. I nodded, still wondering what this was all about. "I'm offering you the chance of a lifetime. When an opportunity like this presents itself, it's always smart to seize it. Am I right?" she asked the boys and girls behind her. They all murmured in agreement. Big surprise.

"I'm offering you a chance to be one of us. You will be standing next to me, talking, chatting, smiling and flipping your hair with me in the hallways and anywhere we go. You will be popular. You will be loved. You have potential, and with the right help, you could be one of us." Her eyes blazed as she said this.

This was my chance! This was what I had been dreaming of! It was obvious there was going to be a catch, but I didn't care. This was going to be the best day of my life. Or so I thought.

"Now. All you have to do is tell me one of Jenny's secrets and we'll start the makeover during winter break." She said it so casually that I knew she was hiding something.

"Why?" I questioned.

THE WORD

What's the difference between gossip and a rumor? These two kinds of backstabbing babble are similar, but **gossip** tends to be more personal and is sometimes based on the truth, while **rumors** can be anything from urban legends (the existence of the Loch Ness monster) to made-up stuff flying around school (Mrs. Bartell only gives As to boys with blond hair). Bottom line? Both gossip and rumors are bad news, so don't pass them along!

Seen It?

MTV's hit show *I Want a Famous Face* features people who undergo **major plastic surgery** to look like a celeb in their quest for popularity. **How far would you go** to be popular?

"Because, we're going to spread it around the school like wildfire and make it the rumor of the year."

She explained that Jenny's boyfriend from the drama club was the guy Rachel liked. (Who knew that Rachel didn't like jocks like most cheerleaders?) Of course it wasn't Jenny's fault, but at the time, apparently with only dust in my head, I thought Jenny was horrible. I convinced myself that Jenny must have known that Rachel liked this boy and dated him out of spite. Bottom line—what I thought *most* about was me being popular. Pathetic, I know.

> **For Real?**
> A recent survey says that **40%** of students admire *other* kids who are popular, while only **32%** of kids consider *themselves* to be popular.

So I agreed. I agreed because I wanted that taste of popularity. I agreed because I was now cold in the heart with selfish greed. I agreed and became one of them.

Over that winter's break I was changed into someone completely different. Hair, makeup, clothes, even my personality.

> **For Real?**
> **Gaining popularity** might seem like the most important thing in your life right now, but you'll be happy to know that researchers have found that **being unpopular** as a teenager doesn't mean you'll have the same results as an adult.

When winter recess was over, I proudly walked into school by Rachel's side. I felt bolder, like I was on top of the world. And it felt great right until Jenny snatched my arm and screamed, "How could you?" She rambled on about true friendship and betrayal for another thirty seconds before Rachel pulled me away.

"Do we know you, loser?" Rachel asked as she flipped her hair and we started to walk away. I turned to see Jenny's eyes filled with hate. Then my heart started to sink. I felt horrible. But I soon forgot when everyone started crowding around me, chatting constantly. *This isn't bad,* I thought. Compliments filled my head, and soon I even became more popular than Rachel. Everyone loved me, but what good was that?

Weeks later, I had no *real* friends. I had people follow me like dogs, not friends. I mean, where were my "friends" when I was feeling down? Where were they when I needed someone to talk to? They were only around to shop and to make me look popular.

I passed Jenny occasionally in the hallway. She never looked at me once. She now had a new best friend who was definitely a better friend considering how disgustingly I had treated her. Being loyal was what being a true friend was all about. I trashed that and walked all over it.

Yeah, being popular was all I ever wanted, but who knew that behind all the smiles were cold, empty hearts? So *this* was what it was like to be truly popular. I still remember those days when Jenny and I would talk on the phone constantly and laugh and joke about silly things. Where was that now? It had disappeared, just like my true identity. I hid all the things I wanted to say

CONSIDER THIS . . .

Researchers show that even though **teens** become part of **cliques** or **groups** to help gain a sense of identity, most feel like others' perceptions of them aren't right anyway.

and smiled as if everything was always okay. What was I now? Sure, being popular was cool at the beginning, but after the initial excitement, where was this going to take me? Nowhere. I wished I could take back all that I did. I was rude and mean, and most of all I lost my only true friend. Actions have consequences, and mine were the worst of all. I lost my true happiness and settled for a cold, meaningless existence. For the next year in school, I lived miserably, a smile plastered to my face.

Now life is different. I have learned greatly from my mistake of choosing social acceptance over a true friend. I would never betray a friend again after what I have done. I've met new people, made new friends. Some people still regard me as the one who changed drastically and became popular, but that's all behind me now. My new friends are truly the best that I can ever have, and we are closer than anything in the world. We love each other for who we are, not by our social status in school. Nothing will ever tear us apart. Not even an opportunity of rising to the top because, let's face it, even the top isn't as great as everyone says it is.

Demi Chang, Age 15

I'M GOING TO SHARE AN EXCERPT from my seventh-grade language arts composition book dating back to . . . well, let's just say it was a long time ago. The piece is titled "Friends."

Friends

In all these books I read, the characters always get home from school and call up a best friend on the phone. Then they go over to their best friend's house. As I look around me, everybody has a best friend. Well, almost everybody. When I was four years old, a girl named Gretchen moved in next door. We got to know each other, and we got to be best friends. We continued to be best friends from kindergarten to sixth grade. Then her parents started thinking about being separated. On a Monday morning, while Gretchen's dad was at work, the mom, the kids and the dog left. After that I started to meet more girls. Soon I had loads of friends, but no **best friend.** Well, I explained this to my mom and she said, "Just be patient. You'll find a best friend this year just like Shelly [my sister] did." And to this day, I am still being patient.

For Real?

Can you believe that advertisers had to pay **$2 million** just to have one 30-second commercial air during the series finale of *Friends*?

Okay, it's not Hemingway, but you get the point. Throughout middle school, I had it in my head that I would have a super best friend, the kind every girl my age on TV or in the movies seemed to have. Someone to talk with about crushes until the wee hours of the morning. Someone whose mom would be my second mom, their home my second home. We would never fight. And, of course, we would share the same size and trade clothes. High school

Read It?

Ann Brashares' popular novel *The Sisterhood of the Traveling Pants* tells the tale of four friends **bound together by** the ultimate pair of **jeans.**

would be a whirlwind of double dates and our boyfriends would themselves be best friends. She and I would be each other's maid of honor at our weddings . . . the whole works. I just knew that's the way it was supposed to be.

Not.

I spent so much time trying to turn my friendships into something more than they were that I usually ended up disappointed. I eventually did find a friend who I called my best friend. We did trade a few clothes, although we didn't wear exactly the same size. I did sleep over a bunch of times, but it never did feel like my second home. We double dated once or twice, but it never turned out as great as I imagined. She came to my wedding, but then we lost touch.

So now I've stopped trying to force my relationships to fit a mold created by a Hollywood film. Those movies are fiction for a reason; reality isn't always so glamorous. Not everyone has a picture-perfect best friend. The only way to define a successful relationship is to see how you feel in it, not how well it holds up to what you see on the silver screen.

Oh yeah, and now I have two rockin' best friends, and our relationships are far better than any screenwriter could ever imagine. And besides that, they're real.

CONSIDER THIS . . .

What is it **that makes a friend a BFF? At the top of most teens' lists of BFF qualities are** trust, loyalty, understanding **and a** good sense of humor.

Lonely

I wasn't scared when I walked into my high school for the first time. I sat in my geometry class and picked out a friendly face and started talking. I did the same in my subsequent classes. I sat with these girls during nutrition and lunch. It became a routine.

Yet something was amiss. The girls I sat with were perfectly nice. But it didn't seem like I was their friend. They went out and about the city at night.

I did not.

I was neither invited nor included. My Friday nights were spent at Blockbuster renting movies with my mom.

Middle school was never this lonely.

Things changed that summer. I became friends with kids from the more visible social scene. (I refrain from using the word popular because high school is not a TV show. Popular to whom? Themselves? Social boundaries are not always crystal clear.)

We hung out together. I had friends who acted like friends. However, I did not act like myself. I was acting like them. I dressed in more provocative clothes. I wore makeup. I was myself trapped inside someone else's body.

I ignored this feeling until they adopted this group of total losers—several boys who gallivanted about drunk and idiotic.

I didn't want to feel alone again. I asked if we could get a bite and talk after school. It seemed fine with everyone and we agreed on a meeting spot. Someone

CONSIDER THIS . . .

Because schools are becoming more diverse, many **cliques** are now being formed on **ethnic lines** rather than just fashion and attitude.

CONSIDER THIS . . .

Have you ever heard the **advice** to "just be yourself"? Well, when it comes to making friends, that just might be the **best advice** you could ever get. Pretending to be somebody you're not can get exhausting after a while . . . just ask Peter Parker.

invited the guys. They all now acted like I didn't exist.

It was the last straw and I stomped off.

The next day I sat with my "friends" from ninth grade. I was miserable. I wished that I didn't have to go to high school.

Swim season started that next month. I made some new friends. It took every ounce of courage in my body to walk toward where they sat at lunch and ask if I could sit down. I did. High school didn't seem so bad anymore.

I could act however I wanted around them, and they would still be my friends.

They still are.

My rapid social shifts in high school were painful. But in the end, they were worth it. High school isn't bad with the right friends. You just have to find them.

Kimberly Menaster, Age 17

OUTSIDE THE BOX

Looking to make some new friends? Try out some of these ideas:

- Join an after-school club or sport.
- Ask a classmate to study with you for the big final.
- Sit at a different table in the caf once a week.
- Say "hi" to one new person every day.
- Be open and approachable.

IF YOU WERE TO READ INSTRUCTIONS in some manual about how to make and keep friends, no doubt one of the first steps would be to do things that you enjoy—playing a sport, singing in the choir, writing for your school paper—and befriend someone who shares your interests. A common ground or shared interest can be a great foundation for a friendship.

But sometimes instruction manuals don't provide all of the answers. In fact, sometimes, you can find great friends in the oddest of circumstances. Look at Han Solo and Chewbacca. Wilbur the pig and Charlotte the spider. What makes two people decide to spend their time together doesn't always make sense. And if you're not open to it, you might miss out on a great friendship that's right under your nose.

HOW ABOUT YOU?

Do any of these famous pairs remind you of your relationship with your BFF?

- ❍ Bert and Ernie
- ❍ Charlotte and Wilbur
- ❍ Laverne and Shirley
- ❍ Joey and Chandler
- ❍ Will and Grace

So how about having friends who are from different cliques or social circles? Can it be done? Is it worth the price? I think so. And here's why. Just as having friends of the opposite sex can give you a fresh way to look at things, so can same-sex friends from different social groups.

At the end of the day, it's friends who like you for who you are that are the ones worth keeping around. The ones where you don't have to act or be like someone you're not. If we only hang out with friends who, on the outside, seem like they're just like us, the pressure to conform, dress and look a certain way can be all-powerful.

Seen It?

The Breakfast Club (1985) is a classic comedy about kids from **different cliques** coming together for one *very* long Saturday detention. In the process, they all come to the same conclusion: Everyone's dealing with some kind of baggage . . . just not a matching set.

On the other hand, friendships that cross those clique barriers can be freeing. When you know someone isn't hanging out with you because you look or act a certain way, you can spend less time worrying about keeping up appearances and more time being yourself.

We're Different, That's Enough

I first met Michael in junior high school. I was in seventh grade, he was in eighth. I had joined the school's Drama Club at my mom's persuasion. She thought my quiet ways were unhealthy and said that extracurricular activities would be good for me. As it was my first day, I mostly kept to myself like I always do. Not that I was being rude—I just didn't like talking with other people. I eventually started daydreaming while others were doing improvs and monologues. Then, hearing a torrent of laughter, I looked up to see a scrawny, dark-colored boy, about a foot taller than me, performing a monologue as Richard Simmons.

Later on, I found out that he already knew who I was. He was friends with my brother Nicholas, who had quite a large group of friends of his own. I saw Michael several times after that, at Drama Club meetings and when he came to visit my brother. Mike was loud and full of life, completely opposite of my personality. On more than one occasion, he reminded me of a comic relief character from some show, coming up to people with a laugh and a grin. Still, though, his presence in my life did not make that much of an impact. At least not yet.

Our first real one-on-one encounter happened three years later. It was a week after my birthday, in my sophomore year of high school. I had answered the phone and, upon hearing Mike's voice, immediately gave the phone to my brother, assuming the call was for him. After a moment, the phone was given back to me, my brother saying that the call was for me. Confused, I took the phone and heard the sentence that would change me and my life.

"Hey, a bunch of us are going to hang out at Stephanie's house. Wanna come?"

This was the first invitation to a group party I had ever received. I had been invited to visit other friends before, but always just with one person. I never had the courage to go to a gathering with a group of people before. I didn't want to sound rude, so I agreed. Once there, I was shocked at how easily they accepted me into their little group. Afterward, Mike gave me his number, saying, "We should definitely hang out more."

HOW ABOUT YOU?

Some people think that complete opposites actually make the **best of friends** because each person contributes something different to the friendship. What do you think?

Soon after that, Mike and I began to see each other more often. I was wary at first. I figured that his attitude toward me was based on the laws of association and that the reason he wanted to be my friend was because he was friends with my brother. With time, however, he demonstrated that he wanted to be friends with me, Chris, and not just "Nicholas' brother." This meant a lot to me. While I never felt any contempt toward my brother, I did feel like I was seen as just a relation to him at times. Mike made me feel like an individual, like he liked me for the things that made me who I was. This was the major impact he had on my life.

Soon, Mike became one of my closest friends. We would visit one another constantly and spend the day playing video games, watching anime or just talking about school. One thing did bother me, though. The more we talked, the more I found it strange that we were friends. While he was outgoing and energetic, I was reserved and mostly kept to myself. A typical day between us would consist of Mike talking

WHERE DO YOU STAND?

Are you open to meeting new friends?

Your nice, but *geeky,* lab partner wants to study together after school. Would you do it?

___ NO WAY! (0 points)
___ HEY, YOU NEVER KNOW. (1 point)
___ TOTALLY! (2 points)

A kid you've never noticed before smiles and says "hi" to you in the hallway. Would you return the greeting?

___ NO WAY! (0 points)
___ HEY, YOU NEVER KNOW. (1 point)
___ TOTALLY! (2 points)

While talking to friends over IM, the new kid in school sends you a random message. Would you write back to him?

___ NO WAY! (0 points)
___ HEY, YOU NEVER KNOW. (1 point)
___ TOTALLY! (2 points)

Add up your points:
0–1 = Private party.
2–4 = Never say never.
5–6 = The more the merrier!

while I listened for most of the time. The idea that he would want to be friends with someone like me baffled me.

This became more of a concern when I saw how other people reacted around him. People loved hanging out with Michael—he was the school's social icon, the one everyone wanted to know. He could sit down with anyone and become friends with them in a heartbeat. But instead, he chose me. And for a long time, I just kept wondering, why?

"I enjoy spending time with you. When I'm with most people, I have to be careful of what I say or do, because they get offended or hostile. You don't really judge me or anything. You just listen to what I have to say. Around you, I feel like I can really be myself," he explained.

He just said it out of the blue one day, while we were talking in my basement. That last phrase—"I feel like I can really be myself"—was the one thing I wanted most of all. Even though all I could do was listen to his problems without being able to offer advice, that was enough for him. I was someone he could turn to when he needed to get something off his chest. My friendship was important to him, and that made a world of difference for me.

Michael and I are very different; that much is obvious. It wasn't until that talk in my basement that I realized it was our differences that made our friendship tighter. I relied on his extrovert personality to draw me out of my social shell. This helped me gather the courage to make other friends and even get a girlfriend (going on six months now). In turn, I offered my ears and opinions whenever Mike needed someone to talk to about his problems. Our flaws cancelled each other out.

If someone told me that I would be friends with Michael on the day I met him, I probably would have given them the "You crazy?" look. Now, Mike's one of my best friends, and I wouldn't have it any other way.

Christopher Boire, Age 17

For Real?

A study shows that most teens think it's **okay to lie** to their parents to avoiding hurting them or stay out of trouble. Only 1 out of 3 teens said lying was never okay.

WE ALL GET INTO TROUBLE WITH OUR PARENTS at some point in our teenage lives. No matter how great our relationship might be, there are bound to be times when we do something that doesn't meet with mom and dad's approval. I'm extremely familiar with this phenomenon. Out of my group of friends, it seemed I was always the one who got in trouble for everything. Getting sent to my room after dinner happened so frequently that I had practically worn a path in the carpeting leading from the table to my bed.

Punishment? I could handle that. It was when I didn't get punished for something bad I'd done, usually at the prodding of my friends, that I knew I'd *really* screwed up. Those were the times when my parents were *disappointed* with me, and the look in their eyes, that sadness that totally deflates you, was punishment enough. I've only seen that expression a few times, and when I did, I was

Consider This . . .

Parents who try to **prevent** their kids from being friends with someone they think is a bad influence may be doing **more harm than good**. Studies show that "forbidden friendships" can become more attractive to teens.

reminded that my parents were people too, not just "parental units" standing between me and my freedom. But at the end of the day, no matter how badly I'd screwed up, somehow they'd manage to love me. I guess that's their job. And I'm thankful that they were always there to catch me when I fell.

Spotlight On . . . PEER PRESSURE

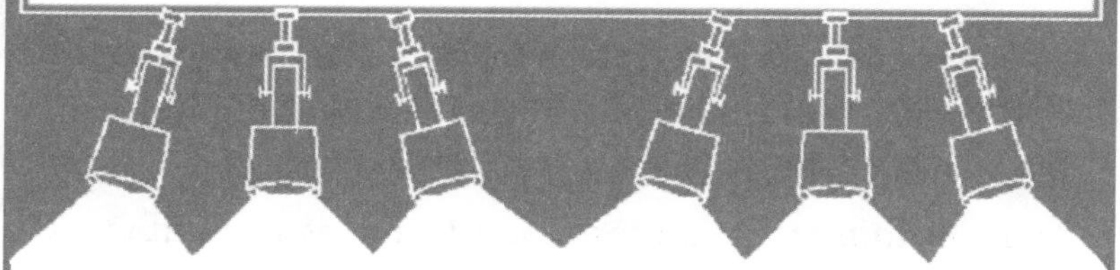

What is **peer pressure** anyway? Since peers are the people around you who are most like you (same age, same status), peer *pressure* is when these people try to get you to do something that you might not do otherwise, like smoke, drink, cheat, gang up on someone and so on. Peer pressure doesn't always have to be bad, either. For example, have you ever seen the "Truth" anti-smoking ads? Created by teens for teens, these ads use the power of peer pressure to show that smoking is *not* cool. A lot of schools use positive peer pressure to combat problems like bullying, too.

You might not have even realized it was peer pressure at the time, but have you ever . . .

- worn a name-brand piece of clothing just because it was popular?
- gone to see a movie you weren't really into because your friends wanted to see it?
- smoked a cigarette or taken a swig of a beer just to fit in?
- let someone cheat off of you in class even though you knew it wasn't fair to everyone, including yourself?
- gone along with the crowd because it was easier than doing your own thing?

As you can see, peer pressure comes in many shapes and sizes. Next time you feel like you're falling victim, ask yourself this question: *If I had my own way, would I still be doing this?* If the answer is "no," you might want to reevaluate the situation and the peers who are leaning on you.

One Wish

Happy birthday, dear Rhea, happy birthday to you . . ." Silence penetrated the room.

"Make a wish," my mom said in a sweet, half-whisper. Her eyes glittered above the white cake. Was she crying? It tore at my heart that she still looked so sad, now that everything was over. I looked around the room filled with my friends, cousins, uncles and aunties, and then finally my mom and dad standing right next to me. I couldn't help but smile.

I wish . . .

• •

The December morning breeze brushed my long, black hair as I stepped towards the large russet doors of Hagenberg High. It was my first day of school. There were students all over, trotting around with heavy backpacks, slamming lockers and running to catch up with old friends. I wondered who *my* friends would be. I was a bit anxious because I was starting school two-and-a-half months late.

For Real?

49% of teens say that they admire their peers who **don't** let themselves be influenced by other people.

In first period English, Mrs. Farley immediately put me on the spot.

"We have a new student." Heart pounding wildly in my chest, I managed a weak smile.

"So, what school are you from?" Mrs. Farley asked, tilting her head.

"At a . . . school in the Philippines," I replied softly, my voice rising slightly as if I were asking if that was the right answer. Only two weeks ago, my parents and I migrated to America, hoping for a bright new life. At that awkward moment in class though, I silently prayed that I would snap out of the bad dream I was in and wake up to the sounds of the sea back home.

CONSIDER THIS . . .

Teenage **immigrants** are caught in a struggle between their parents' traditional values and the **need to fit** in as a teenager in the U.S. Because of this, Filipino teenagers are much more likely than American teens to suffer from **depression.**

"How long ago did you move here?"

"Uh . . . two . . . two weeks ago." I had never stuttered

For Real?

One survey showed that peer pressure causes more **stress** for **teens** today than violence in school.

before, but there I was, sounding as if I learned English only last week.

"Welcome to America . . . Ree-ya?"

"Rhea."

"Ra-ya." Mrs. Farley made herself a little note on the roll sheet. Why hadn't my parents just named me Ashley? Or Mary? All I wanted was to be *normal*. I wanted to be *somebody*.

At home, my parents spoke to me in Tagalog, and I didn't have any friends yet who spoke to me in English. But what was I worrying for anyway? In the Philippines I had many friends, all the teachers knew me, and I had been getting excellent grades.

For Real?

One in ten teenagers **skips** school once a week. Approximately **11%** of students end up dropping out of high school.

Walking through the locker-lined hallways, my dreams shattered like broken glass around me. I was alone, roaming the halls like a lost little kid. I unknowingly avoided interacting with anyone because I was afraid they'd laugh in my face. When my English was better, I decided, I would finally come up to people and maybe manage to say, "Whussup?"

Finally in gym class, a friendly brown face. She almost looked like me, only happier. Her name was Caroline. At lunchtime we found ourselves enjoying the bland cafeteria food. She wanted me to meet her friends. "Don't worry *Ate* Rhea," she assured me, calling me "sister" in Tagalog. "You'll fit right in."

And I did. It was as if some foreign soul entered my body and made me do things against my will. I found myself drinking beer, smoking cigarettes and skipping school. I didn't even like the taste of beer. The moment it touched my tongue I felt like I had to spit it back out. But I didn't. I couldn't afford to look bad and lose my new "friends." I began to miss at least one day of school a week to hang out with them. Then I missed two, three, even four days in a row.

But while I was out having fun with my "friends," inside I was full of conflict, unhappiness and regret. I stopped practicing my English sentences in front of the mirror and instead practiced, "I don't know *why* the school called, mom. It was probably a glitch in the system because *I did not miss school today*."

WHERE DO YOU STAND?

How comfortable are you speaking up for yourself?

Someone in your group of friends passes you a cigarette, but you've got no interest. Would you give in to save face?

___ DEFINITELY (0 points)
___ MAYBE (1 point)
___ PROBABLY NOT (2 points)

One of the popular kids asks you to keep your test visible for him to cheat off of. Would you do it?

___ DEFINITELY (0 points)
___ MAYBE (1 point)
___ PROBABLY NOT (2 points)

Your group of friends decides to ditch out of eighth period. You don't want to join them, but don't want to look like a wimp either. Do you go along with them?

___ DEFINITELY (0 points)
___ MAYBE (1 point)
___ PROBABLY NOT (2 points)

Add up your points:
0–1 = Joining in is easier.
2–4 = Depends on my mood.
5–6 = I speak my mind.

One day the school counselor called my mom at the house

while I was already at school, and the truth came out. I pushed open the heavy doors of the counselor's stuffy office, dreading the situation I had to face. When my mom lifted her tearful eyes and saw me, I knew I failed her.

CONSIDER THIS . . .

Teenagers who know how to **speak up** for what they believe in are less likely to get involved with drugs and alcohol.

"Why, *anak ko?*" she cried. *Why, my child?* I stood there, swallowing the lump in my throat, but I had nothing to say. I wished she would yell at me, embarrass me or tell me what a bad kid I was. But she didn't. She cried like her only daughter was lost and had run away. My dad flashed me an accusing glare. I looked down—I couldn't bear the hurt in their eyes.

I was so depressed that night—I was sure I had lost my parents' trust and love. But when I was at my lowest point, my parents came through for me, and I realized just how much they loved me, no matter what. My mom was just worried . . . so worried in fact that she looked older, as if the years of raising me had drawn lines on her lovely face.

"I'm sorry, I'm sorry . . ." I cried. I wanted to say I was sorry for the failing grades, for all the arguments . . . for all the lies. But a feeble "I'm sorry" was all I could muster.

HOW ABOUT YOU?

Have you ever gotten **sucked in** with the wrong crowd? How did you handle it?

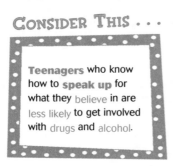

"It's okay, honey. Everything will be okay," my mom whispered. My dad ran his fingers tenderly through my hair. Nothing else mattered at that moment. Not the laughing jokes at school, not my friends . . . not even the familiar teenage longing to be somebody. I was somebody in my parents' eyes.

My parents didn't change how they viewed me, despite everything I had done. They still loved me as their daughter, and I welcomed the forgiveness, understanding and unconditional love in their warm embrace. And now, staring at the yellow candles on my birthday cake, I only have one wish: *That someday, somehow, I can repay my parents for raising me the way they did and for loving me no matter what.*

• •

My mom's voice roused me from my thoughts. "Have you made your birthday wish yet, sweetie?"

I looked at her, and then at my dad, tears of love and gratitude brimming in my eyes. "Yes, mom."

Then I hugged them both very, very tightly.

Rhea Liezl C. Florendo, Age 20

OUTSIDE THE BOX

Is someone putting pressure on you to do something you're really not into? Here are some ways to "just say no":

- Try to change the subject or suggest an alternative plan
- If you're at a party, call your parents on your cell and use a prearranged code word to tell them you're in a bad spot. When your parents come and get you, you can make them look like the heavies and still save face with your "friends."

OUTSIDE THE BOX

- Just say "NO!" If you're clear about your desires from the get-go, there's a good chance your friends will lay off. Plus, the fear of going against your friends' wishes is usually worse than the actual result.

Take the Quiz: WHAT KIND OF FRIEND ARE YOU?

1. After much effort, you've finally become a member of the "it" crowd at your school. But when a new girl tries to sit down at your lunch table, members of your clique don't treat her so well. In fact, they're being downright cruel. You . . .

___ A. join in with your friends and tease the new girl. There's no point in jeopardizing your status over someone you don't even know.

___ B. don't actively make fun of the new girl, but you don't stand up for her either. You managed to work your way into the clique without any help, why should you bend over backward for her?

___ C. tell your friends to simmer down and give the girl a break. It's gotta stink being the new kid in school and not even know who's who or where to sit. If they're really your friends, they'll respect your opinion.

2. You walk into biology class, and instantly members of the "it" clique are all over you. They've heard a rumor about your best friend, and they want you to tell them if it's true or not. This is

the first time anyone from the populars has ever bothered to acknowledge you even exist. You . . .

___ A. see this as an opportunity to boost your social status, so you confirm that the dirt is true.

___ B. get nervous and neither confirm nor deny the rumor, not wanting to sell out your friend, but not wanting to detract from the attention you're getting.

___ C. stand up to the populars and politely tell them to mind their own business. The attention of the "it" crowd isn't worth jeopardizing your friendship.

3. You've been looking for an opportunity to talk to Rachel one-on-one so you can invite her to the upcoming school dance, but when you finally do, Rachel's only interested in finding out more about your best friend, Jack, who you happen to know also likes her. You . . .

___ A. tell Rachel that Jack isn't looking for a girlfriend right now, hoping that she'll turn her affections toward you.

___ B. are clearly thrown off, but collect your composure and try to steer the conversation back to you. If Jack is so interested in Rachel, then he should tell her so. It's not your place to get in the middle.

___ C. realize that there's no point in getting in their way and tell Rachel that Jack likes her back—they should go for it! If Rachel's not into you, what's the point of pursuing her?

4. You and your BFF (Best Friend Forever, natch) have been invited to a party where the "it" crowd will be. Once you get there, you find out that everyone's drinking, and you and your friend are being pressured to join in. You know your BFF doesn't want to drink, but you're not sure how to say "no" and save face at the same time. You . . .

___ A. convince your BFF that one drink won't kill anybody and maybe she should break out of her shell a little bit.

___ B. decide to drink just a little alcohol, despite your friend's wishes. After all, if she doesn't like it, she doesn't have to have any.

___ C. realize the situation makes your BFF really uncomfortable, so you suggest you both leave the party and catch a movie instead.

5. You've got a really important track meet after school, and even though you know your BFF has a really busy schedule, you expect him to be there for you, just like you were there for his big basketball play-offs a few months back. At the end of the school day, you see your friend heading home instead of out to the bleachers. You . . .

___ A. accuse your friend of being selfish. After all, you would have been there for him.

___ B. tell your friend that you're bummed out he can't make it and harbor a grudge for a few days.

___ C. give your friend a break. Just because you expected something different doesn't mean your friend has to do exactly what you want.

How'd you do? Give yourself 10 points for every A, 20 points for every B and 30 points for every C. Look below to find out what kind of friend you are.

50–70 points = Looks like you could use a few tips on how to be a good friend, as most of the time you're more concerned with making yourself happy than keeping your relationship in good shape. If you don't make some changes, you might find yourself with very few friends left in your posse.

80–120 points = Most of the time you know just how to be the perfect friend, but sometimes situations come up that challenge your sense of what's right and wrong when it comes to the key people in your life. A good bet to making the right choices is to ask yourself how you'd feel if the roles were reversed.

130–150 points = You're the kind of friend anyone would be lucky to have. You're loyal, trustworthy, and you know that to have good friends you need to be a good one in return. Keep up what you're doing and you'll never find yourself alone.

CHAPTER 2

EVERYDAY LIFE

While a lot of issues relating to school life fit neatly into categories like sports or studies or stress, what about those little aspects of the daily grind that are a part of every student's experience? I'm talking about things like waking up on the wrong side of the bed, losing homework, being moody, experiencing everyday embarrassments and being overwhelmed with all the baggage that comes along with being a student in today's schools. Well, that's what we tried to capture in "Everyday Life." Sometimes it's the little things, like the sounds and sights that are a part of school, that are the most memorable.

I'M STILL NOT A BIG FAN OF MORNINGS, but when I was a teenager, they were definitely the worst part of my routine. Just about every day started off as a bad day. How could it not when it began at the ungodly hour of 6:15 A.M.? I mean, clearly, the sun wasn't up for a reason, right?

For Real?

Because it's a high-energy food and takes a while to digest, eating an apple in the morning **is actually better at keeping** you **awake than drinking caffeine!**

While I didn't particularly like waking up to my mom's singsong voice, it was better than the alternative—an alarm clock. I used one of those primitive mechanisms until I proved it was no match for my hand, which had developed a brain of its own and learned how to hit "snooze" every nine minutes while the rest of my body was still asleep. Not to be outwitted by my bionic hand, my parents moved the alarm clock across the room, until I demonstrated my newfound skill of sleepwalking. Oh, and then there was the plastic cap my dad taped atop the snooze button so no matter how hard I hit the thing, it would keep on buzzing. To that device I say, *It's amazing what you can sleep through when you're really tired!*

Eventually, I would get out of bed, and then the *real* daily nightmare began. Fighting for bathroom time with my older sister, trying to throw together a decent outfit from my very limited wardrobe, making sure I had what I needed for track or volleyball or whatever after-school activity I had that day,

HOW ABOUT YOU?

What is your technique for getting through **a really bad day?**

being teased at the bus stop by the neighborhood kids or running so late that I had to sprint up the hill and jump on the bus winded and sweaty, a thirty-minute bus ride in which I'd occasionally get pegged in the head by some sort of flying object, not usually intended for me, but instead just thrown by someone with poor aim.

For Real?

Do you have **trouble waking up** for school? Hate the sound of your alarm buzzer? Check out these unconventional alarm clocks:

- The Sunrise Clock mimics the rising of the sun by making your room brighter and brighter.
- The Sonic Boom alarm uses flashing lights and a bed vibrator.
- The Natural Sounds alarm eases the sleeper awake with nature sounds like rain, the ocean and wind.

All that, and school hadn't even begun yet. *Sigh.*

In reading the next poem, I realize that the trials and tribulations of my daily morning routine were probably pretty typical. Some days are bearable, while others start off so bad that any sane person would want to throw in the towel. But like everything else in life, bad days, too, come to an end.

BAD DAY

The alarm is sounding,
Beep, beep, beep!
Hop out of bed,
I trip over my books,
Hardly awake.
If I don't hurry, I'll be late!

WHERE DO YOU STAND?

Everybody has them, but what equals a "bad day" for you?

The pipes at your house freeze in a big snowstorm so you can't shower before school.

- I could stand it.
- Depends on my mood.
- The worst!

When you sit down to take a quiz in biology, you realize you stayed up all night studying the wrong chapter!

- I could stand it.
- Depends on my mood.
- The worst!

Your teacher asks you to read your essay aloud at the front of the room right after you spilled tomato soup all over your sweater.

- I could stand it.
- Depends on my mood.
- The worst!

The guy you've been scoping on for months asks your best friend to be his date to the autumn dance.

- I could stand it.
- Depends on my mood.
- The worst!

Rush to the shower,
Where's the hot water?
I sadly realize,
This is not my day.

Now I'm running late,
I can hear the bus coming.
Running out with only one shoe on.
The bus is just leaving.
Now Mom's mad,
I missed the bus again.
I sadly realize,
This is not my day!

I'm late for school,
I missed an important lesson.
So now my teacher's mad,
This day is really bad!
I rummage through my folder,
I can't find my homework!
I sadly realize,
This is not my day.

Monique Ayub, Age 14

Consider This . . .

A **bad morning** doesn't have to equal a **bad day.** Here are three ways to turn a bad day around:

1. **Keep a picture** of your dog, your cat, your best friend or a happy moment in your notebook. When you look at a picture of something that brings back happy memories, your brain will remember the feeling and change your emotional state of mind.
2. **Breathe!** Close your eyes, inhale slowly and deeply, and exhale at the same rate of speed. Repeat ten times. Do this any time you feel stressed or upset. It really clears your head!
3. **Take a moment** to think of one thing you're thankful for, even if it's just the fact that there's a new episode of your favorite show on tonight. Even in the worst of days, remembering the good in our lives can be a great mental boost.

WHEN I WAS IN HIGH SCHOOL, my parents were *so* out of touch. My dad would try to help me with my math homework using a slide rule. My mom's advice about boys was always something simple like, "Well, if he doesn't like you, then he doesn't know what he's missing." They didn't understand why I wanted to tease my hair to look like the lead singer of The Cure or why wearing boxer shorts to track practice was actually fashionable.

Yet my parents insisted they could totally relate to everything I was going through, that they had once been teenagers themselves. And I had to wonder, *Could that possibly be true?* So now, twenty years later, I find myself wondering the same thing. Has high school really changed since I was there?

The same issues that I was dealing with are definitely still a part of everyday life: peer pressure, cliques, pressure to do well on the SATs, the stress of being too busy, teachers who don't get it. These seem to be the universal truths of the high school experience.

The labels on the clothes worn by the "it clique" may have changed, but the feeling that goes along with not being part of the crowd remains the same.

My mom used to tell me to "just hang in there" when I found myself at wits end with the daily grind of high school life. She'd say that things weren't so bad and that I wouldn't realize until after I graduated just how great high school actually was. I didn't believe her at the time, and I don't expect you to believe me now, either. I know how tough it is . . . the emotional ups and downs, the pressure, the feeling that nobody understands. But I also know I wouldn't be the person I am today if I hadn't gone through each and every one of those experiences. When I think of it in those terms, I can look back at high school and smile. And I guarantee you—someday you'll be able to do the same.

Read It?

Fifteen-year-old author Zoe Trope wrote the gritty and highly controversial book *Please Don't Kill the Freshman* (2003), in which she talks about life as an **"outsider"** in today's high school.

For Real?

The band **The Cure,** which made a big comeback in 2004 with the release of their new album, *Three Imaginary Boys,* was originally called **Malice.**

PEOPLE ALWAYS TELL ME, "IT'S JUST HIGH SCHOOL!"

Cliques
Jocks
Preps
Geeks
"It's just high school."

Relationships
Cheating
Jealousy
Regret
"It's just high school."

Girls
Two-faced
Backstabbing
Social climbers
"It's just high school."

Weight
Anorexia
Bulimia
Exercise
"It's just high school."

Grades
Exams
Homework
Projects
"It's just high school."

For Real?

42% of people believe that today's teenagers have more challenges to face while growing up than their parents did.

Seen It?

Degrassi: The Next Generation is hailed as one of the **most realistic** glimpses of the high school experience on television. The Canadian drama has won awards for tackling serious issues like **drugs, sex** and **dating.**

HOW ABOUT YOU?

Have you ever looked at your parents' high school yearbooks? If so, what **surprised** you the most about what you saw and read about your parents?

Identity
Insecurity
Naive
Self-conscious
"It's just high school."

I just can't wait to grow up . . .

Allison Kueffner, Age 16

For Real?

16% of teenagers say they feel a lot of **pressure** to look a certain way, while **45%** of teens say they don't feel any of this pressure at all. Where do you clock in?

HOW ABOUT YOU?

Everyone's **felt humiliated** at school at one time or another. What happened to make **you** feel this way?

SEVENTH GRADE WAS FULL OF MANY, MANY MILESTONES. My first training bra. My first kiss (it was only a peck, but it still counts, doesn't it?). And undeniably my worst school day ever.

It was a Tuesday morning, and our section had just played a lively round of dodgeball in Mrs. Bressler's gym class. Afterward, we were in the tiny locker room changing when suddenly my friend Michelle whipped out a Polaroid camera and snapped a picture of me, topless and *without* that training bra I mentioned earlier. And did I happen to tell you that I didn't actually *need* a training bra in the first place?

Anyway, a second later, Michelle's camera spit out a picture of me, eyes wide open in shock. No, Michelle wasn't getting back at me for anything or following up on a dare. She told me she was putting together an album of her close friends in embarrassing situations, just for fun.

Why did I believe her? Why didn't I rip the photo out of her hand and flush it down the toilet? Okay. Good point. Polaroids can't be flushed down the toilet. But certainly I could have come up with something else, something other than agreeing to let her keep the photo as long as no one else saw it.

Yeah, right.

Apparently, Michelle had told this impossibly tall and obnoxious boy named Brian about her impromptu photo shoot, and halfway through the next period, Brian had lifted the picture from her bag. By lunch, the entire school had seen me. *All* of me. It wasn't until the guidance counselor called me to his office during seventh period that the tears came.

The guidance counselor had somehow gotten a hold of the photo and ceremoniously cut it up in front of my eyes, assuring me that the scandal was over.

But I knew it wasn't. My horror was just beginning. How in the world was I to walk through those double doors ever again and look anyone in the eye when I knew they had all seen me half-naked? (I can't emphasize enough how flat I was—I was practically inverted.) But my parents insisted that I go to school the next day, telling me that the whole thing would "blow over" in no time. Easy for them to say. But for once, they were right. It did blow over pretty quickly. I guess my profile wasn't that "memorable."

CONSIDER THIS . . .

Renowned author Kurt Vonnegut says **high school** "is closer to the core of the American experience than anything I can think of." **What do you think?**

For Real?

Did you know that the first Polaroid camera, **capable of taking and printing pictures in 60 seconds, was invented in 1947?**

For Real?

Would you believe that 2,000 years ago, Roman and Greek women strapped a band around their breasts to make their chests **look smaller?**

I'm sure you have your own "worst moment ever"—it's all part of being a teenager. But look on the bright side. At the very least, you'll have something great to write about and laugh at later on in life.

THE TEENAGE YEARS

It's never easy
the hassles and disappointments and delays
the hopes and fears and dreams and nightmares
always pulled back
never ahead of anything
weight, looks, money, smarts
friends that only judge you
people that only use you
embarrassment and foolishness
being awkward and misunderstood
becoming something, anything
grasping at a figment of who you want to be
losing prospects and gaining insight
things that come and go in a fraction of a second
it all goes so fast and so slow at the same time
it's never easy
but who said it would be?

For Real?

Did you know that the **law** in the United States says that **all teens** under the age of 16 **must attend school?**

Sara J. Reeves, Age 16

Consider This . . .

Over the years, kids have gotten pretty **creative** when it comes to **making excuses** for lost homework or a missed assignment. Have you ever used one of these doozies?

- The dog ate it (a classic).
- I donated it to charity.
- Someone offered me $100 for it, and I needed the money for my mom's kidney operation.
- I thought it was optional.

THE TRANSITION FROM MIDDLE SCHOOL TO HIGH SCHOOL is a big deal. It's kind of like going from twelve to thirteen. Once you turn thirteen, you're officially a "teenager," which is way cooler than being a preteen or a tween or whatever other label they want to stick you with. Middle school is like a dry practice run for the real event—high school is where things are really supposed to happen.

Surely, the immature boys from middle school will suddenly become handsome, sensitive young men. Cool high-school parties will be rampant, and you and your friends will hang out together, dancing every Saturday night with 100 of your closest friends, making memories that will last a lifetime. You and your significant other will be the hottest couple in school, being crowned prom king and queen, the envy of all your friends.

Not.

It's no surprise that once you've made the leap and find yourself squarely in your high school life, it's not all you thought it would be. Let's face it . . . you probably had some pretty high expectations.

How About You?

Did you have unrealistic expectations about what **middle school** or **high school** would be like? How **different** was it from what you thought?

Consider This . . .

Is high school **really** that **different** from middle school? Here are just a few of the things that make the **transition** to high school challenging:

- tons more students
- bigger classes
- a lot more homework
- more cool classes to choose from
- pressure, pressure, pressure!

That's not to say that a lot hasn't changed. There's definitely more homework in high school, and the excuses for why your essay didn't get finished back in seventh grade don't work so well anymore. You've got more selection for your classes, which is cool, but that also leads to more division between you and your friends, all of whom might be scattering in different directions. Sure, homecoming and prom could be great, but who's to say that the perfect date is going to be available, just waiting for you to grab his or her arm? There might be more parties, and while these are fun, they also confront you with some of the most difficult situations you've had to face in your life so far—like saying "no" to drinking or getting in a car with someone you know has been drinking.

Perhaps someone should write an instruction manual on how to handle all of these situations. It would undoubtedly be on the top of the *New York Times* best-seller list. But stick with it. After a few rough months as a freshman, you'll start to get the hang of it.

For Real?

The average number of **students** per class in 2002 was **23** for every one teacher.

TIMELINE: School in the United States

1809 The first blackboard was used in a public school.

1870 Paper was mass produced so students could take work home with them.

1910 First standardized tests were administered to rate students' IQs.

1926 SATs (Scholastic Assessment Tests) were introduced.

1930 Public school students were separated by class, race and gender.

1939 Television was first used in the classroom.

1952 Elementary students were required by law to go to school.

1954 Segregation in public schools was deemed unconstitutional in *Brown v. Board of Education*.

1966 Detroit public school students boycotted high school, saying the standards of education were too low.

1972 Title IX , which bans discrimination based on gender in public schools, was passed.

1980 First charter schools are born.

1990 Channel One TV, which broadcasts news and ads, first began appearing in public schools.

The Real World

High school. The place that gets us ready for the "real world," or so they say. But as I looked around on my first day of eighth grade, the world seemed pretty darn "real" to me. *Huge* was one way to describe it, and not just the school. Oh no. The twelfth-graders that towered over my five-foot, six-inch

Seen It?

Surprise indie hit *Napoleon Dynamite* (2004) presents a **realistic**, and **funny**, glimpse of **high school life.**

stature looked like mountains. My neck eventually gave up trying to see past the clouds and into their eyes.

The day wore on, and I nearly got dragged on the bottoms of peoples' shoes. The hallways were so crowded I began to wonder how anyone could breathe in this place, never mind learn what we needed to know. Locker combinations, teachers' names and eight different classrooms of terror spun in my mind as I shakily asked for directions and got no reply whatsoever in return.

I wanted my elementary school back. You know, the safe place where no one could possibly get lost because it only had five hallways, and where everyone from grades one through seven knew your name, phone number and address because there were only four hundred kids in the entire school? Yeah, I longed for that.

High school wasn't exactly what I expected, to say the least. In pictures you only see the good things: smiling cheerleaders, straight-A students and great-looking

WHERE DO YOU STAND?

How well do you handle the pressures of school?

Three of your teachers all schedule their midterms for the same exact day! You . . .

___ SHRUG YOUR SHOULDERS (0 points)
___ WRINKLE YOUR BROW (1 point)
___ BLOW A GASKET (2 points)

It's only the second day of school, and you get lost on your way to algebra. The late bell just rang! You . . .

___ SHRUG YOUR SHOULDERS (0 points)
___ WRINKLE YOUR BROW (1 point)
___ BLOW A GASKET (2 points)

Used to being a straight-A student, you get back an essay test and receive your first D. You . . .

___ SHRUG YOUR SHOULDERS (0 points)
___ WRINKLE YOUR BROW (1 point)
___ BLOW A GASKET (2 points)

Add up your points:
0–1 = I take it in stride.
2–4 = I guess I'm a little stressed.
5–6 = I need help!

student body presidents. What you don't see are the lies, plots and deception that tear those people apart, piece by piece. Not everything was pretty, perfect and fun like I thought it would be.

For Real?
Mount Everest is **29,035** feet high—that's almost 6 miles!

Eventually I began to warm up to my new school and make new friends, as well as catch up and build stronger relationships with old ones. But every day was a new battle, and not just fighting for the cinnamon bun with the most icing or battling about who your gym partner was. Each day of the week was a ferocious war with friendships crushed, piles of homework as tall as Mount Everest and hoping that the day was almost over even though it really wasn't.

Consider This . . .

Everywhere you look, there are plenty of **media images** of high school surrounding us, telling us just what it should look and feel like. How **realistically** do you think these shows portray the high school experience?

- *Everwood*
- *Beverly Hills, 90210*
- *Degrassi High*
- *Saved by the Bell*
- *7th Heaven*
- *Freaks and Geeks*

School got tough. I wasn't doing so well in my classes and didn't join any school teams, even though sports were practically my life. One day I looked at my social studies mark and the fat C+ under my name nearly leapt out and smacked me across the face. A C+! I had never gotten a C+ in my life! After all, I was Stephanie Fraser, straight-A student, valedictorian of my graduating seventh-grade class and Student of the Year award winner. How could this be happening?

When I realized I had a C in math, I knew things had to change. Changing my homework and study habits made a difference, but adjusting my attitude and perspective helped more than anything.

For Real?

44% of teens feel a lot of pressure to get **good grades.**

With my grades steadily improving from Cs to As, I, too, improved and repaired who I was. My confidence seemed to jump miles high, and I was no longer being pushed to the side of the hallways, ashamed to be in the way of bigger, better people. I realized that they weren't better—I was just as important as they were. I grew taller, too, not only in height, but in spirit.

The year ended as quickly as it had begun, but I was forever changed into a person I loved, a person that I wanted to be. Looking back at that first year of high school, my

Consider This . . .

Many of **life's** disappointments can be attributed to unrealistic expectations. If you're **anxious** about the **transition** from middle school to high school, here are some ways to make it go smoother:

- Talk to a high school student (older sibling, friend's older sibling), and ask all the questions you can think of about what to expect.
- Attend an open house for the school prior to the start of the year.
- Understand that unless they've been abducted by aliens and had their brains reprogrammed, the kids who were obnoxious in eighth grade are still going to be that way in ninth.
- Keep a journal so you can go back and look at how far you've come in so little time.

friends and I laugh at all the crazy stuff we did and said. We reflect on the good and attempt to put the bad as far behind us as possible.

HOW ABOUT YOU?

What is your **least** favorite, and **most** favorite, aspect of **school?**

I came into ninth grade with dreams as big as oceans and questions following behind me for miles, but I'm ready. Ready for what this year will bring and what it will take away. Ready for answers and thoughts clogging up my mind into madness. Ready to volunteer my shoulder for someone to cry on and for others to do the same for me. Even though I'm only in ninth grade and have a long way to go until the doors open to the "real world," I feel more real than I ever have before. Even though I didn't know I was lost, I found *me,* and the *me* I found was who I had unknowingly been searching for all my life. And now, when I see a small, terrified eighth-grader in the hallway, I don't shove them to the side. Instead I answer, "Yes, room 102 is right down the hall."

Stephanie Fraser, Age 14

I WAS ONE OF THOSE STUDENTS who was always trying to find a way to get out of class, and on many occasions I succeeded. I started off my day by skipping homeroom because my friend and I spent the first twenty minutes every morning reading the announcements over the school's intercom system. Then, during at least one of my morning classes, I would get a case of the hiccups, and by leaving my mouth open and relaxing my diaphragm, I could make them so loud that the teacher would ask me to step out into the hallway to get a drink of water. This excursion could take up to five minutes if I walked slowly enough. By senior year, my best friend and I had befriended our new, young principal, and somehow he'd given us an open-ended pass to get out of class for "official school business," and we would go hang out in his office and give him the scoop on the students' perspectives on just about anything.

For Real?

More and more schools are **eliminating** homeroom from their daily schedules, mostly because of **pressure** they feel to have **every spare moment** of time spent at school be used for academic purposes.

By the time I graduated, I had perfected the art of "class skimming"—making the day-to-day more bearable by "redefining" my schedule a bit. I share all of these things because I think I know how the author of this next piece entitled "Prison" feels. School can be rather confining, to say the least. But just like prison, there is safety inside those walls. There's the security of knowing what to expect every

Seen It?

The indie film *Super Size Me* (2004) sparked controversy when it showed that the same companies that provid unhealthy meals in prisons also provide **meals** in public school cafeterias.

day—classes, socializing, a warm meal (or one made up of a grab-bag of sugar goodies). Once it's over, life starts to get a little less predictable. And while that unpredictability can sometimes be a good thing, every now and then you'll still get a hankering for a chocolate milk and some Twinkies.

Prison

In some ways, I'd rather go to prison than go to school. In truth, the two institutions are shockingly similar. A student, or inmate, is held captive in either one. Luckily for the criminals, in prison nobody has to sit and watch a dull old man ramble on about a dull old theory for two full hours that seem like four. Nor do the prison inmates have to worry about their GPAs. They know their lives are on hiatus for the next few years. My life seems to keep going without my consent.

I ask myself if prison would bore me. Then I realize that however boring prison is, school is equally boring. The only difference is that prison doesn't have that weird mix of boredom and stress. That's something only found in the classrooms.

For Real?

Did you know that today there are **93,000** public schools across the country, while there are **2,000** federal and state prisons? The number of students attending school every year is nearly **48 million,** while the prison population is just over 2 million.

In some ways, prisoners have more freedom than high school students. For example, in many prisons the toilets are right in the cells. A prisoner can relieve himself whenever he feels the need. In school, a student's bathroom breaks are limited to the ten minutes between classes. Not only that, but the toilets are shared with hundreds of other inmates . . . er, students.

For Real?

Prison inmates who **never graduated** from high school are required by law to take **GED classes** (General Education Development) for at least 120 days.

Also, most prisons are single-sex. Women in prisons don't have boy problems. They don't worry about whether they will get asked to the next school dance or whether they will get kissed before they graduate. No female prisoner has ever stolen another woman's boyfriend in a single-sex prison—that's reserved for high school.

Of course, the female inmates probably get sick of each other every few days and start fights just because they're bored. Actually, a full-fledged fistfight would be a relief compared to what I go through. I have never met a teenage girl who fights with her fists. Teenage girls are smarter than that. They know that the body heals, so they go straight for the soul. I know what pain feels like. There is not a high school student who doesn't.

Some days my life feels so overwhelming that I wish I really were in a prison. Then I stop to think (a rare occurrence, but it happens). Prisoners don't get to experience those sweet little moments that students do. The moments where teachers seem human and students seem to care. And I realize that it's those moments that make school worthwhile.

Jody Schechter, Age 15

Take the Quiz: HOW MUCH DO YOU KNOW ABOUT THE HISTORY OF SCHOOL?

If you think public school in the United States hasn't changed that much over the years, think again. Take this quiz to test your knowledge of just how different things really are.

1. In today's schools, the start of the day, the beginning and end of classes, and the end of the day are signified by an electronic school bell blasted through the school's sound system. Do you know what schools in the 1800s used instead?

___ A. A rooster

___ B. A handbell

___ C. A horn

2. The first blackboards were used in 1809, but they didn't look like the blackboards of today. Can you guess what the original blackboards were made of?

___ A. Eggs and potatoes

___ B. Sand

___ C. Concrete

3. Today, students who get in trouble might get a suspension or detention, but most physical punishment is taboo. This isn't true of the schools in the 1800s, when students who were troublemakers were disciplined with one of these instruments. Do you know which one?

___ A. A Ping-Pong paddle

___ B. A chalkboard eraser

___ C. A cane

4. Schools today use all kinds of high-tech instruments to teach their lessons, but these weren't always available. Can you guess what the predecessor to the overhead projector was called?

___ A. Posterboard

___ B. Stereoscope

___ C. Holograph

5. In today's schools, teachers hand out tons of homework, sometimes totaling five to six hours worth of work a night. But back in the 1800s, homework wasn't really an issue. Can you figure out why teachers didn't give their class homework?

___ A. Students had too much work to do on the farm.

___ B. Books hadn't been invented yet.

___ C. Few students went on to college, so what was the point?

Answer Key:

1. **B**. Handbells were typically used by teachers who would stand inside the doorway and ring the bell.
2. **A**. Believe it or not, the first blackboards were made up of pine lumber that was covered with egg whites and the ash from burnt potatoes.
3. **C**. Wooden canes were used in the classrooms of the 1700s and 1800s to discipline unruly students.
4. **B**. Slightly different from the overhead projector, the stereoscope could project three-dimensional images on the wall.
5. **A**. Most students in the 1800s still had major responsibilities on the family farm, so they couldn't take time out for homework.

CHAPTER 3

THE OUTSIDER

At some point in our lives, we've all felt like an outsider. Maybe you've been the new kid at school and just wanted to fade into the background. Or maybe you've been the last person chosen for the team during phys ed. Maybe it seems like everyone else has a close group of friends and an incredible social life, while you're left out in the cold. If you've ever felt this way, hopefully reading "The Outsider" will show you that, at the very least, you're not alone. Read on for some heartfelt writing from teens who've bared their souls and shared their innermost feelings about life on the fringe.

WHEN I WAS IN SCHOOL and someone used the word "bully," visions of tough gangs wearing leather jackets and chains, teaming up on scrawny kids to steal their lunch money came to mind. I didn't know then that bullying could mean any number of things: verbal abuse, intimidation, even exclusion.

For Real?

15% of all students are **bullied** on a regular basis. Most of these students are victims of verbal bullying as opposed to physical.

Today, bullying is a huge problem in schools, and what's most surprising is that there are many more girl bullies than when I went to school. *Girl bullies? For real?* Unlike boys, who tend to pick on both boys *and* girls, girl bullies usually pick exclusively on other girls. And whereas boys are much more physical in their bullying, girls overwhelmingly rely on things like name calling, rumor spreading, gossip mongering, teasing and manipulation. Yeah, okay. Name calling, gossip spreading, now *that* sounds familiar. But apparently, girls are bullying like this today more than ever. What's *that* all about, anyway?

As recently as thirty years ago, many girls in school were soft-spoken, taking a back seat in the classroom by staying quiet and fading into the background. Some people think that girls are bullying more today because they've been encouraged to speak out for themselves, and maybe they've taken it too far.

Read It?

The second most popular kids' book of all time is still *The Outsiders*. The book, which pits the "greasers" against the "socs," was written in 1967 by S. E. Hinton when she was still in high school.

Perhaps if we looked at the reasons *why* kids bully, things will become clearer. According to researchers, kids bully because they're angry, have low self-esteem, want to gain popularity or

Seen It?

In one episode of Cartoon Network's *The Powerpuff Girls,* Blossom, Buttercup and Bubbles face off with the Gang Green Gang who're bullying around the other kindergarten kids.

are attempting to make themselves feel better. Hmmm. All those reasons have nothing to do with the victim and *everything* to do with the bully. Yet it's the victims who end up feeling inadequate, persecuted and insecure. Unless, of course, they're like the author of this next essay, "Like Water."

Like Water

I'm in phys ed class, freshman year. I'm wearing my stupid fuchsia gym pants. I feel self-conscious. I'm the short, nerdy girl in the ugly clothes. I'm embarrassed by myself. I scratch my head and yawn. More than anything, I wish this class were over. For good.

I stare at the clock and wonder if its hands could move any slower. The teacher comes in and we automatically start running around the gym. That is our routine exercise. We only stop when the teacher blows his whistle, but he's really slow today. I wonder if he forgot to look at the time or if he's just torturing us on purpose. A little while longer and I might start hyperventilating. Finally, the shrill sound pierces the air.

Consider This . . .

Would you be interested in starting or signing an **antibullying** campaign at your school? Check out Dr. Phil's Web site and print out the Antibullying Pledge (*www.drphil.com*).

We sit down in our squads as the gym teacher and his student instructors take attendance. Today is elective day. We have a choice between basketball and volleyball. I stand up and walk toward the cart of basketballs. I reach in and take a good, bouncy one. Suddenly, a pair of hands seizes the ball from me, and maniacal laughter sounds. I look up to see a big, scary sophomore girl. She grins evilly at me. "My ball!" she says. Her big, scary posse cackles.

For Real?
Many schools don't have mandatory physical education anymore. The Surgeon General says this is a major cause of the **increase** in **adolescent obesity.**

I've seen lots of movies where the bullies pick on nerdy kids. I just never thought it would happen to me. I've always liked to think of myself as brave. Not daunted by anyone. So here's my chance. That girl stole my basketball. Am I just going to let her bully me like that? I take a deep breath. What am I supposed to do? Tell her off? Steal my ball back? Punch her in the face?

Talk about a slow reaction . . . the mean girl and her posse have already run off laughing before I even have a chance to do anything. By now, half the gym class has seen what happened. I feel like a horrible coward. I tell myself to think happy thoughts. Stay calm. Be like water. Don't let the ripples disturb you. I imagine myself punching that girl in the face. I feel a little better.

For Real?
Bullies are getting more and more technologically advanced. "Cyber bullying," where kids **IM** other **kids** with **taunting** words and threats, is becoming a real problem.

I'm dribbling another basketball. It is very flat and hardly bounces. I look up and I wonder if my eyes are deceiving me. That mean girl is running toward me. Maybe she's coming to apologize, beg for forgiveness. Suddenly, she comes up and grabs my basketball. Again. I clench my teeth. Enough is enough. The time has come for her to get what she deserves.

"Hey," I said. My brilliant comeback. "Stop!" She rolls her eyes psychotically at me and runs off to her friends, who are roaring with laughter. The other kids laugh, too.

HOW ABOUT YOU?

How would you handle it if you were **teased** in front of your friends?

I try not to cry. If I were someone else, someone who actually had courage, this would have turned out differently. Only a nerd would get pushed around like that.

Someone tugs at my arm. It is Sarah, my gym partner. Silently, she hands me another basketball. Gym class goes on. I survive it.

What happened in gym that day might not seem like a big deal. And no, it wasn't necessarily one of those crucial, life-changing moments. But I did learn something. I realized that no matter what kind of person you are, there are bound to be hard times in life when others are mean to you. No one is perfect; no one is immune to teasing and bullying. There are bound to be people bigger and tougher than you. It is how you deal with them that matters. When you learn to respect yourself, others will get the message to do the same.

Address Book

Are you a **victim** of **bullying** at your school? Check out these Web sites for support.

- Bullies to Buddies (*bullies2buddies.com*) is a support Web site for young victims of bullying.
- Bullying.org (*www.bullying.org*) provides tons of information for victims of bullying.
- Kids Help Online (*www.kidshelp.org*) points you in the right direction to antibullying groups and provides a chat room and online counselor.

Today, I'm a junior in high school. I don't think school is that bad anymore. The psycho girl and her gang have not given me any trouble since freshman year, and I hardly see them. I still wear my fuchsia gym pants. They've come a long way, and I've grown attached to them. I don't care what I look like or what I wear. I'm not embarrassed that I'm short, or that I don't have name-brand clothes, or that yes, sometimes I have acne flare-ups. Isn't that part of life? I realize that feeling self-conscious and pressured to fit in is not healthy at all. I have learned to be glad of who I am.

Jean Huang, Age 15

OUTSIDE THE BOX

Have you ever been the victim of bullying? It's hard to know what to do when you're in that situation. Here are some ideas for how to combat bullying when it gets personal:

- Try to avoid confrontation with the bully in the first place. Stick close to friends; have a parent pick you up after school.
- Although you'll be tempted, don't retaliate, either physically or verbally. Retaliation generally results in a worse situation.
- Lean on your friends for support and don't get down on yourself. It's not about you. It's about them.
- If the bullying is threatening or physical, tell an adult: a parent, teacher, coach or guidance counselor.

GRETCHEN WASN'T JUST MY NEIGHBOR for as long as I could remember, she was my best friend. We started kindergarten at the same time, waited for the school bus together and fended off insults from the older kids on the street. We hung out after school, doing gymnastics, playing kick the can, and launching ambitious ventures like the "detective agency" we set up on my front lawn.

Throughout elementary school, we were inseparable, and I thought things would continue that way as we moved up to middle school and beyond. But then

CONSIDER THIS . . .

Considering how **difficult** it is **to move,** imagine how much tougher it is when having to deal with the breakup of a family at the same time.

the summer before sixth grade, Gretchen confided in me that her mom was planning to leave her dad. Part of me didn't believe they would actually go through with it, but just in case, we made a pact that Gretchen would call me and give me a warning when, and if, the day arrived.

By the time we started middle school a few weeks later, I had figured the plan was off and looked forward to settling into a new school with my best friend by my side. Then one day, I called Gretchen to see if she wanted to hang out, but her father told me, "Gretchen doesn't live here anymore." *Huh?* I hung up the phone, numb. This couldn't be happening. But it had. Gretchen and I spoke that night, and she filled me in on all the details. She would now be attending Reading High, a much bigger school, and they were going to be staying with her aunt, *indefinitely*. We made a plan to see each other that weekend and said good-bye.

For Real?

Changing schools and leaving friends behind can have serious **psychological effects** on teens, including mood swings, depression, tension within the family, headaches and loss of sleep.

Gretchen and I vowed to stay best friends, and for a while it looked like we would. But as the months wore on, it became harder and harder to keep up with each other's lives (granted, this was in the stone age, long before cell phones and instant messaging). And even though we caught up on the phone, we each fell into new groups of friends. With each visit, we realized that we were moving in very different directions. Calls eventually became few and far between. By the time we graduated from our respective high schools, we had completely lost touch with one another.

Looking back on that first year of middle school, I can only imagine how difficult things must have been for Gretchen. At the time, I could only think about my own loss and how deserted I felt. But for Gretchen, everything had changed. School. Teachers. Friends. Routines. Home life. Everything. If you've never been the one who's had to move, read on. You'll see that being the new kid in town is one of the toughest things a teen can go through.

IMAGINE

Imagine a world
Where wind blows so soft
And laughter and joy
Are heard frequent and oft.

Imagine a world
Where the work is like play,
And the sun smiles warmly
On you every day.

With your best friends around you,
You're never alone
And each day after school,
You all talk on the phone.

Where you know if you're sad,
There are places to go;
A soft shoulder to cry on
As you let your pain go.

Now imagine that world
On a bright summer's day

THE WORD

Depression is an illness that affects the way a person thinks and feels about things. Here are some of the signs:

- feeling sad
- feeling hopeless
- losing energy
- having no appetite
- having a hard time concentrating

As you stand there and watch it
All get torn away.

After three months of mourning,
You're in a new school
Where you're youngest and dumbest;
You feel like a fool.

There used to be good days
And bad days were rare,
But now that's reversed,
And you're too cold to care.

For the warmth that you loved
Has blown off on the breeze;
Now you're shivering and cold,
Always ill at ease.

Your heart's in your throat
And the fear's in your mind,
But where to go now
When the world's so unkind?

You flee from the lunchroom
And dash for the stairs
Knowing no one will miss you
Because nobody cares.

And as tears streak your face
At noon every day,
You wonder if ever
You won't feel this way.

HOW ABOUT YOU?

When you see a **new kid in class**, what's your typical reaction? Do you say hello? Ignore him or her until you find out what others think? Investigate what he or she is all about?

Imagine a world
Of deception and fear
Of lies, drinks and drugs
That don't belong here.

And imagine my friend,
Just what would you do?
If this new scary life
Thrust itself upon you?

And so that is why
Sometimes I won't talk;
Why I flee class so anxious
And go for a walk.

I need you right now,
So please stay with me, friend
Through this nightmare of change
Until we reach the end.

Ashley Yang, Age 15

Seen It?

Ryan Atwood knows what being an outsider is all about in the hit Fox drama *The OC,* as he **struggles** to **fit in** with a crowd and community that couldn't be further from his past.

OUTSIDE THE BOX

Walking is one of the best ways to eliminate stress, as it gives you time to think, process and vent. If you're feeling anxious and stressed out, here are some other things you can try:

- Listen to music. Blasting your favorite tunes can be a great way to let loose.
- Laughing. Rent a comedy or watch reruns of Friends.
- Get distracted. Do something like go to the movies or play arcade games with a friend.
- Meditate. This can mean anything from sitting alone in your room like Buddha or going for a hike to get back in touch with nature.
- Eat well. Diets heavy in sugar and fat might make you feel good while you're eating, but the crash afterward can add to your stress.

THE WORD

Immigrants are people from one country who leave to permanently live in another. Currently, there are 33.7 million immigrants living in the United States (that's 12% of the population).

MANY TEENS SUBMITTED ESSAYS for this book about the horrors of moving—packing up and making a fresh start in a new school, new city or even new state. But what about those students who not only moved out of their happy home, but crossed international borders to do so? I'm talking about *immigrants*. There are thousands of teenagers from other countries living in the United States today. Are you one of them?

The most intercultural experience I had at my small school in eastern Pennsylvania was hanging out with Michela, an Italian exchange student, and giggling at her adorable accent. I learned a lot more about other cultures in college, where I volunteered as an ESL teacher, or English as a Second Language. Don't ask me how, but I ended up teaching a class of adult Russian immigrants who didn't speak a lick of English. That experience showed me just how difficult the exchange of information can be when a language barrier exists.

For Real?

Did you know that **30%** of the U.S. population is an ethnic minority (African-American, Hispanic, Asian-American, Pacific Islander, etc.), and that number just keeps getting **bigger** and **bigger?**

So I can't even imagine how tough it must be for immigrant students who barely speak English to be thrust into a classroom where it's the only language spoken. As if social studies wasn't boring enough, listening to a teacher drone on in a language that you have to struggle to understand must be a certified form of torture.

But thousands of kids do it every day. And it's not just the language difference immigrant teens are up against. It's having different customs, clothes, religions, traditions, cultures, appearances. To top it off, if you think your parents are tough on you when it comes to grades, studies show that immigrant students might have it doubly hard, as many of their parents expect them to be super students. Talk about pressure!

Seen It?

The movie *In America* (2002) authentically tells the story of an Irish immigrant family **adjusting to life** in present-day New York City.

For many immigrant teens, the stress can get to be too much. But sometimes, as you'll read in the following story "On Language," that pressure can work to their advantage, resulting in teens who are empowered, bilingual and pretty darn smart to boot.

For Real?

Being an **immigrant** can be especially tough on teens because they often find themselves separated from loved ones who are still in their native countries.

On Language

According to James Baldwin, language is one of the epitomes of life, a source of connection to or divorce from the face of the public. Anyone who has had to navigate through the plethora of tongues around the world knows that the revelations of the Tower of Babel are true—it is very hard to understand and to be understood. I know this truth firsthand because I've lived through it. I stood at the bottom of the tower and had to find a way to climb up, around and over. Language, my fear of it, my embrace of it and ultimately my delight in it, turned out to be my weapon in the battle to be heard.

Consider This . . .

James Baldwin is a famous American writer, best known for his works about the **civil rights** movement.

I grew up in the Philippines, a wonderful stew of thousands of languages and cultures and islands, scented by billowing pollution and noncirculating traffic, beautiful landscapes and tropical delights, and a population in transition. Most of the populace speaks Tagalog. It was my first language. I was also fortunate enough to learn the basics of English as I grew up, catching a phrase here or there, grasping that it was a language that was valuable to know.

THE WORD

Did you know that Tagalog is the second most common Asian language spoken in the U.S.? (Chinese is the most popular.)

When my family emigrated to the United States, I was in the second grade. Tagalog was no longer "good enough," no longer the currency I needed to navigate the world. I had to get my hands on English. I was resentful. I felt like my native tongue was robbed from me, all because we had come to America, the land of opportunities. I didn't understand why this evil place, this monster America, didn't appreciate the singsong beauty of Tagalog, the language of my parents and my grandparents and me. In America, it was worth nothing.

For Real?

There are more than 400 different languages spoken by student immigrants in the United States!

People who knew English had a distinct advantage. I learned this right away. Without that magical skill, I felt powerless. In class, where I had always been the star back home, I was no longer able to impress my American teachers with my talent and knowledge. My hand didn't shoot up like a rocket to answer every question. Instead, I sat silently, thinking in Tagalog in my head, refusing to dive into English, viewing it as the language of the enemy. I was perceived as a shy

CONSIDER THIS . . .

Less than **1%** of the U.S. population is made up of Native Americans. You know what that means? That's right: Most of us are here because our ancestors immigrated to the United States. Do you know where your ancestors came from?

little girl in the corner, sitting on a rickety chair too small for her but not complaining about it, squinting behind her slanted eyes to see the blackboard, chatting to herself all the "Asian" thoughts nobody in America wanted to hear.

I was always getting in trouble for writing on the table, chiseling the words "I hate here," my broken English not capable of conveying the rage I felt for being silenced, for losing my language. Although I was only seven, I had a sense that it would get better as I grew up. My parents and older sister seemed to be getting along easier than I was. However, I still had to spend some time sitting back, staying quiet and staring at the classroom ceiling until I had the skills to say what was on my mind.

For Real?

Did you know that **10%** of all U.S. students are **immigrants?** The majority of them live in California, Florida, Illinois, New York and Texas.

My classmates would talk about how Chinese I looked, a skinny girl with pigtails gripped by colorful Popsicle clips, with white skin and slits for eyes. I wanted to scream at them "I am not Chinese! I AM FILIPINA," and punch them, but I didn't dare, mostly because I didn't know how to scream such an affirmation in a language they would understand. I kept myself confined within a social wall, unable to cry for help, scared of trying anything. It took a long time for me to realize that I had to jump in, get over the fear of being wrong, sounding wrong, and tackle the Tower of Babel one English syllable at a time.

Now, so many years later, it is hard to remember how frightening all of it was to me. I've become a California girl, with tanned skin and wider eyes. As for the all-powerful language, I have tamed that scary monster. I'm on the speech team in my school, and I write poems and stories and essays—even a novel. One of the few things I am not afraid of is language. I'm a word person. It is who I am.

Read It?

The popular novel *The Joy Luck Club* (1989), by Amy Tan, tells the story of four Chinese **immigrants** in San Francisco.

Consider This . . .

Most teens in **Europe** and **Asia** speak more than one language, while many American teens speak only English. But don't think that speaking a foreign language isn't important. Here are just some of the **benefits** of knowing another language like **Spanish, French** or **German:**

- Bilingual students are better problem solvers.
- Mastering another language also makes you better at other things, like math and writing.
- Knowing another language opens up many more job opportunities down the road.
- When you're older and traveling the world, you'll have an easier time communicating with the locals.
- Speaking another language is a quick way to impress people!

Language has helped me evolve and rise above the fate of so many disenfranchised immigrants, to join the melting pot and find a way to put my unique imprint on it. It has given me my voice and will ultimately guide me toward my future. To bring the journey full circle, I am working on a creative piece in Tagalog, hoping to reach out to other Filipinas who haven't crossed the English bridge yet.

James Baldwin thought that the privilege of language could be fatal, a Pandora's box that, once opened, could lead to strange and surprising results. That has been my experience with language, some of it good, some scary and some bad. I'm glad I had the determination to persevere, to learn a new language. It has led me on an interesting path. I plan to learn other languages and to encourage everyone to do the same. The world may get bigger or smaller, but we will always have a need to talk to one another.

Lovely Umayam, Age 17

CONSIDER THIS . . .

Expert psychologists say that washing kids' mouths out with soap to deter them from **swearing** doesn't work. Instead, parents should just **ignore** their kids' foul language and not give it any sort of attention, good *or* bad.

I WAS JUST A THIRD-GRADER the first and only time I had my mouth washed out with soap. The neighbors were over for dinner, and the four of them, plus my parents, sister and me, were at the table in our yellow and green wallpapered dining room. Steve, the older neighbor boy, said something to tease me as usual.

Without even thinking, I told him to shut up, followed by a bad word.

Punishment was instantaneous. My mom marched me back to the bathroom, where she grabbed a bar of Ivory soap, lathered it up, and inserted it into my mouth. If you've never had your mouth washed out with soap before, may I recommend that you do everything in your power to avoid this fate. It's not fun.

After that night, I learned very quickly that the spoken word could get strong reactions. One slip of the tongue, and you can find yourself doing a taste test of cleaning products. I defended myself back then, saying I had learned the swear words in the back of the bus, which wasn't really my fault because if my parents drove me to school in the first place it would never have been a problem. That didn't work. My other argument (and this is one I would use for years) is that there was no such thing as a "bad" word, that a word is just a collection of letters and it's people

WHERE DO YOU STAND?

Do you unknowingly turn people off with the things you say? Would you do any of these things?

Call the costumes your music teacher wants you to wear for the big concert "retarded."

___ NEVER (0 points)
___ MAYBE AS A JOKE (1 point)
___ ONLY TO MY FRIENDS (2 points)

Pass along a great "blonde joke" that you heard the other day.

___ NEVER (0 points)
___ MAYBE AS A JOKE (1 point)
___ ONLY TO MY FRIENDS (2 points)

Use a racial slur when kidding around with your friends.

___ NEVER (0 points)
___ MAYBE AS A JOKE (1 point)
___ ONLY TO MY FRIENDS (2 points)

Add up your points:
0–1 = You know the power of words.
2–4 = Be careful what you say.
5–6 = Your words are a turnoff.

themselves who that make them bad. That one didn't fly either. But despite getting in trouble time and time again, my mind didn't change. I just didn't see anything wrong with using bad words.

It wasn't until many years later that I realized that the words that so carelessly came out of my mouth could actually hurt people, even if I didn't intend them that way. My wake-up call came when I was in college and, without even realizing it, used a word in conversation that directly offended the person I was speaking with. I was horrified at my gaffe. How could I have said something so insensitive? How many times had I thrown words like that around and never thought about how they might be interpreted or who I might be hurting as a result? That incident happened many years ago, but I can say that to this day, I think before I speak and continue to appreciate the power of words.

HOW ABOUT YOU?

Have you ever **said** something **without thinking** and then **regretted** it later?

For Real?

The reason your **bar of soap floats** in the bathtub is because in 1878 too much **air** got into a batch of Procter & Gamble's soap. Customers loved the floating soap, and so from then on, air was added to the ingredients.

The Hallway

The cruelest lies are often told in silence.

—Robert Louis Stevenson

A group of high school students is gathered in the hallway during break period.

A handsome boy in a red and silver varsity jacket, with his backpack hanging off his arm, leans against a wall of lockers. "We've got a game against Caldwell tomorrow."

"Caldwell High?"

"Yeah, heard their point guard's good."

His girlfriend hangs onto his arm. "You're gonna beat them good, aren't you, Luke?"

Luke shrugs and runs his hands through his hair. "I dunno . . ."

Luke's buddy, a boy named Stephen, gave him a friendly shove. "Come on—that school's gay. You can beat 'em blindfolded."

His girlfriend nods with a laugh. "Yeah, you can beat a fag school, can't you?"

While they're talking, a kid passes by, studying his biology notes. He's mostly just weaving past the loud, heavy crowds in the hallway, trying to recall the definition for photosynthesis, but he can't. Frustrated, he flips back to his notebook to check. Most

THE WORD

Tolerance is all about *respect*, that is, respect for other people's beliefs, practices, lifestyles and ideals.

Address Book

Tolerance.Org (*www.tolerance.org*) is a Web site dedicated to **fighting hate** and **promoting tolerance** among teenagers.

of the time he'd find the definition, scold himself for forgetting it and then go back on his way. But then he overhears what Luke and his friends are saying, repeating "gay" and "fag" and laughing, and he stops in his tracks, right in the middle of student traffic. The notebook was now forgotten, hanging loosely from his grasp. Now it didn't matter anymore what photosynthesis meant.

Read It?

The gripping novel *Speak* (1999), by Laurie Halse Anderson, tells the story of a girl who learns the importance of making her **voice heard.**

All of a sudden it feels like there is a hole in his chest, where those kids had just ripped out a part of him. *Gay, fag, gay, fag.* It all churned in his mind, how those words were such a bad thing, and yet that bad thing was somehow part of him, was him. He was confused and sad and angry and a whole lot of other things, all because of a few words. He wants to stomp up to that group, tell them off, but what to tell them, he doesn't know. Then he just gives up, knowing that it's hopeless, totally hopeless, like everything in life is.

He lets out a little sigh and trudges down the hallway to his biology class.

I know. I've been that kid at least a dozen times.

Cristina Bautista, Age 15

Consider This . . .

Have you ever **witnessed** someone being **intolerant** of another student because of their race, gender or sexual identity? If it happens again, do your part to stamp out intolerance:

- Refuse to participate in intolerant dialogue.
- Speak up and tell the intolerant person that his or her attitude isn't cool or okay.

MUSIC IS INCREDIBLE STUFF. Scientists now know that music has the power to increase or decrease heart rate, lower blood pressure, aid in learning, increase memory capacity, and dilate a person's pupils. And those are just some of the physical effects. The emotional effects are even more incredible.

Don't believe me? Watch a horror movie like *Scream* and turn off the volume during the really intense parts. See what I mean? Without the ominous background noise, slashers seem more silly than scary. Or how about when you're in the middle of a workout, and you don't think you can take another step on the treadmill or lift one more hand weight. Pop in some tunes (like the theme from *Rocky*), and you'll get through the rest of your workout feeling great.

While you may have listened to music all of your life, there's something about being a teenager that goes hand and hand with music. It's the whole reason for MTV's success! What is it about some musicians and songwriters that enables them to tap into the very core of who we are and make us feel as though they understand what teenage life is all about?

Consider This . . .

Sometimes **soundtracks** to **movies** can be just as memorable as the movie itself. Have you seen any of these movies with awesome soundtracks?

- *O Brother, Where Art Thou?*
- *About a Boy*
- *The Wedding Singer*
- *Love Actually*
- *Pulp Fiction*
- *8 Mile*

For Real?

MTV was first launched in New York City in 1981. The very first **music video** ever played was "Video Killed the Radio Star," by The Buggles.

HOW ABOUT YOU?

What's the **one song** that can **pick you up** when you're really down?

I listened to all kinds of music when I was a teenager: pop, punk, rap, new wave. But there was one artist who most impacted me more than anyone else as a teen—Billy Joel. Okay. I know you're probably rolling your eyes right now, but believe me when I say that Joel's older albums—*Turnstiles, The Nylon Curtain, Glass Houses*—were works of genius as far as I was concerned. He wrote with such honesty about real emotions like pain and suffering, love and confusion . . . life. I spent countless hours every night in our rec room listening to cassette tapes blasted over the speakers, absolutely positive that Billy Joel knew exactly how I felt at every moment. This was a comforting thought. It made me feel like if he had gotten through all the difficulties I was facing, then I could, too.

For Real?

Studies show that most **teens** spend more than ten hours every week listening to **music.** Are you one of them?

When you find singers or songwriters who connect with you this way—Sarah McLachlan, Ashlee Simpson, Avril Lavigne, Usher or Linkin Park—embrace them. Music really can get you through the tough times and even help you to look at things with a new perspective.

THE WORD

There's actually a real science just for studying music. It's called **musicology**.

Lyrical Ponderings

On my first day of high school, I found myself squeezing my body through the sardine-like crowd of students. I was the little fish trying to maneuver through the masses. A hoard of arms and foul words swept past me.

"Hey, Tubby! You're going the wrong way. Cafeteria is in the other direction!" a boy said. I heard snickers in the throng of people closest to me. My attacker was hidden by the multitude.

For Real?

20% of children ages **6–19** are considered **overweight,** more than triple the percentage in 1980.

He probably only made the remark to relieve some pent-up frustration or insecurity he was feeling, but it still stung me. I tried to act like it was nothing more than a mosquito bite. I brushed it off and kept squeezing my way to my next class, but in the back of my mind the comment was awakening a long dormant fear.

Consider This . . .

An article in *The Wall Street Journal* reported that **teens** who **diet** might actually be setting themselves up to gain more weight, mostly because **diets don't last,** and they're often followed by **binges.**

By lunch, the comment was still gnawing inside me. I've always been a thick girl, and in elementary school some of my classmates teased me about my weight. At recess, I didn't want to play with the other kids because I was scared they would throw rocks at me and call me names.

After a while, I tried to hide what I considered to be my physical flaw by feeding my brain. I became dependent on books. In my fifth-grade year I managed to read the entire school library and started searching for more things to nurse my hungry mind. I thought that if I could pretend to be smart and hide behind my books, people would forget about the rest of me and see only an intelligent young lady.

This game worked for a while, until middle school came and the pressure to be thin increased. I did what most girls in my position do, I started starving myself. I learned to live with the hunger pains, but then I would succumb to my grumbling stomach and binge. It wasn't a healthy habit, and I knew I had to stop. The more weight I gained, the less confidence I had, and the more I tried to hide behind my books. I was spiraling down into a pit, the lose/gain cycle was affecting more than my health; it was affecting my grades.

THE WORD

Bingeing is an eating disorder where a person eats more food than would be considered normal. Like other eating disorders, bingeing is much more common among girls than boys.

In the span of three weeks, I had gone from a straight-A student to a B student. This was another blow to my self-confidence since I had always been an honor student. To help ease the stress, I started writing poetry. The poems were dark and morbid, but they helped me get out my anger and insecurities. Poetry became my refuge for over four years, and it worked until I started losing interest in my writing. I lost pleasure in releasing my thoughts to the world. It became more of a chore than an outlet.

So, on the first day of high school I found myself in the cafeteria not eating. Thoughts flooded my brain. *Why do people always have to look at me? If I get something to eat, maybe they'll stop staring, but what if I give away that I'm hungry and I eat too fast or I eat too much?*

Their eyes bore into me, scrutinizing my flaws. I made one last attempt to make myself feel more secure. I closed my eyes and imagined getting smaller and smaller until I was an insignificant speck. If I was that small, no one could see me, and no one would judge me, right?

> **For Real?**
> Teens who are **overweight** are more often **teased** than other teens, and research shows this makes overweight teens much more likely to be depressed, have low self-esteem and **suffer** from eating disorders.

Finally, lunch ended, and I went back to my classes, still frustrated. I couldn't understand why I was always falling victim to some idiot's remarks. Old doubts about making it through the day came back, and I was starting to panic. What if I really wouldn't make it in high school because I couldn't get over my past? The school day ended with that thought churning in my mind.

When I got home, I felt like I was slipping into a warm bath. I quickly made my way up to my room and shut my door. Finally, I could be somewhere safe. My problems vanished in my room. My fears were not allowed in. This time though, I was troubled by

> **For Real?**
> Did you know that the band **Linkin Park** is named after Lincoln Park in Santa Monica, California? They changed the spelling so they could get the Web site address with their name (*www.lincolnpark.com* was already taken!).

For Real?

If you don't believe that **music** can have a powerful effect, think again. Termites chew through wood twice as fast when they're listening to **heavy metal.**

the day's events, and I worried that depression would once again start the all-too-familiar lose/gain cycle. In times like this, I used music to blast my pain away.

So I turned on the radio, and I was immediately engulfed by angry, soul-searing lyrics—lyrics that ignited in me a calm wave of understanding. I sat in the middle of my bed and closed my eyes, letting the song draw a picture of hurt and realization in my mind. The song swirled around me, then soaked me with its meaning. I felt like this song, "Breaking the Habit," was made for me, but then Linkin Park had always written songs that helped put things in perspective. I could piece the puzzle together now. The words penetrated me, ". . . you all assume I'm searching in my room, unless I try to start again, I don't want to be the one the battles always choose, cuz inside I realize that I'm the one confused . . ."

As the song died down, I ran some ideas through my head. It didn't matter how much I tried to cover up my feelings or flaws. They would always shine through. I couldn't get rid of them until I understood them. It was okay to feel confused and beaten down as long as I brought myself back up. The key to breaking my self-destructive swaying between dieting and bingeing was to understand and appreciate my inner self before I could begin to work on my outer self. I

Read It?

In his book *Songbook* (2002), author Nick Hornby presents a collection of **essays** about what his favorite songs mean to him.

realized that the kids weren't the problem because I would find ignorant and immature people no matter where I went. I had to work through my pain and move on.

I fell asleep with one last thought: The next day would be better. It would bring out a new girl. I would not hide anymore, and if someone made a comment, I wouldn't let it get to me. I would remember that it was only a comment, and I had the power to reject it. The boy who teased me didn't know me, but I was getting to know myself better and better. That night, I chose to seek out self-respect rather than focus on ignorance. From that point on, the battles didn't choose me. I took my power back.

Coral Lozada, Age 14

For Real?

You might think that **school uniforms** are just for private schools with wealthier students, but they were actually first used in sixteenth-century England at charity schools for poor children.

THERE ARE MANY REASONS phys ed can be considered a form of cruel and unusual punishment. First off, there are the uniforms, often so hideous that they look like they've been designed in the 1960s. Could they *be* any more unflattering? Then there's the whole sweating-in-the-middle-of-the-day thing. Everyone knows that showers after gym class are a pain in the butt, so the next best option is peeling on clean clothes over sticky, sweaty skin, and that's just not a good thing for anybody. And how about

Seen It?

The movie *Rudy* (1993) is about a scrawny boy who defies all the odds by making his dream of playing college football a reality.

the activities these gym teachers come up with. Badminton? Wiffle ball? Bowling with hollow plastic pins? Come on, now.

But possibly the worst aspect of phys ed is the whole component of "picking teams." No matter what the activity, be it crab soccer or volleyball, it's always the super-athletic eager beavers who are chosen as team captains and then are given the task of handpicking his or her team, the goal being to select members who will be sure to decimate the opponents. So when someone is the last person chosen to be on any given team, the message is, *You're no good. In fact, I don't even want you on my team, but there's no one else left to pick.* And unfortunately, that message gets through to everybody present, loud and clear.

THE WORD

Outcast means someone who is excluded from society. (Not to be confused with the hip band Outkast, who couldn't be more "in.")

If you've been the one to be picked last before, take solace in the fact that you're not alone. At some point in our lives, we've all been the last one to have our name called, the one standing on the outside looking in.

OUTCAST

A boy sat alone at recess watching others play
He wanted to play basketball or football
He wanted to have friends
He wanted to be noticed by all the popular kids
Instead of sitting on sidelines watching
A still stone who'd amount to nothing

No one ever thought of him
Didn't recognize his
existence
Waste of space and breath,
Time and money.
It wasn't that kids made
fun of him
Just that no one took time
to say "hello"
Never making the small
efforts that
go a long way

Cold wind raked rough
fingers through his hair
But not as cold as the
engulfing loneliness
Athletes dunking,
constantly glancing to
see who's watching them
Jump-roping girls
chattering like squirrels
Cliques merging at
imaginary lines only
to separate to spread
their gossip
He'd seen the routine
Glory-seekers march forth trying to gather every ounce of
attention
Until rejected by those supposed to be impressed

WHERE DO YOU STAND?

Ever made someone
feel like an outcast? Find out.
Have you ever . . .

completely ignored someone who was trying to join in a conversation you were having with friends?

___ NEVER (0 points)
___ SOMETIMES (1 point)
___ USUALLY (2 points)

imitated the way someone talked, walked or looked to make your friends laugh?

___ NEVER (0 points)
___ SOMETIMES (1 point)
___ USUALLY (2 points)

told someone you were "saving the seat" next to you for someone else just so they wouldn't sit down?

___ NEVER (0 points)
___ SOMETIMES (1 point)
___ USUALLY (2 points)

Add up your points:
0–1 = No, you're very accepting.
2–4 = There's a good chance.
5–6 = Yes, you've hurt people's feelings.

He had often tried
To be like them
Lining up for the picks at basketball
The captains forgot he was there
Looking for a "group" he might take after
He was little more than a shadow
Anger, sadness, loneliness
Horrible emotions to live through
Choking his seed in the soil

Joseph Workman, Age 13

OUTSIDE THE BOX

Are you feeling depressed? If you are, here are some things that might help you deal with it:

- Talk to someone about how you're feeling: a parent, a friend, teacher, someone from your church.
- Be patient with yourself. A bad mood can take a while to snap out of.
- Take time to exercise or be social. The participation can help your frame of mind.
- Keep a journal so you have a place to express yourself freely.

Above all, depression should be taken seriously. Don't be afraid to ask for help.

For Real?

There are more than 1 million **homeless teens** living on the streets in the United States.

WHEN I LIVED IN NEW YORK CITY, I volunteered at a shelter for homeless teens. These were teenagers who had been living on the streets for years, many of them forced to leave home because their parents went to jail or their mom couldn't take care of them anymore because the family ran out of money. These teens had it tough, and their life experience couldn't have been further from mine.

In the two years I worked with these teens, I learned a lot about what it feels like to be an outsider. To most of society, *they* were the outsiders: shunned by most, ignored by others. To them, *I* was the outsider—this dorky white girl who obviously wasn't streetwise. And I knew that no matter how hard I tried, I would never know exactly what it was like to be in their situation.

Seen It?

In *A Walk in Your Shoes* on the teen television network The N, **teens trade places** with someone else to **experience life** from a different perspective.

At some point in their lives, everyone feels like the outsider, everyone has moments where they're just sure that no one else could possibly know how they feel or what life is like for them. And you know what? It's true. No one but you can truly know your personal experience.

One of the Team

I looked down in dread, my stomach tightening. "We're running up this thing?"

Justin, the team captain, grinned, "It feels good! What're you scared of?"

"Right," I shot back sarcastically while I took quick, regular steps to even out my heart rate and waited for Bora and Lindsay to catch up. Most members of the boys' team were already there, panting on the pavement, but the other girls were still a few blocks behind.

For Real?
29% of teenagers say that their ethnicity or heritage **impacts** their self-esteem.

They showed up soon enough, followed by Coach Mark, a short, stocky, blond-bearded guy who wore shorts year round. We were going to do hill sprints, he explained, and ignoring the groans he led us to the bottom of the hill and pointed out the correct form—taking quick, measured steps, keeping the back erect, and using only the upper half of the foot (heaven forbid your heel touch the ground). As we lined up, tense excitement filled my lungs like it always did before a whistle blast. Sprints were a vicious cycle—the almost fatal, heart-in-your-throat last seconds before the whistle and then suddenly the whoosh of feet and harried breathing and burning flames in your legs. And all of this performed in ritual silence—no one speaks until a set is over.

HOW ABOUT YOU?
Have **you** found yourself in a situation where you felt like an **outsider?**

The top of the hill was the only relief because once you started making your way to the bottom you were already dreading the next sprint up. So we would dawdle at the top and stare intently out at the foggy bay as if thinking about something terribly important, or we would stretch and re-stretch our calves—perhaps there was a sore tendon or an unhealthy ache (sore tendons were always "bad pain" but a plain old ache was usually "good pain" and encouraged by Mark, our coach).

"Last one!" shouted Mark, "then back to the park to stretch out." We followed orders and I loped back to the park with Sean, a freshman who was just about my speed. Traffic was heavy but asphalt was better for running than cement so we chose to dodge the cars all the way back to the park.

"You coming to the meet this Saturday?" Preston, another freshman, asked me while we were doing arm circles on the grass.

"What?"

"I said, are you coming to the meet this Saturday?"

"No, I don't think I'm gonna make it."

Seen It?

Chariots of Fire, which won the Academy Award for best picture in 1981, tells the true story of a world-class sprinter who **won't** run on the Sabbath.

"How come?"

"Family get-together thing—it's a big deal." My face was reddening.

"Oh, that's annoying. I heard they give out trophies at these meets."

"There's another one in two Saturdays," Sean piped up, "You could earn a trophy then." I tied and retied my shoe and was silent, avoiding the subject. We finished stretching and I walked off the grass to where Lindsay and Bora were chatting with the coach next to his red pickup truck. "So Rachel," Coach Mark said easily, unlocking his truck, "you making it this Saturday?"

"Well, no, I'm actually not gonna be able to." My voice was very small.

"Oh, too bad . . . these meets are fun. Thursday meets are pressured, but Saturday's are laid back, and you can win awards and stuff. Well, you'll come to the next one."

THE WORD

Sabbath is a word for **"day of rest."** In the Jewish religion, it goes from sunset Friday until sunset Saturday.

For a moment I imagined myself at Saturday's race, running in the sunshine with all of my teammates, but then I steeled myself. "Actually, I can never run on Saturdays—it's my Sabbath." I stared at the ground without seeing it, wishing Lindsay and Bora were somewhere else.

"You're Jewish?" Coach Mark asked thoughtfully.

"Yeah."

"Hmm. You know my grandmother was Jewish."

"Really?" I hadn't expected that.

"Yeah, she had the number on her arm and everything. I was real scared of it when I was a kid." He got in his truck and rolled down the window.

Read It?

The famous true story *The Diary of Anne Frank* (1959) was written by a 13-year-old Jewish girl hiding with her family from the Nazis in World War II.

"Remember ladies, 3:20 sharp at the track field tomorrow." Then he drove off.

"It's so horrible what happened there," Lindsay said later as we walked home together. "I saw these pictures of a concentration camp and it looked like a jail."

"Yeah, it was pretty bad," I replied. There was really nothing else to say. I always felt uncomfortable when others tried to relate to me like they knew what it was like to be me, to be

Jewish. We continued on in silence.

As we came to the corner where we usually parted ways, Lindsay asked, "So I'll see you at practice tomorrow?"

"Yeah, sprints at the track field. Oh goody," I answered sarcastically. We both groaned, and then grinned. I didn't know about Lindsay, but I was excited to get on that field tomorrow. All of us together, as a *team*.

Rachel Berman, Age 19

For Real?

The Jewish population in the United States is **decreasing**, possibly because fewer and fewer parents are passing down the faith to their children.

IT'S A FAMILIAR PLOT FOR HOLLYWOOD ROMANTIC COMEDIES. Girl goes to school. Girl has braces, acne, a bad hairdo, a bad figure and bad fashion sense. Girl is ridiculed at school. The boy the girl likes wouldn't be caught dead near her.

Flash forward ten years.

Girl is now woman. Gorgeous. No braces. Flawless skin. Perfect hair. Great figure. *Model.* Girl's former crush runs into her at reunion and obnoxiously hits on her, not even recognizing that she is the

Consider This . . .

The "ugly duckling" transformed into **beauty queen** is a popular plot in Hollywood movies. Have you seen any of these recent movies with "ugly duckling" themes?

- *America's Sweethearts* (2001)
- *The Princess Diaries* (2001)
- *My Big Fat Greek Wedding* (2002)
- *She's All That* (1999)

"ugly duckling" he didn't have time for as a teen. Girl decides to play trick on boy and get revenge. Hilarity ensues.

If you're like me, I'm sure you've seen that movie at least half a dozen times. But what is it trying to say, anyway? That it's okay to be an ugly duckling as a teenager because when you grow up and look phenomenal, you'll have oodles of fun waging war against those who dared to tease you?

What I take away from those movies is the fact that when we get older, the way we looked in middle school and high school isn't so important. Everyone, and I mean *everyone,* goes through big changes between twelve and twenty-five. Baby fat will have come or gone. Skin will have cleared up or gotten worse. The queen bees may go from the hottest thing in school to absolute nobodies. To base your self-esteem on how you do or don't fit in physically with the rest of your teen peers just sets you up for unnecessary heartache. These years are just a snippet in time, and who you are on the inside will never age.

CONSIDER THIS . . .

When reflecting on her high school days, super-star celeb Jennifer Garner describes herself as **"a happy nerd."** Boy, have things changed!

The Ugly Duckling

Finally the day I had anticipated all summer long arrived: the first day of high school. A week before, I had spent an entire day at the mall shopping for an updated wardrobe. It was time for a whole new me. I had on my favorite pair of new blue jeans, topped with my new pink hand-sewn sweater. I had bought a new pair of glasses, which my mother told me enhanced my light brown eyes. And it didn't even bother me that I still had braces because they only showed if I smiled a certain way, and I had practiced in front of the mirror a million times to smile so that you could barely see them. Yet, as I stood on the front steps of my school, I sensed that something wasn't quite right and felt my stomach twist into a tight knot. I wanted a fresh new start and hoped that my haunting past would no longer follow me like an everlasting shadow.

Read It?

The classic fairy tale *The Ugly Duckling* was written by Hans Christian Andersen more than 100 years ago.

Suddenly in the distance I heard the school bell go off. I looked at my watch. It was 8:15. I had spaced out for only a couple minutes and already I was going to be late for my first day of school. I burst through the heavy doors and ran down the hall, clutching my schedule in my clammy hands as I tried to find room 302. Apparently this massive building had been built as a maze to fool incoming freshmen like me. Finally, after what seemed like forever, I found myself approaching my first class. I took a deep breath before I swung open the door and felt my cheeks burning up as the eyes of every student in the room fell on me. I mumbled an "I'm sorry I'm late" to the teacher, but she just rolled her eyes and told me to hurry up and take a seat.

For Real?

No wonder teens are so concerned about **beauty.** More than half of the ads in a typical teen magazine are for fashion or beauty products.

As I walked quickly to the only empty desk left in the room, somebody whispered loudly, "Hey look, it's the ugly duckling!" He said this just loud enough for the entire class to hear, but not enough for the teacher to notice. In a span of about three seconds the whole class had burst into tiny giggles. I slowly sat down in my seat near the window, trembling, and felt great big droplets of tears welling up in my eyes.

For Real?

63% of teenagers say that they are somewhat satisfied with the way they look. Only **6%** say they **aren't** satisfied with their looks at all.

Suddenly, it all came back to me. The giggling and the laughing and the whispers as the popular kids yelled out "Ug-ly duck-ling! Ug-ly duck-ling!" Students along the hall pointing at me and whispering evil comments just loud enough for me to hear as I passed by. Not one person willing to help me as I ran down the hall, tears in my eyes, to the nearest bathroom where I would stay, crouched in a corner, for the rest of the day.

Seen It?

The dark comedy *Welcome to the Dollhouse* (1995) tells the story of an **ugly duckling** seventh-grader trying to survive school and home life.

Nevertheless, as I sat in my seat I decided to hold back my tears and stay strong. There was no way those same people could still think the same way about me. Anyway, in such an immense school with such a vast student population, there was bound to be someone who sympathized with me. There was bound to be someone who would be my best friend for the next four years and stand by me no matter what. High school was supposed to be the best four years of any teenager's life, and I wasn't about to let a petty incident in my first class on the first day of school ruin my entire high school life.

But the minute I walked into the lunchroom I knew there would be a problem. Who was I to sit with? This could determine my status in high school forever. I quickly glanced around the room, only to find that everyone was already sitting with a friend and no one seemed to have room for more. I grabbed my lunch and bravely took a seat near one of the window seats where no one would notice me. Maybe tomorrow I'll be early and find a new friend to sit with at lunch. But for now, eating alone wasn't too bad.

For Real?

70% of students say the caf is the place where social boundaries are most visible. To combat that, millions of students participate in the annual "Mix It Up at Lunch Day," sitting at new tables in the lunchroom to connect with new people.

As I decided to use this free period to spend some quality time reading, a group of sophomores passed behind me. Before I even had a chance to turn my head around to glance at them, I felt hard little pellets hit me from above. I instinctively shut my eyes to keep whatever was hitting me from going into my eye, but instead the unidentified flying objects banged against my glasses and bounced off. It turned out that as an evil joke, one of the sophomores had poured a whole bag of sour Skittles on my head. This time I couldn't stop the giant balls of tears from rolling down my cheeks. I could hear the giant roar of laughter coming from them, and it made the tears fall even harder. By the time I made it to the bathroom, I was shuddering uncontrollably. I couldn't believe this was happening all over again. All I wanted to do was to go home, jump in bed and have a good, hard cry.

I remember that first day of high school like it was yesterday. Now, sitting in my dorm room freshman year of college, flipping through the pages of my high school yearbook, I come across a picture from ninth grade. The memory came rushing back to me, emblazoned so deeply in my mind that I guess it never really went away. The pain and the hurt sometimes come back so overwhelmingly that I feel like I still need to cry it out, to relieve my aching heart.

HOW ABOUT YOU?

Do you sometimes **wish** you could snap your fingers and **get a fresh start** at your school?

It's true when they say beauty is skin deep. Because somehow, somewhere between high school and college, I "blossomed." People who had once ignored me were suddenly willing to become my best friend without ever truly knowing me. I guess those are the benefits that come with being pretty, yet I found that finding a best friend when you don't have tons of options is far more precious than becoming friends with everyone who comes along in your life.

At first I was overwhelmed by this new interest in me, and I couldn't get enough of it. But I soon saw through the façade and chose instead to make a true new friend anytime I saw a lonely girl being picked on. I always found their beauty, not just on the outside but especially where it was most hidden—on the inside.

Diana Chang, Age 18

Take the Quiz: HOW CONFIDENT ARE YOU IN WHO YOU ARE?

1. You've just started high school and discover very quickly that your older brother has quite a reputation around school, and not a good one, either. Every time a new teacher finds out you're related to your brother, he or she makes a negative comment, judging you before you've even uttered a word! You . . .

___ A. shrug it off with a chuckle. You know that once the teacher gets to know you and sees your work, you'll blow his or her socks off.

___ B. get slightly annoyed and concerned, but decide to give it some time. If you don't judge your teacher right off the bat, hopefully they'll do the same for you.

___ C. go home from school devastated, begging your parents to let you transfer. There's no way you can survive high school riding on the coattails of your disliked older brother.

2. Your chemistry teacher hands out a semester-long project and announces that he's already broken the class up into pre-assigned groups. As he calls out the names, you realize your group is made up of you and two of the most beautiful and popular girls in school. You . . .

___ A. sit down with your group in shame and embarrassment, suddenly feeling completely self-conscious about your clothes, hair, skin and just about everything else.

___ B. nervously get to work and hope that they like you for who you are, although the next time your group meets you might pick out a better outfit.

___ C. smile, take a deep breath and get to work. These girls don't even know you, and who cares what they think of you anyway?

3. It's the first day of school, and you've got no one to sit with at lunch. You approach a group of kids and ask if you can join them, but they simply snicker at you and give you a look that says, *You? Are you kidding me?* You . . .

___ A. lose your appetite and run off to the bathroom, convinced that no one at school is going to like you.

___ B. are shaken by their rudeness and decide to sit by yourself today. Maybe you'll try to sit with someone else again tomorrow.

___ C. say "Oops, sorry. Wrong table," and move on to another one. Who wants to sit with those guys anyway?

4. You're psyched when the phys ed teacher announces you'll be playing soccer today, but are surprised when neither team captain acknowledges how good you are by picking you to be on their team until the very end. You . . .

___ A. are totally bummed out and get angry at the captains, spending the next hour trying to prove how awesome you really are.

___ B. are surprised that you're picked last and hang back during class. You've got to give your ego time to recover.

___ C. decide it doesn't matter . . . it's just gym class, anyway. You love playing soccer, and that's what counts.

5. You've spent all weekend thrift-shopping for clothes: perfectly faded jeans, retro vests, hip shoes. But when you confidently walk through the school doors on Monday wearing your new threads, you're confronted with teasing from the populars, who ask you if your family can't afford new clothes. You . . .

___ A. go home that afternoon and pack the clothes away, never to wear them again. Good thing they didn't cost much in the first place.

___ B. self-consciously reexamine your look and decide to make it more mainstream next time you wear your thrift clothes.

___ C. ignore the teasers. At least you have some flair and individuality in the way you dress.

How'd you do? Give yourself 10 points for every A, 20 points for every B and 30 points for every C. Look below to find out how confident you are:

50–70 points = Most of the time you feel like a total outsider and it hurts. You let others determine how good you feel about yourself, which ends up not feeling good at all. If you look for areas in your life where you are confident and try to expand on those experiences, you'll be surprised at how quickly you can turn things around.

80–120 points = Sometimes you hold your head high, but other days it's just too hard to keep your chin up in the face of adversity. Try to remember how good it feels when you believe in yourself. Soon you'll forget to care about what others think.

130–150 points = You should feel great because you're comfortable in your own skin. Being confident in who you are can have a powerful and positive impact on everything you do in life.

CHAPTER 4

THE GROWN-UP FACTOR

From parents and caregivers to teachers and coaches, dealing with adults is a part of life. There are the coaches we love to hate, the teachers who inspire and challenge us, and the overprotective parents who smother us or the ones who try to be our best friends when all we really want is some guidance. What is it that makes some adults "get it," while others couldn't be more clueless? Why do some adults who aren't even related to us take a special interest in who we are and what we're doing? In the following stories and poems, you'll hear from teens pondering these relationships with adults.

CONSIDER THIS . . .

When it comes to **support** from adults, would it surprise you to know that studies show teenagers **rely** the most on their **parents?**

HAVE YOU EVER NOTICED THAT SOME PARENTS HAVE "RADAR"? I'm not sure how it works, but there are some moms and dads out there who just seem to know when things are going on that shouldn't be going on, even while many other parents are oblivious. Well, my parents not only had radar—they had the equivalent of night vision goggles with telephoto lenses. It seemed that out of all of my friends, I was the one who got in trouble for everything: breaking curfew, not being where I said I was going to be, for hanging out with the wrong crowd, the list goes on and on.

No matter what the plan with my friends was, my parents drilled me with questions: who, what, where and when? Come to think of it, they never asked why. I guess they figured that one out on their own. It used to drive me crazy, how my fate on any given day was determined by whatever mood my dad happened to be in, because once he decreed a "yes" or "no" to my request, there was no changing his mind.

I tried different methods to get the results I was after: asking after dinner, before dinner, after I'd done something great like clean up around the house, approaching my mom first and trying to get her to go along with me, reminding my parents that "all my friends were doing it." Might I add that that last method—the one where I said all my friends were doing it—was a bad move. It never worked.

CONSIDER THIS . . .

77% of teenagers are comfortable talking with their parents about school and friends, and studies show that the more **involved parents** are in their teens' lives, the more confident the teens are.

Seen It?

Talk about a close relationship, Lorelai and her daughter, Rory, are often mistaken for sisters on the hit TV show *Gilmore Girls*, which leaves lots of opportunity for humor and drama.

At the time, I found all of this parental interference extremely bothersome to say the least, but now I know that they were just doing their job. Their interest in what I was doing was actually their way of showing an interest in me.

EXCUSES, EXCUSES

It's my friend on the phone,
Mother, can I go?
I don't like that tone,
No, I don't think so.

Every day it's the same,
Mother, can I go?
What's his or her name?
These things I need to know.

She's still waiting,
Mother, can I go?
Hang on, I'm still debating,
You've got homework you know.

It's only two hours long,
Mother, can I go?
Okay, I hope I'm not wrong
Come home after the show!

Alicia Jaynes, Age 21

For Real?

70% of teens feel that their **freedom** is too restricted by adults, and **22%** said they would be happier if their parents gave them **more freedom.**

HOW ABOUT YOU?

44% of teenagers say they will be less strict with their own children when they have them. How about you?

CONSIDER THIS . . .

46% of teenagers feel that they need to earn respect from their parents, while the other **54%** feel their parents should automatically respect them until they give them reason not to. If you want to earn your parents' respect, try following these tips:

- Tell your parents the truth, no matter how difficult.
- Be where you say you'll be.
- Be responsible.
- Follow the family rules.
- Communicate with your parents.

THERE ARE TIMES IN EVERY TEEN'S LIFE when it seems like adults *just don't get it.* Often, at the top of the list of clueless adults are mom and dad. Why is there such a disconnect between teens and their parents? The problem seems to be *communication,* or should I say, the lack of it. What might have been a simple conversation a few years ago suddenly has the potential to turn into a full-fledged fight. One wrong look and there might be a blow-up. Parents often don't know how to relate anymore, so they talk to their kids like they're strangers.

Read It?

Jay McGraw's best-selling book, *Closing the Gap: A Strategy for Bringing Parents and Teens Together* (2001), talks about ways to forge the **ideal relationship** with your parents.

Other parents act like their kids are their best friends, but that doesn't work either because, let's face it, most teens already have a best friend, and he or she doesn't have gray hair and the same last name as they do. Yet other parents retreat and leave their kids alone, or try too hard and end up sounding like some wacky psychoanalyst.

Yet despite the fact that a communication gap between teens and their parents exists, most teenagers want their parents to talk with them and show an interest in their lives more than ever before. Getting the job done is the hard part.

This next essay is written by a teen looking for a way to communicate with her parents, and so she wrote her words in the form of a letter, which she hasn't sent. Perhaps one of these days she'll put the letter in the mail and open up the dialogue.

CONSIDER THIS . . .

43% of parents want to be their kids' best friend. But many teens are looking for something different from their mom and dad, like **guidance** and **boundaries.** What kind of relationship do you want with your parents?

The Seal to a Letter Unmailed

Dear Guardian,

You think they're just tears I'm crying, but they're not. My tears are the pieces of me that I shed; they're pieces that I lose along the way. I cry them for you—*because* of you. I cry because it is the only

Seen It?

In *Mean Girls* (2004), **"it"** girl Regina has a mom who goes out of her way to act like "one of the girls," and it drives her daughter **crazy.**

WHERE DO YOU STAND?

Even though you might not admit it, studies show that teens really do want to talk with their parents about serious stuff. How do you feel about discussing these topics with your parents?

Dating and sex

___ YIKES . . . NO WAY! (0 points)
___ I MIGHT BE OPEN TO IT (1 point)
___ I'D WELCOME THE TALK (2 points)

Feeling insecure

___ YIKES . . . NO WAY! (0 points)
___ I MIGHT BE OPEN TO IT (1 point)
___ I'D WELCOME THE TALK (2 points)

Being bullied or teased

___ YIKES . . . NO WAY! (0 points)
___ I MIGHT BE OPEN TO IT (1 point)
___ I'D WELCOME THE TALK (2 points)

Failing a class or test

___ YIKES . . . NO WAY! (0 points)
___ I MIGHT BE OPEN TO IT (1 point)
___ I'D WELCOME THE TALK (2 points)

Problem with a close friend

___ YIKES . . . NO WAY! (0 points)
___ I MIGHT BE OPEN TO IT (1 point)
___ I'D WELCOME THE TALK (2 points)

Add up your points:
0–1 = It sounds like torture.
2–4 = They'd have to bring it up.
5–6 = I want to spill the beans.

way I know how to say what I need to. It is impossible to have words when one cannot speak, let alone know what to say in order to express one's feelings and have them understood.

Do you hear the pain in my tears? Do you even listen anymore? The pain has become so frequent that I'm not sure if you hear it but then just close your ears instead. You think that maybe if you aren't listening I will stop screaming through my silence. You think I'm quiet? Really? Because I have more to say than time can allow for. I say what I know and what I know you will understand. But it is through the quiet that I tell you my true thoughts—expose the most inner core of my being. It is through the silent sobs of my mourning soul that I give you a hint as to the desperation and depression deep inside of me. Do I not share enough with you already that you think there is more? You think there are things I keep from you? No. It is all there. It lies before your eyes, deep in my own, and it lingers in the slow, methodical breaths that I breathe when that is all I can do—just breathe and nothing more.

HOW ABOUT YOU?

Would you go to your parents with a **serious problem?** How would you tell them about it?

I keep nothing from you. It is you who chooses to hear what you do, and it is you who refuses to understand what you don't. Who am I in this moment? You can't expect me to give you all of me when I don't even know what that means. I suppose I am a girl, a young woman if it suits you to say that. In my head I am a child. I see things in a way that others don't, and I am amused by things that others have ceased to take pleasure in. I am a frail girl, insecure and immature in the ways that many outgrow. Just like a baby, I have yet to find a way to express myself through words and with the language that most people choose to communicate with. All I can do now is speak through silence and through tears and hope that those listening will recognize and understand what each cry or unspoken word means. Sadly, not many people do, and if they get close, sometimes I confuse them by speaking words that alter the true meaning of the cry of my heart. So no, it's not just tears that I cry, I am crying me and it's all over you.

Sincerely, Sarah

Sarah Brook, Age 17

OUTSIDE THE BOX

Can you read minds? Well, chances are your parents can't either! If you're having trouble getting through to your parents about something on your mind, why not try one of these approaches?

- Write your parent a letter—and send it!
- Send your parent an e-mail.
- Ask your parent to spend some one-on-one time with you, at the mall, going to lunch, playing a sport.
- Do something unexpected (clean up the kitchen after dinner, take out the trash) to get their attention and then bring up the subject.

MR. FARENBACH WAS A LEGEND AT MY SCHOOL. Everyone knew him as a tough, eccentric teacher who wore V-neck wool cardigans, pocket protectors and thick-rimmed glasses. He walked briskly through the halls, waddling like a duckling trying to catch up with the rest of the pack. Mr. Farenbach taught language arts, otherwise known as English, although his approach was a little off the wall.

You see, Mr. Farenbach was obsessed with mythology. You know, Greek and Roman gods and stuff: Zeus, Hera, snakes for hair, flying horses, all that stuff. Don't

CONSIDER THIS . . .

Mother's Day, Father's Day, Grandparent's Day . . . now there's National Teacher's Day! Celebrated the first Tuesday in May, this is a day to honor teachers for the impact they've had on our lives. Do you have a teacher to **thank** on National Teacher's Day?

ask me what mythology has to do with English, but it was the former that we were drilled and tested on over and over.

Mr. Farenbach was intimidating, not because of his stature (he couldn't have been more than 5 feet, 6 inches) but because of the rapid-fire pace he'd go around the room, querying the baffled students about which god or goddess did what and why. Wrong answers could result in spending a whole class holding piles of crusty old dictionaries in the corner. (Did I happen to mention that I developed strong biceps over the course of the seventh grade?)

What I didn't realize then, but totally get now, is that Mr. Farenbach covered grammar extensively throughout the the class. Prepositions, conjunctions, possessives, participles. I know these like the back of my hand today, because although the quizzes appeared to be testing our knowledge of which mythological character spent eternity pushing a rock up a mountain only to have it roll back down again (it was Sisyphus, by the way), in reality we were proving that we knew the difference between "its" and "it's."

Mr. Farenbach may not have been the most inspirational teacher I've ever had, but through him I did learn that the impact grown-ups have on our lives can be everlasting. Even today I can dissect the different parts of a sentence in a heartbeat. And crossword puzzle clues about mythology? Just try and stop me.

For Real?

Spanking a student, washing their mouth out with soap, forcing him or her to stand for long periods of time, all of these equal what's known as **"corporal punishment."** Today, 28 states have **outlawed** any type of corporal punishment in schools.

English Teaching Wonder

Mrs. Seley, my seventh-grade English teacher, was the loudest, most obnoxious, put-you-on-the-spot teacher I had ever met. She was crazy, goofy, dramatic, quiet, serious and outrageous, all in the first five minutes of class. No wonder I liked her.

To be honest, I wasn't sure about her at first. She seemed pretty tough, and I didn't do well with particularly tough teachers. And even though I had been a star student in English in elementary school, my grades in her class fell. I went from low As to Bs, then from low Bs down to Cs.

For Real?

The National Teacher of the Year Program, which has been around since 1952, **honors** one person every year as the best teacher in the public school system.

But that wasn't the only class I was having trouble in. Due to personal problems at home and a demanding school schedule, I was becoming more and more stressed out. My grades were suffering. I wasn't sleeping well. I was talking back to my family and becoming so irritable that I was spending less time with my friends. Straight As turned into Cs, Ds and dreaded Fs. ("F" I found out, doesn't stand for "Fantastic.") In fact, the only class I was able to keep an A in was science, which for me was nothing more than a daily nap.

HOW ABOUT YOU?

How many books do you **read** each year?

One day near the end of the semester, Mrs. Seley pulled me

Seen It?

In *Mr. Holland's Opus* (1995), Richard Dreyfuss plays a music teacher who shares his passion with the students in his band.

aside. She explained to me that I needed to get my butt into gear, and that she wasn't afraid of failing me, regardless of how smart I was. She reminded me that the personal goal I had set to read eight books during the semester was a long way from being met. I had read only two. Either I needed to have a serious cram session or Mrs. Seley would see me again next year. She certainly wasn't subtle about it.

When Mrs. Seley had finished explaining that I might need to start making friends with sixth-graders, she asked me a question that I hadn't expected. She wanted to know if what I had written in a previous assignment was true. Two months earlier we had been asked to write about a meaningful time in our lives. Most people wrote about their vacations to Hawaii or the Bahamas or France, but I interpreted the word "meaningful" differently than everyone else. So I didn't write about a vacation. I wrote a story about the problems that were happening in my life right then. When I write, I write from the heart. Nobody wants to hear about some heartfelt trip to Canada.

Tears came when I thought about all the awful things I had written, and then confirmed to her that they were indeed true. Not out of pity, but out of understanding, she decided to help me with my grades. She cut my reading from eight books to four so I had enough time to finish them before grading time came.

Read It?

The best-seller *Tuesdays with Morrie* (1997), by Mitch Albom, tells the story of an unconventional and inspirational student/teacher relationship.

I realized then that Mrs. Seley understood what it was like to be a teenager like no other teacher I had ever met. She didn't help me because she felt sorry for me. She did it because she remembered things that happened in her own life. And she wanted to give me a chance.

That chance made all the difference to me. I had to admit that I couldn't rely on myself to do everything that needed to be done. Sometimes I needed help, and with just a little bit of it, I could pick myself back up and start over again. The stress of that time in my life may have long-term effects on my body (I developed lactose intolerance and irritable bowel syndrome, or IBS, and I am still recovering from my "breakdown"), but the long-term effects on my mind were worth it. I learned more than just nouns and verbs in English that year. I learned that I wasn't alone in the world.

Nicole Poppino, Age 14

HOW MUCH DO YOU KNOW . . . About Teachers?

Sure, you see them every day, but just how much do you know about those people who are planted at the front of the class?

T F 1. Teachers must have a master's degree in the subject they are teaching.

T F 2. The average salary for a public school teacher in the United States is $44,000 a year.

T F 3. To teach in a high school, one must be at least 25 years of age.

T F 4. Over one-third of new teachers have recently made a shift from a different career.

T F 5. Once they become teachers, most people stick with the career for life.

How'd you do?

1. **FALSE**. Master's degrees aren't required, although 75% of public school teachers have them.
2. **TRUE**.
3. **FALSE**. There are no age requirements for teachers.
4. **TRUE**. Many teachers become teachers after deciding their initial career path wasn't for them.
5. **FALSE**. More than 20% of teachers leave the profession within the first three years.

WHEN I WAS IN HIGH SCHOOL, track and field was my thing. The hurdles, to be exact. I was a decent 100-meter and 300-meter hurdler, but I wanted to be even better, and so I spent countless hours after school, even off-season, working out and doing everything I could to be in better shape by the time spring track rolled around.

It was because of track and field that I saw one of my teachers, Mr. Bankert, in a completely different light. By day, he was kind of a fuddy-dud teacher with an odd sense of humor and an all-business attitude. He never

HOW ABOUT YOU?

Do you have a teacher who doubles as a **coach** or **club advisor?** How has it changed your relationship with him or her?

thought my jokes in class were very funny, or at least he didn't let on if he did. When I found out Mr. Bankert was an assistant track and field coach for the boys' team, I was surprised to see him taking such an interest in the students. And then one day he took an interest in me.

Seen It?

The Rookie (2002) stars Dennis Quaid as a high school baseball coach who is supported by his team to try out for the major leagues if he coaches their team to victory at districts.

It was winter of my sophomore year, and I was working out in the abandoned hallways after school when Mr. Bankert walked out of his classroom to head toward the exit. He noticed me doing strides up and down the length of the hallway and came over and started giving me tips. Good ones, too. Then he went back to his classroom and came back with a book on track and field technique, giving me drills to help improve my hurdling technique. I was floored. This teacher, who I'd assumed didn't even like me very much, was going out of his way to give me pointers.

And it didn't end there. Over the next few months, Mr. Bankert spent about an hour after school a couple of days a week working on hurdle drills with me. I never asked him too—he just saw a need and made himself available.

For Real?

Cheerleaders should be taken seriously, both as athletes and as students. In fact, **83%** of cheerleaders have a **B average** or higher, while **62%** of them are also on another sports team.

Spring track came and went, and that year I set personal records in both of my events and regularly finished in the top five in the county. I know that my success that spring in part had to do with Mr. Bankert's extracurricular efforts, but the impact his actions had on my life have lasted season after season.

Inside Out

Trying to ignore the butterflies inside my stomach, I reached for my toes and counted to ten. In every direction, girls were perfecting their jumps, mouthing the cheer or hitting their motions. Miss Neuhaus thought I belonged here, but that didn't keep me from feeling like I had stepped too far out of my comfort zone. The thought of jumping up and down yelling "Go, team, go!" didn't exactly appeal to me. As an active member of various organizations throughout the school, I worried that trying out for cheerleading would affect my image as a respected student, plus I wasn't sure that I possessed the coordination or ability to fit the mold of a cheerleader.

> **Address Book**
>
> **Verb** (www.verbnow.com) is an excellent site for fitness and sports info. You can even find a place to play your sport near you through a zip code search.

But Miss Neuhaus wouldn't take "no" for an answer. She recognized my potential and at the same time allowed me to see it, too. She hounded me for weeks to try out for the squad. At first I thought she was kidding. But when she wouldn't let up, I knew that at least I had to try. So I found myself in the gym facing the crowd. I hesitantly lined up behind the other girls, visualizing standing in front of the judges and praying that I wouldn't make a fool of myself.

> **For Real?**
>
> According to *The Wall Street Journal*, **cheerleading** is the most popular girls' sport in the country. But did you know that the first cheerleaders more than 100 years ago were men?

Read It?

We've Got Spirit: The Life and Times of America's Greatest Cheerleading Team is a great book about all the hard work these athletes put in to be the best.

Spiriting into the gym, I smiled so hard that I could feel the grin freezing on my face. I stepped up when my name was called, did my two jumps, and performed the required cheer and chant as close to perfect as I could, carefully remembering each motion. I left the gym both relieved and satisfied, knowing I had done my best. Even though I felt I had done well, it still came as quite a shock when my name was announced to be a cheerleader for the following year. By that time, I was looking forward to next year, knowing that Miss Neuhaus would be my constant source of support and confidence.

Miss Neuhaus knew me from the inside out. She understood me not as I appeared to everyone else. Instead, she saw straight through me. When we talked, it was as though she could read my mind or explain the feelings brewing inside me that I couldn't verbalize myself. My dreams became her dreams, and she never stopped encouraging me. Cheerleading was just one of the many possibilities Miss Neuhaus inspired me to consider. She helped me to see past my doubts toward the bigger picture, set goals and aim for higher aspirations. She gave me room to grow and the opportunity to learn from my mistakes.

Seen It?

Bring It On (2000), starring Kirsten Dunst, shows the competition between cheerleading squads as being fierce and impressive.

Breaking down the walls of my comfort zone was a slow process, but it was worth it, as it helped me gain a new perspective and open up to new things. The demands of cheerleading were not any different from many other aspects of my life. Taking risks was no longer out of the question. By the end of my eighth-grade year, the uneasiness was gone and I didn't feel so out of place. I realized that cheerleaders were not ditzy prima donnas, but hardworking performers who strived to combine the art of athletics, dance and gymnastics with superb grace.

I became secure in my new role. My fellow classmates expected me to be a model of enthusiasm and optimism, and over time these traits became a natural part of my character. Although separating myself from the stereotypes of cheerleading and dealing with the perceptions I once had was no easy task, I developed a love for cheerleading that took me a step further. The next year, as I prepared to leave middle school, I decided that I wanted to try out for the high school squad.

CONSIDER THIS . . .

For some reason, **cheerleaders** often get a **bad rap** and aren't taken seriously as students or as athletes. But these negative stereotypes didn't seem to hurt some of these famous people. Check out this list of former cheerleaders!

- President George W. Bush
- Mandy Moore
- Paula Abdul
- Samuel L. Jackson
- Katie Couric
- Madonna

Smoothing my hand over my carefully pulled-back ponytail, I took one last glance at the end of the hall where Miss Neuhaus stood, reminding me to smile and point my toes. It was then that I realized her faith in me had been the foundation for much of my success. I slipped through the doors and entered the gym, trying not to be intimidated by the large number of girls there. I went into the tryouts just as I had the year before, perhaps with even greater confidence than I expected.

With the news of making junior varsity, I ran across the gym and threw myself into Miss Neuhaus's warm embrace. While my arms stayed tightly wrapped around her, Miss Neuhaus expressed how proud of me she was, and I felt like I could do anything. As I embark on my high school years, I am thankful for the careful guidance Miss Neuhaus provided for me. I continue to approach life, its obstacles, new experiences and challenges, with all I have because I realize that when you think you can't, there is always someone who believes you can.

Maryanne Lee, Age 14

CONSIDER THIS . . .

Teachers even impact Hollywood! Actor James Earl Jones couldn't have created the memorable voice of Darth Vader if a high school teacher hadn't drawn him out of his shell when he was a boy.

OUTSIDE THE BOX

Are you trying out for a sport this year? Try some of these methods for keeping your cool when it's time to shine.

- Listen to tunes that put you in a positive mood before your tryouts.
- Visualize yourself performing the routine, lay-up, pitch, sprint, whatever, perfectly.
- Take five deep breaths before you begin.
- Wear something that makes you feel comfortable and confident.

FOR MUCH OF MY LIFE AS A TEENAGER, I was constantly following in my sister's footsteps. So when I went to the same college as she did, no one was surprised that I decided to major in film, just like her. Yet when I went to speak with the head of the film department, he spent the next hour telling me why I shouldn't bother to major in film. He told me that careers in the film industry were way too competitive, and while it might be a fun major, I shouldn't expect to ever make a living doing anything even related to film. I think his exact words were something like this, "You'll probably end up as a housewife with a film degree, and that will be nice and all, but you won't be working in the industry."

I left his office in tears, *and* I changed my major, both because I was so disheartened by what he said and I didn't want to have to look at his face for the next four years. I don't regret changing my major back then, but I do regret letting someone, someone who didn't even *know* me or what I was capable of doing, influence not only my decisions but also how I felt about myself and my abilities. It took me many years to realize that this person didn't know what he was talking about, and his comments had nothing to do with me, but more to do with his insecurities. Luckily, the author of this next piece, "Write for Life," didn't take years to learn this lesson. And by letting the words sink in, I hope you'll learn it, too.

HOW ABOUT YOU?

Do you think it's okay for a teacher or guidance counselor to **discourage you** from pursuing your dream as a method of "weeding people out" who aren't really dedicated?

Write for Life

When I was younger, I always wanted to be a writer. There was something special in the fact that as a writer, I would be able to influence people, be able to get my voice out there, let the world know my thoughts, opinions and dreams. It was beautiful, the way I could start with a blank sheet of paper and just pour out my heart and soul and end up with this piece of me right there on paper for the world to see, maybe to understand me a little better.

I wrote about everything and everyone. I had journals that contained my life story. Throughout these books my soul was bared: my hurts, the frustrations and betrayals I had felt. Every ounce of pain and longing, every feeling of love and loss, was right there in black and white for me to look back on and relive for the rest of my life. I wasn't afraid of the future; there was no reason to be scared of where I was going because I knew exactly where I came from. I had it all right there in front of me, every little detail of who I was. If I read between the lines, I was sure that it would show me who I would become.

Then, when I became a freshman, I had to talk with the school

Read It?

Have you seen *Teen Ink* magazine on the newsstand? *Teen Ink* is a magazine and Web site that is **written by teens, for teens.** There are no staff writers; all of the writing comes directly from teenagers! Check it out at *www.teenink.com.*

For Real?

84% of all high schools offer print journalism courses, while **32%** teach television journalism.

counselor about my future dreams. I told her I wanted to be in the (very elite) journalism class, and she told me that for them to accept me, I had to have all sorts of qualifications and references. Being a freshman, the teachers didn't know me very well and so they couldn't help me, and my junior high didn't have a newspaper, so I didn't have any references from there.

When I told my counselor that I didn't know of anyone I could use on the application, she gave me some advice, albeit not very good advice. She told me that one out of every hundred people who want to be writers actually succeed, so I would be better off finding a new dream. She said she didn't know whether I had what it takes to be a writer, since it was such a competitive field. As I sat and listened to her, I swore I wouldn't let what she was saying bother me. After all, I needed to get used to criticism if I was going to get anywhere.

CONSIDER THIS . . .

Do you keep a **journal** or **diary?** If not, you might want to consider starting now. Keeping a journal can have many great benefits, including:

- providing a place to write about dreams and ideas
- relieving stress by giving you an outlet for frustrations and problem solving
- helping you see things you've accomplished over time
- letting you get more in tune with your feelings

When I got home from school that day I replayed our conversation in my head, and when I was alone it was a lot easier to believe the things she had said. I went over every little detail of our meeting again and again, and the only conclusion I could come up with was that she was right. Here I was, this inexperienced freshman with such big dreams, and she had been a guidance counselor for over ten years. She had to know more than me, right? That's when I did the unthinkable. I brought out the box of my journals, read through them one last time, and tore them all up. I know I wasn't thinking clearly or I would've realized that it wasn't such a good idea. I would've known that someday I would want to look back at my childish self and reflect on some of those moments. At the time, though, I was so blinded by anger and hurt that I lashed out at what meant the most to me—my writing.

If it had only been better. If I had only been better, I would've gotten into that class. I'm just not good enough.

That line repeated in my head all afternoon long as I tore through every journal in the box. I cried, mentally beating myself up for being so dumb, for not having what it took. Later on, I would be beating myself up for ever caring what one person thought of me.

> **Address Book**
>
> For more information on **journalism** for students, check out *www.highschooljournalism.org*. Here you'll find quizzes, resources, scholarship info and much more.

Junior year of high school I went to a new school where I could finally get into the journalism class, and I started writing with a new zest. It no longer mattered to me whether anyone thought my writing was good or bad—I was in control and that's how I liked it. I remembered why I had started writing in the first place: to give *my* opinion to the world, not someone else's opinion of me. It felt good to get back into the swing of writing, the hectic deadlines, the busy classroom, and finally seeing my name on the byline of all sorts of articles. I was home.

It's been two years since my resolve to become a writer was renewed. I don't know whether I will be the most famous of authors, but in my own little circle, I am loved. I have people hooked on an insatiable writer with a quirky sense of humor and a tad too much sarcasm for her own good. But to me, the few fans I have are good enough for me. They know and love my writing style and have gotten to know me through it, just like I dreamed when I was little.

Tracy Tanner, Age 18

Spotlight On . . . WRITING AS A CAREER

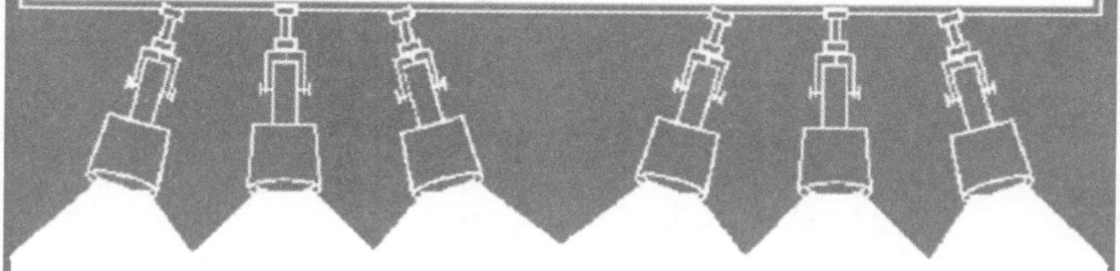

Writing as a career can be competitive, but no more so than most creative professions. According to the statistics there are more than 319,000 writers making a living in the United States today, and more than one-third of these writers are self-employed. Writing as a career can entail anything from editing to being an author to being a technical writer. The fact is, most companies have a need for people with good writing skills. Here are just a few of the kinds of companies that need good writers:

- publishing houses
- magazines
- newspapers and TV news stations
- financial institutions
- nonprofit organizations
- Internet and technology firms

For more information on writing as a profession, check out the U.S. Department of Labor's Web site on the topic: *www.bls.gov/oco/ocos089.htm*.

OUTSIDE THE BOX

Do you have a journal, but sometimes get stuck trying to figure out what to write? Here are some prompts to get you going. Just pick one of these phrases, copy it in your journal, and start writing!

- What is something that really bugs me? Why?
- What is the most bizarre dream I've ever had? What do I think it meant?
- If my pet could talk, what would I want to talk with him or her about?
- If I could change one thing about myself, what would it be and why?
- What trait do I have that others admire the most and why?

THERE'S NOT MUCH WORSE THAN BEING TOLD you can't do something you really enjoy doing. Yet much of our lives are spent experiencing just that. When we're younger, we're told we're too small to ride the big roller coasters or too young to see a really popular movie. When we're teenagers, we can't always sleep in until noon or borrow our parent's car or stay out with our friends until the wee hours of the morning.

But what about those things we're told we can't do just because of who we are? Because we're too short or tall, too skinny or fat, too dumb or smart? This is a feeling many girls are all too familiar with, the thought that girls shouldn't or can't do certain things as well as boys, whether it's debating, solving math problems or playing certain sports.

CONSIDER THIS . . .

What we **tell** ourselves **inside** of our head has a lot to do with **how we feel.** If the message our brain is constantly getting is that we're no good at something, then chances are we won't be. By changing the thought and reminding ourselves of our strengths, the results can be positively **overwhelming!**

I know that when I've been faced with that attitude, I took it on as a challenge. *Oh yeah? You don't think I can do that? Well, just watch me!,* especially when it's an adult doing some of the doubting like in this next essay, "Girl Power." Sometimes I succeeded; sometimes I fell flat on my face. But no matter what the result, I always felt better for having tried.

Girl Power

As Olympus was heaven to the gods, this was heaven to me: the orange court with its three-point line, free-throw line and boundaries. This was where I wanted to be—the basketball court. It was my life, my destiny, my future.

The noisy gym held a bunch of students talking, rapping, eating or just staring into space. Our gym teacher stepped in front of us. "If you want to play basketball, get on the court," he blurted.

As usual, most of the prissy girls were scared that their makeup would smudge or their hair would get ruined, so they went to sit in the bleachers and flirt with the boys. But I jumped right onto the basketball court. Unfortunately, I was the only girl. *Man, should I sit down? Or should I show my moves to these boys? But what if the boys are WAY better than me? I would look like a high school basketball player going up against Kobe Bryant. Oh well, I'll look like a chicken if I sit down now.* With these things in mind, I took my spot on the court.

HOW ABOUT YOU?

What response do little kids have when they're told the word **"no"**? That's right, they usually throw a tantrum. As teenagers, being told **"no"** brings out another reaction: **defiance.** How do you feel when someone tells you "no"?

The game was about to begin. All the teams had been selected, and I was one of the first picks on the blue team. I was thrilled! Then I heard a group of girls snicker, and one said, "The only reason you got picked is because you're the only girl and they felt sorry for you."

That can't be the reason. They chose me to play against the best boys . . . or did they just want to embarrass me?

Resolutely, I strolled to my position when a boy in the bleachers yelled, "Girl, get off that court. Basketball isn't your game." His words ground into me like I was a piece of dust on the gym floor.

The coach blew his whistle, and the game began. *Here I go,* I thought. *I should show these boys my skills and make them EAT my dust.*

I tried blocking passes, but the guys just shot over my diminutive body and swooshed the ball in. I tried to guard them, but they pulled some tricky moves and I felt stupid as I spun around looking for the ball. One boy crossed over me, bounced the ball between my legs and shot a three-pointer. Then another did a fake pump, acting like he was going to shoot the ball, and when I jumped up to block it, he dribbled around me and slam-dunked it. Yet another boy held the ball in the palm of his hand and kept fake passing it to other players. You name it, they did it.

CONSIDER THIS . . .

Have you heard of **Title IX?** This legislation was passed in 1972 to give girls an equal opportunity to participate in **sports.** And, boy, has it had an impact on the state of sports today! Before Title IX, only 1 in every 27 high school girls participated in sports; today, 1 in every 2.5 do.

Finally, I stole the ball. I was shocked to see the orange sphere in my hands. I was so excited that I didn't even move until everybody shouted, "Run! Run!" The ball was mine. It was my chance to shine, my opportunity to make the people who doubted me look dumb. I knew that witnessing my skills would silence the teasing, but I had to do this right.

I ran across that basketball court like a tornado destroying a city, and *BAM,* I tripped. I couldn't believe it. How had it happened? I couldn't even hear myself think because there was so much laughter coming from the bleachers. It was then that I realized that my Nikes were untied. *Oh my goodness,* I thought. Here I was trying to make myself shine, but I made a fool of myself instead. The same boy from the bleachers chuckled, "Ha, you silly girl! Now you know you can't play, so get off the court."

Consider This . . .

Most schools **allow** girls to compete on a boys' sports team if that sport isn't offered for girls. For example, if your school doesn't offer female wrestling, the boys' team might allow girls to participate, too. How do you feel about boys and girls **competing against each** other in sports?

Had the team lost? I wasn't even paying attention because I was so busy trying to hide from the crowd. I looked down to see the basketball court beneath my feet. Oops! I was still on the waxy court, and the other team had already started to shoot. So I tied my shoelaces and hopped off to the side. I planted my bottom on the first row of the bleachers, even though I wanted to crawl under them so that no one could see me. The prissy girls, obnoxious boy and even the coaches were smirking and laughing at me. How was I going to get through this humiliation?

Seen It?

Love & Basketball (2000) tells the story of Monica and Quincy and how **basketball** impacts their lives.

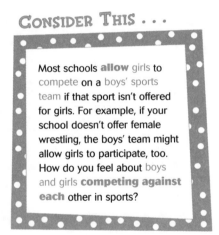

An hour later, the laughter had slowed down, but I knew that it was still in their memories. If I didn't do anything, by the end of the day the whole school would know about my little incident. No one would know what really happened because people were bound to exaggerate the story to make it funnier. I knew I had to do something to prove I was competent.

"Coach, can you put me in the next round?" I asked.

"You want to go in the game? Come on, Araz," he said.

"I want to play," I countered.

"You'll hurt yourself. Just let the boys finish off what they started."

"No, I want to do this." I stood firm.

"Alright, then. It's your decision, but don't come whining to me if you get hurt," he mumbled.

HOW ABOUT YOU?

What is the most **embarrassing** thing you ever did in your phys ed class?

So I went back in. This time I played for the red team. The spectators' eyes rested on me. I felt the pressure to show them everything I could do. The game started with a tip-off. I got the ball, dribbled it down the court, crossed a boy over, and made a layup. "Ohh," the crowd cheered. I did the same thing when I got the ball again, except this time I did a reverse lay-up. Again I heard the crowd roar. I felt like I was in control of a ball of fire. This was the attention I craved. I wanted people to notice me for my talents, not my mistakes. I was doing all different types of

For Real?

The Women's National Basketball Association **(WNBA)** has only been around since 1996!

moves on these boys. You name it and I did it. The roles had switched. Maybe Michael Jordan had entered my body. By the end of the game, I had beaten just about every boy on that court, and people were coming up to me and complimenting me on my playing.

CONSIDER THIS . . .

Even the **pros** trip and fall. Where do you think all the material for those **sports blooper** specials comes from?

I had done it. I had done what had seemed like the impossible. Even though I felt like hiding in the bathroom and never getting on the basketball court again, I dusted myself off and tried again. Something told me to get back on that court and prove everybody wrong. Just like the basketball, people tried to knock me down, but I bounced right back up.

The best part of that day was when a certain boy, that same one who had made fun of me, came up to me and said, "Nice game! You played great. Most girls would've given up as soon as I teased them. You got back on that court and played like Jordan. It sure is hard to break you down. Next time, I want to play you one-on-one." That put a smug smile on my face for the rest of the day. I felt like a true achiever.

Araz Garakanian, Age 14

Take the Quiz:
ARE YOUR PARENTS IN TUNE WITH YOU?

1. When you and three other students turn in an essay test with the same exact answers, all four of you are accused of cheating. You're in shock because you've never cheated in your life. You later find out that the other three students managed to copy your work. The school has already called your parents. What do your parents do?

___ A. Go to you immediately and take your word for what happened, promising to stand behind you as you straighten things out at school.

___ B. Believe what the school says until you manage to convince them that you didn't cheat, although you can still sense they have some doubts.

___ C. Call you down for a family meeting and proceed to make the same accusations the school made, assuming you're in the wrong.

2. Your curfew is set for eleven o'clock on the weekends, but you break it on Saturday night because the party you were at was just getting started. When you do get home at one in the morning, you lie to your parents, telling them that your ride's car broke down. How do they react?

___ A. Your parents can sense that you're lying and encourage you to tell the truth.

___ B. They have a feeling that you're lying about your reason for being late, but want to be "cool parents" so they shrug it off and tell you not to do it again.

___ C. They take your word for it; the thought that you might lie to them never crossed their mind. Plus, they're too tired to deal anyway.

3. You got a ride home from school with a friend who smokes, and when you walk in the front door of your house, your mom takes one whiff and realizes you smell like an ashtray. You've never smoked a cigarette in your life and think the habit is pretty disgusting, and you tell your mom so. What does she do?

___ A. Agrees with you about smoking being a nasty habit and knows you're telling the truth.

___ B. Finds it hard to believe that this much smell can come from just being in the same car as a smoker, but decides to give you the benefit of the doubt, *this* time.

___ C. She doesn't believe you, and tells you so. Since she tried smoking when she was your age, she just assumes it's something all kids do.

4. A big study comes out in a magazine that says that one-quarter of all high school students have had sex. When your parents bring it up in conversation at the dinner table, you tell them the truth—that you are committed to waiting to have sex until you're married. How do they respond?

___ A. They know that you take things like this seriously and are proud of the choice you've made. They know that if the situation ever changed, you'd feel comfortable enough to speak with them about it.

___ B. Your mom and dad would like to believe you, but are concerned that the temptations as a teen are difficult and you might not stick to your plan.

___ C. Your parents would rather be safe than sorry, so they insist on having the "birth control" talk with you, whether you say you need it or not.

5. Your older brother is an amazing athlete and rules the field in soccer and baseball. You've never been much into sports but aren't sure how to tell your parents that you don't want to follow in your brother's footsteps—the thing that really lights your

fire is music and band. What do your parents do when it's time for soccer tryouts?

___ A. Sensing that you have other interests, your parents don't assume you want to join soccer with your brother. Instead, they ask you what kinds of things you'd like to explore.

___ B. Are surprised to find out that you don't want to play soccer, but are willing to help you find out what you'd like to pursue instead.

___ C. Your dad pushes you to get involved in soccer. After all, good playing skills are obviously in your genes! He feels strongly that in time you'll grow to love the sport.

How'd you do? Give yourself 10 points for every A, 20 points for every B and 30 points for every C. Look below to find out how in tune your parents are with you:

50–70 points = Your family knows how to communicate, and that has paid off big time. Not only do you feel comfortable opening up to your parents, their trust in you is a given.

80–120 points = Your parents have always felt in tune with you, but as you've become a teenager, they find themselves filled with more and more doubt. They're concerned with making a mistake, but want to trust you at the same time. Take the initiative and open up to them. It will be well worth it.

130–150 points = Let's face it: Your parents are pretty clueless when it comes to knowing who you are. But I bet they'd be interested in finding out more if you were willing to share with them. Start slowly . . . but start.

CHAPTER 5

TOUGH STUFF

More than any other chapter, "Tough Stuff" was, well, *tough* to put together. We received so many submissions from teens that fell into this category that it became clear that life for teens in school is more challenging today than ever before. Many of the stories and poems we received dealt with the kinds of subjects that people just don't seem to talk about, but are such a big part of teenage life, like drinking, cutting and depression. These are difficult issues for anyone to deal with, let alone teens who are already emotionally maxed out with the stresses of surviving school and dealing with surging hormones. We think it's about time these tough issues get talked about.

APRIL 20, 1999, was a day that will forever be marked as one of the saddest days in American high school history. On that fateful Tuesday, the town of Littleton, Colorado, was forever changed by the Columbine shootings.

For Real?

Even though more than **35%** of teenagers say they feel **unsafe** in school, it is actually the **safest place** to be.

Do you remember where you were when you first heard the news that two teenage boys had gone on a shooting spree in their suburban school, killing twelve students and teachers before turning the guns on themselves? I remember feeling that what those two teens did seemed so unimaginable, so horrific.

THE WORD

School violence doesn't just mean guns and knives. Everything from **bullying** to **fist fights** to **verbal threats** and **extreme teasing** fits under the definition of school violence.

Eric Harris and Dylan Klebold, the two boys behind the Columbine shootings, were outcasts, according to other students at their school. Most people figured they had planned their violent attack because they felt angry about being isolated by the students at school, where they were frequently targeted by bullies. When you consider this, it might seem like tons of kids could be ticking time bombs. How many kids are victims of bullying at your school? How many kids are treated like outcasts by the rest of the student body?

For Real?

Many teens feel **drugs** are a bigger problem at their school than violence.

For Real?

In October 2004, two teenagers in Texas were arrested for planning to recreate the Columbine shootings at their school.

The day the news about Columbine came out, a sense of helplessness spread across the rest of the country. The big question became, *Could anything have been done to prevent this tragedy?* There's no way of knowing whether something or somebody could have changed Eric's and Dylan's minds. But it's never too late to prevent it from happening again somewhere else.

For Real?

17% of all teenagers think that **school violence** is a very serious problem at their school, while more than half of African-American students say it's the most **serious problem** they face.

Spotlight On . . . SCHOOL VIOLENCE

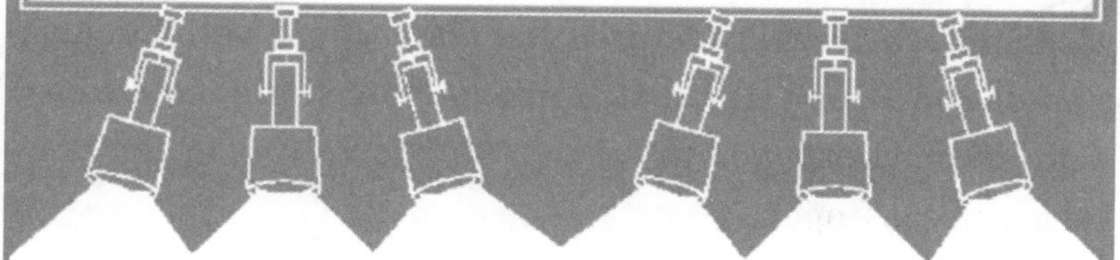

Why do teenagers get violent? No one knows exactly what pushes some teens to act out with violence, but researchers often tie it to low self-worth, feeling the need to gain attention and being the victim of abuse as a child. While most of the time gossip or rumors should be avoided at all costs, if the rumors involve someone talking about threats or wanting to harm someone at your school, it's time to speak up. You don't have to feel helpless about school violence. If you want to play a role in preventing it, here are some things you can do:

- Start with yourself and don't give in to violence or carry a weapon.
- Report any suspicious activity or violent behavior to an adult.
- Mentor a younger student and be a good influence on them.
- Set up or join a Student Crime Watch.

Dangerous Depression

"Blah, blah, blah, blah, blah . . ." was all I heard while my Spanish teacher lectured the class about verb conjugation or something like that. Someone raised his hand to ask a question. I struggled to keep my eyes open. *You need to listen to this,* I thought to myself. Our teacher went off topic, *again,* and started telling us a really interesting story that had nothing to do with learning Spanish. I looked at the clock. There were still thirty minutes of class

HOW ABOUT YOU?

To combat the issue of **weapons** on school grounds, a lot of schools use things like metal detectors and security guards. Do you believe they should have these things at your school?

left. But a minute later, the bell rang. It couldn't possibly be the dismissal bell.

Is there an earthquake or fire drill today? I thought to myself. Usually the teachers forewarned students about drills, but this bell rang longer than it should have. There could only be one reason that a bell like that would ring: a lockdown drill.

For Real?

7% of teenagers report they had brought a weapon with them **to school** at least **once**.

THE WORD

A lockdown means **"no one in, no one out."** In the case of a school lockdown, the doors to the building are locked and no students or teachers are permitted to leave, nor is anyone other than law enforcement authorities permitted to enter until the lockdown is over.

After locking the classroom door, our teacher immediately called the office to ask them what was going on. They didn't know, but they did say that the bell was not for a lockdown *drill* but for an actual *lockdown!* Everyone in the class got scared. The students began to talk among themselves, including me. One girl, Joyce, had to go to bathroom really bad, but no one was allowed to leave class. An armed gunman could be walking the halls for all we knew. Before I knew it the dismissal bell rang, but we couldn't go to break because no one could leave class. Joyce just couldn't hold it anymore. So our teacher asked for an administrator to escort one of her students to the restroom—it was an emergency. It wasn't too long

Seen It?

The movie *Pay It Forward* (2000), starring Haley Joel Osment, puts the spotlight on violence in schools.

after Joyce came back that a girl in my class got a cell phone call from her friend, and we found out what was going on.

In room 309, another classroom just two halls away, a boy stood up with a loaded gun, pointed it at the teacher, and started talking about how horrible his life was and how stupid his family was. While he was speaking one of the teacher aides snuck out of the classroom with about five students and ran to the office. It was then that the lockdown bell rang. The boy with the gun waved it around while the teacher and his friend tried to calm him down. The boy pointed the gun at a student named Greg. His friend saw this and, although terrified, jumped on the boy. Greg, seeing that the boy was distracted, immediately grabbed the gun. An administrator came in, and soon after the police arrested the boy.

I called my parents and left school early that day, along with half of the school.

HOW ABOUT YOU?

What would you do if you **heard** someone was going to **bring a gun** to school?

CONSIDER THIS . . .

Did you know that your chances of being struck by lightning are much **greater than** your chances of being killed by school violence?

Address Book

- **Report It** (*www.report-it.com*) is an anonymous **24-hour tip line** for students to report violence or threat of violence at their school.
- **Safe Youth** (*www.safeyouth.org*) has tons of online resources for info on violence in school, along with a toll-free hotline: **1-866-SAFEYOUTH**.

The students from room 309 went to counseling for the next few weeks, which brought them behind in their classes.

The boy with the gun is now in jail; he will never participate in a graduation ceremony. However bad his life was, it cannot be worse than it is now. I wish he knew there are other ways to cope with trauma than by using a weapon on yourself or others. Help is always there.

Rosie Ojeda,
Age 18

WHERE DO YOU STAND?

Many teens suffer from depression, but the illness is clouded with misconceptions. To find out how much you know about depression, take this true/false quiz.

1. Everyone suffers from depression at some time in their lives.

__ T __ F

2. People who are genuinely depressed don't often talk to their friends about their feelings.

__ T __ F

3. The majority of people who attempt suicide do it just to get attention.

__ T __ F

4. People who are wealthy and smart rarely get depressed.

__ T __ F

5. Sufferers of anorexia nervosa may eventually become depressed.

__ T __ F

1. **False.** Studies show that fewer than 20% of people experience serious depression at any point in their lives.
2. **True.** Many people feel uncomfortable opening up to friends and family about their feelings, which leads to further depression.
3. **False.** While many suicide attempts don't succeed the first time, most people who attempt suicide are genuinely hoping to kill themselves.
4. **False.** What they say is true—money can't buy happiness. Victims of depression come from many different economic backgrounds.
5. **True.** Sometimes the effects of anorexia, including loss of sleep, fatigue and excluding oneself from friends and family, can lead to serious depression.

PERHAPS ONE OF THE MOST DIFFICULT THINGS we all face in life is losing someone we care about. The death of a family member or friend can leave a lasting imprint on who we are and challenge us in ways we never thought possible.

But even the death of someone we didn't know all that well can hit us hard, especially when that person is someone we've seen in school for as long as we can remember. That person who we've sat behind in just about every class, if for no other reason than his or her last name came before ours in the alphabet, is part of what makes up our daily experience. And if that person were to suddenly disappear, especially as a result of a deadly accident or a serious disease, his or her absence would be felt deeply.

If you've experienced the loss of a friend or loved one, you know there's no right or wrong way to handle the emotions you feel. Perhaps, like this next author, you'll be inspired to write about your experience, both to help yourself heal and to keep another person's memory alive.

Address Book

All Kids Grieve (*www.allkidsgrieve.org*) is a Web site devoted to **helping kids,** teachers, parents and counselors **cope** with death in the classroom.

Derek

On the first day of sixth grade, all of my classmates and I were sorted into classes. Just like we had hoped, my best friend Hannah and I were in the same class. Lots of other friends were, too, including Derek, a boy I've known for a long time. I knew class would be great now, and *fun*. Derek was the kind of guy who brought excitement into anything and was nice to everyone, regardless of their "status."

For the first few months of school, Derek was, well, *Derek*. He wore his Maple Leaf jersey to school almost every day because that was his favorite NHL team. He spent all of fall and most of winter playing soccer with the other guys, guarding the net even in a big snowstorm. Once, he brought seaweed to school for lunch. Somehow, he convinced me and Hannah to try it. I spit it out right away—it tasted disgusting! But Hannah kept it in her mouth a little longer—until the seaweed turned her tongue blue. Derek, who actually enjoyed the stuff, laughed at our revolted expressions, revealing a bright, blue tongue as well. Derek always had the best lunches, full of stuff like Pringles and Airheads, his favorite foods. He never finished what he brought, so he would throw the candy in the air and whoever caught it could keep it.

For Real?

Statistics show that **90%** of high school juniors and seniors have **lost** a loved one.

Then, a few weeks before school ended for the Christmas holidays, Derek stopped coming to school. I didn't think much of it at the time—I just kept following my busy schedule.

But on the morning of December 19, 2001, my French teacher announced to our class that Derek was very sick and in the hospital. She said he probably wouldn't be back at school until after the holidays.

That night Derek died. I went to sleep not knowing about it.

The next morning, our class was excited because it was the second-to-last day of school before vacation. We planned to do pretty much nothing all day.

Then as we settled down into craft-making, game-playing and chatting mode, our English teacher walked into the class. Her nose was bright red, and I could tell she had been crying. I stopped midfold in an origami Christmas tree. Then the school principal, who was also crying, walked in. She was followed by a bunch of people carrying Kleenex boxes. I later found out they were from the funeral home.

CONSIDER THIS . . .

Steven Spielberg's Starbright Foundation is creating a new program to **help teens** who have life-threatening diseases cope with their feelings of facing the possibility of death.

Our principal moved to the front of the class and we immediately fell silent, wondering what possibly could have happened.

"I have some very bad news about Derek."

Suddenly, I knew. I knew in my heart what happened, but I prayed to God I was wrong.

"Last night, Derek died."

A mourning silence fell on the class. No one moved. For a second, there was complete stillness. Then, suddenly, everyone was crying. The counselors moved around the room, attempting to comfort us and hand us tissues.

One counselor approached me and led me out of the room and into the library. I just sat there, crying for Derek. The counselor hugged me like my mom would have had she been at school. Then Hannah came into the room, and we clung to one another in disbelief.

One by one, a lot of other students entered the library. Some kids wrote or drew pictures on the big sheets of paper laid out on the table, while others ripped up the paper in anger and confusion. I just sat there, sobbing my heart out.

Derek, I miss you. I hope Heaven is just like I believe it is because it will be the perfect place for you.

Around lunchtime, I went home. I didn't want to be at school anymore, so the secretary called my dad, and he came to pick me up. He was sad, too, even though he never knew Derek personally. He knew that to lose someone at such a young age was painful for everyone.

I went to school the next day, but I was still numb with pain. *I don't understand why you had to die, but you probably do. I think you get smarter and wiser when you die.*

Christmas passed by the same as usual. Well, almost the same. I knew that part of me would never be the same.

As the months passed, I continued to miss Derek with all my heart. *He will miss out on so many things. He won't graduate, get a job, marry, raise a family.* It made me feel like I had to live life as much as possible . . . live for him.

For Real?

The top three causes of **death** in teens are:
1) motor vehicle accidents,
2) homicide and
3) suicide.

On December 19, 2002, exactly one year after Derek's death, I went to school as always. And just like the year before, our class was excited and happy that school was almost out for the holidays.

I brought my journal to school and wrote in it, oblivious to all the Christmas cheer. My teacher took me out to the hallway and asked me what was wrong. And that was it. I started to sob.

The next year was much the same. It seems like I'm the only one at school who continues to be so upset every year. Not that other people don't care, but they just don't seem to show their pain in the same way I do. I don't understand why I've reacted so differently. Derek and I weren't that close, but his death has affected me in such a deep way. Though the pain lessens a tiny bit with each passing year, I know that I will never completely forget him. I will never completely heal.

Then, one day, I had an idea.

Derek, I have an idea. I'll write a story. Your story. Maybe that will help me heal.

But this story is different. Unlike all the other stories I write, I have no control over the ending. That part is not up to me. It's up to God.

Karina E. Seto, Age 13

Spotlight On . . . DEALING WITH DEATH

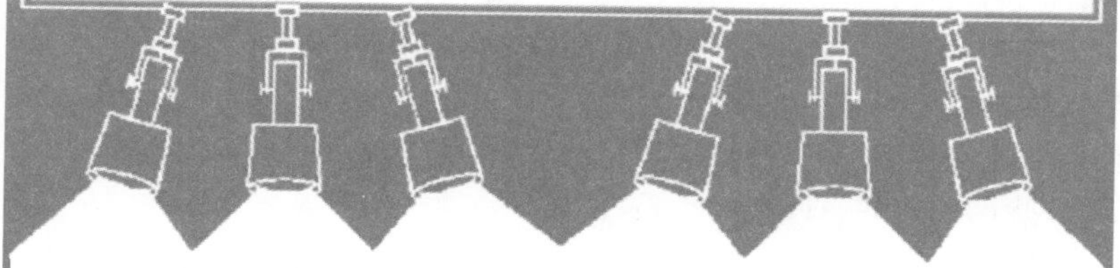

Have you ever experienced the death of a friend or classmate? Here are some ideas for dealing with the emotions that death brings up in all of us:

- **Talk about it.** Keeping your emotions and thoughts bottled up will prevent you from getting over the pain. Talk to friends, siblings, parents, teachers and other supportive people in your life.
- **Get support.** There is power in numbers, and chances are there are others in your circle who are feeling the same way you are. Get together with friends and create a support group where you can be and express yourself.
- **Be patient.** Don't expect the sadness you're feeling to disappear overnight. Painful feelings that go along with losing someone can stick around for a while—give yourself time to recover from the loss.
- **Keep the memory alive.** Make a scrapbook, frame a special picture or write a poem in honor of the one who's passed on. Even if it's painful now, eventually looking at those keepsakes will stir up happy memories.

I DIDN'T FIND OUT THAT MY OLDER SISTER had been slicing or "cutting" herself until after she'd moved out of the house and gone to college. She kind of mentioned it to me one day, real casual like, when referring to a time in her life when she'd been depressed. I didn't make a big deal of what she'd said, partly because I didn't really know what cutting was in the first place and partly because I didn't want to put her on the spot.

I asked her about it again the other day, and she says that back when she was doing it, she didn't know there was even a name for her habit or that anyone else had even thought of cutting themselves, too. She had felt so alone in her world of razor blades. Luckily, the times have changed.

I'm not sure if cutting has become more prominent or if people are just talking about it more now, but it seems as though everywhere you turn there is a story or an article or a storyline with a television character that focuses on cutting. Hopefully, this once "dark secret" will be brought to light. Not only to let cutters know that they're not alone, but also so there will be attention focused on finding solutions for teens who don't know where else to turn.

For Real?

Self-mutilation, like cutting or picking, has been nicknamed the "new age anorexia," in part because it has become so prevalent among teens. In fact, experts say 1 teen girl in every 200 regularly self-mutilates.

Seen It?

In 2004, **"cutting"** garnered national attention, being the focus of special features on *The Today Show* and *The Dr. Phil Show.*

Slice the Way to Happiness

For Real?
Cutting isn't just something girls do. More than 11,000 boys in the United States cut themselves to **relieve** stress and anxiety.

Everybody has problems. Some people aren't athletes. Others aren't Einstein. Some people don't like their parents. Some can't stand their little brother. I mean, growing up these days puts a lot of weight on a thirteen-year-old's shoulders. Parents either want their kids to be mature little adults or want to keep them as their babies forever.

When you were little, did you call a cut a "boo-boo"? Well, in my life, three of my friends have "boo-boos." Many, many boo-boos. Too many to count. You see, they like to make their boo-boos themselves. They slice their way up their arms, down their legs, on their stomachs. Everywhere they can think of, there's a small gash.

It's hard to handle life's pressures, but who would think that cutting yourself would help? My friends would say, "I know where the pain is coming from and I know that I can control how much there is." They think cutting helps their depression. But it just hurts them worse. And they're not the only ones who hurt. I cry every night, knowing what they do. It's not fair to have to worry day in and day out if your friend has any blood left.

Once, I tried it. My friends seemed to be helped by cutting in some way, so I thought that maybe it would help me, too. I never hurt worse in my life. I couldn't handle that feeling.

Consider This . . .

Teens who **self-mutilate** might not be who you expect. They're usually not outcasts or teens who outwardly show depression. Instead, they are your **"everyday" teen.** They get good grades, have good friends, are involved in after-school activities, come from good families. So if they've got all of this going for them, why do they do it? Often times it's a matter of these teens **not** having healthy ways to deal with conflict and so they bottle their emotions up inside. Cutting and other types of self-mutilation give them a way to **release** their **stress.**

In slicing myself, I betrayed them. I did what I had vowed to never do. But worst of all, I betrayed myself. I got a rag and stopped the blood. That's when it came to me. My friends think they know where the pain is coming from, and that slicing dulls the pain inside. Not true. It just makes the pain inside stronger. They're feeding it. But they still think the opposite. They think they're slicing their way to happiness.

Chelsea Oakes, Age 13

I mentioned earlier that I went to a really small school, so it's probably not a big surprise that there wasn't much diversity to speak of. Although I grew up not too far from Philadelphia, my town was a small one, and everyone pretty much looked

Seen It?

In *Save the Last Dance* (2001), Julia Stiles plays a new white student at an all-black school, where she's challenged to overcome being an outsider and racial stereotyping.

For Real?
72% of students feel that division along racial and ethnic lines **isn't** an issue at their school.

the same. To dine out at the only Chinese restaurant around seemed like an exotic experience. My high school was just as white bread as the town; there was only one African-American student there (and he was adopted) and two Korean students (also adopted). Most everyone else came from German stock and had last names like Schmidt and Kauffman.

I didn't experience diversity until I went away to college and then moved to New York City, a city that's about as diverse as one can get. And while I thought I understood the challenges of being stereotyped based on religion or race, I don't think I really "got it" until I was older and started to see how it affected people on the receiving end.

For Real?
New York City is **jam-packed** with people—more than 26,000 per square mile, compared with an average of 400 per square mile in the rest of the state.

In this next essay, "Small Girl Learns a Big Lesson," the author shares a story of unexpected racism at her school, and in the process reminds us that big change comes in small steps.

Small Girl Learns a Big Lesson

Auden, my dear grandmother, passed away in 1992. I was only five years old, too young to remember enough about her. But one important life lesson she taught me remains unforgettable.

CONSIDER THIS . . .

There was a lot of **anti-Semitism,** which is another word for prejudice against Jewish people, in the United States from the 1920s through the 1940s.

When Auden was a high school senior in 1940s Chicago, there was a "must-go-to" party after the prom. My grandmother was invited and was eagerly anticipating the big event. That is, until a few days later when she found out that Jennifer, one of her best friends, hadn't received an invitation. Auden's excitement quickly turned to anger when she discovered the reason for the exclusion.

Jennifer wasn't invited because she was Jewish.

Understand, this wasn't just a big party, it was *the* party of this senior class's high school *lives*.

No matter. My grandmother didn't take this sitting down.

"I didn't want Jennifer, or anyone, to feel left out," Auden said. If Jennifer wasn't welcome, then Auden wouldn't go either. Instead, she invited Jennifer over for their own small party. A two-person party . . . that turned out to be *the* party of the Class of 1940s young lives as more and more classmates decided to do the right thing.

"Injustice," I remember Auden telling me more than once, "is everyone's battle."

I was only a kindergartner, but I listened, I learned and I remembered.

For Real?

Even though there is the same level of **crime** in today's schools as thirty years ago, **suspensions** among students have doubled.

• • •

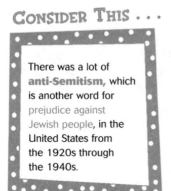

As I have grown up, racism is something I have read about in history textbooks, something that happens to other people, in other times, in other places. Certainly I never thought I would witness something so ugly in my small hometown in Southern California. My middle school was largely white, but with a healthy minority mix of Hispanic, Asian and a few African-American students. I have been brought up to notice skin color only the way I might notice someone's red hair or freckles or dimples. I just see people. Human beings. My classmates. My friends.

Read It?

The novel *Snow in August* (1997), by Pete Hamill, is a powerful story of a young Irish Catholic boy and an older Jewish rabbi living in 1940s Brooklyn.

But one morning I arrived at school to find out my friend Damien had been suspended for getting into a fight with another student. I was shocked. Damien was a kindhearted, gentle person, an honors student, even voted "friendliest" by his eighth-grade classmates. He always smiled and said "hello" when you passed him in the hallways. He was popular with the cool kids and also with the less-cool kids because he was nice to everybody. Damien was the last person I would suspect of being suspended.

THE WORD

Schools everywhere have begun practicing a policy called **zero tolerance**, which means that any student breaking school rules or the law will be immediately suspended or expelled, no questions asked.

Throughout the day, the details of Damien's suspension leaked out. At first I was shocked, then perplexed, then, as I gradually pieced together the whole story, furious.

This is what happened. Damien was waiting for his ride home after school when the school troublemaker, a white kid who had already been suspended numerous times and was just a few missteps away from juvenile hall, sauntered up to him, sneered a racial slur (Damien, I should mention, is African-American) and began to push him around. Damien first tried to walk away, then tried to defend himself. When an administrator finally noticed the scuffle and rushed over to tear them apart, it looked as if both boys had been involved in the fight. Both were suspended immediately. Even when the few witnesses said that Damien was just defending himself, school administrators remained firm. Damien had been involved in a fight with another student, and therefore he was suspended.

For Real?

In 1998, **17%** of students were African-American, so it makes sense that 17% of those suspended would be African-American, too. Instead, more than **30%** of suspended students were African-American.

"Zero tolerance," they said, unaware of the irony. "No ifs, ands or buts about it."

Not only did Damien have to miss school for a few days, as a student who had been suspended he was also barred from any of the remaining school functions: dances, the end-of-the-year field trip to the beach, even the eighth-grade graduation ceremony. To me, this seemed unbearably unfair, especially since Damien had merely been defending himself.

I talked to the principal. She remained steadfast in her stance. I passed around a petition at school and drummed up

WHERE DO YOU STAND?

You might not even be aware that you are doing it, but do you give in to stereotyping? Answer the following "yes" or "no" questions to find out.

___ YES ___ NO At a school dance, you see an African-American student dancing with a crowd around him and figure that he's such a good dancer because he's black.

___ YES ___ NO Your preassigned partner in science is a blonde cheerleader, and you immediately figure that you're going to do all the work because this girl can't be that smart.

___ YES ___ NO The new kid in school dresses in out-of-style vintage clothes, and you guess that her family must not have much money.

___ YES ___ NO Your locker partner is a senior who has lots of tattoos and piercings and hangs out with a rough crowd. You assume he is bad news and avoid making eye contact.

___ YES ___ NO Both of your friends' parents are lawyers and you are surprised to find that they live in a simple house in a not-so-great neighborhood. You assumed they would live in the rich part of town.

If you answered yes to any of these questions, then you've made judgments based on stereotypes.

support from more than 400 students, nearly the entire eighth-grade class. The administration remained stubbornly firm behind the suspension.

On the day of graduation, Damien sat in the audience instead of onstage with the other graduates. As class president, I was allowed to give a speech at the ceremony. I stood at the podium, tears welling up in my eyes at the sight of

HOW ABOUT YOU?

Expulsions in schools have skyrocketed in the past ten years, but many object to **expelling** students for nonviolent offenses. They argue that expelling more students only increases the number of adults without high school diplomas, which isn't good for anybody. Where do you stand?

Damien sitting amid the crowd of parents instead of onstage with his classmates and friends.

I cleared my throat.

"When I was very young," I began, "an incredibly wise lady, my grandmother Auden, taught me a valuable lesson. 'Injustice is everyone's battle,' she used to say. And I say that it is an injustice that Damien is not up here onstage with us today . . ."

I wish I could tell you that our principal was affected by the ovation Damien received and invited him up with us. But she didn't. This battle against injustice was lost.

Or maybe not. The smile on Damien's face told me he didn't feel completely left out.

It is now four years later. When I see Damien in the high school halls, he still sometimes thanks me for what I did.

In truth, he should thank my Grandma Auden.

Dallas Woodburn, Age 17

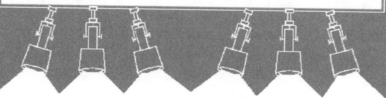

Spotlight On . . . SOCIAL ACTIVISM

If you feel there is social injustice going on in your school or community, don't feel as though you have no choice but to stand by and watch. Petitions can be very powerful tools in raising awareness and promoting change.

What is a petition, anyway? A petition is a collection of names and signatures of people who support your position. The more names you can collect, the more powerful your petition can be. Don't forget to write what your petition is all about at the top of each sheet of paper.

Remember, even if you don't get the results you were hoping for through your petition, you'll undoubtedly show that you and others feel strongly about taking action, which is bound to get people's attention.

For more information on social activism, check out Barbara Lewis' book *The Kids' Guide to Social Action* (1991).

OUTSIDE THE BOX

Teenagers who are intolerant of people from other cultures or ethnic backgrounds often don't even know much about their own heritage. Have you ever explored your family's history? Try finding out the answers to these questions:

- When did your ancestors come to America?
- What were their reasons for coming to the United States?
- How many different cultures and ethnicities make up who you are?
- How is life different for you than it was for your grandparents when they were teens?

NEW YORK CITY IS SOMETIMES CALLED a "melting pot" because so many different people from all walks of life live together in one place. Most of the time, they find a way to get along.

Well, in many ways, school is like New York City, but on a smaller level (and with fewer skyscrapers). Even if your school isn't made up of a blend of students from different racial backgrounds, everyone brings their own unique perspective and experiences to school with them every day. You can't tell by looking at someone what their family life is like, what religion they are or what their sexual orientation is. Yet these are the kinds of things that define who we are, how we view life. Becoming comfortable in who we are takes time and, sometimes, courage. But the sooner we can "get real" with ourselves, the sooner we can really start life.

For Real?

Did you know that the population of New York City—more than **8 million**—is made up of people from more than **fifty** different countries?

Out

The moment I entered the high school for the first time, I knew that things were going to be rough. Everyone seemed very similar, which as you know, is horrifying. I felt like every color and difference in this new world had been blurred together by a giant smudging eraser. I felt alone and unimportant, feeling my heart thumping in my ears at the thought of being the one student all the other kids took turns beating up after school.

The first quarter of freshman year was where the real learning took place. I began to notice things about the students, how they acted, how rumors spread and what kind of people were absolutely hated. One of the loudest statements that the mob of three thousand teenagers made was, *We hate gays.* Although it seems to be a trend to call things that you despise "gay," the kids around me weren't just calling objects and subjects and ideas "gay." They would talk about the gay kids in our school, literally torturing them each and every day with their words.

For Real?

Gay, lesbian and **bisexual** teens are more likely to get depressed than heterosexual teens, mostly due to the fact that many are **treated** like social outcasts by their peers.

Being gay, I was horrified. It was "their" domain, a place that I obviously didn't belong. I knew one "out" gay person at school, a senior. Later I would learn that on Senior Awards Night at the end of the year, he was nominated as "the most stereotypical." That was when he dropped off the face of the

Earth and left me alone, like a snowflake floating in the middle of a hailstorm. Early in the year he had been a bright shining beacon of "If you do not like who I am, I couldn't really care less." I envied him, and yet I walked wordlessly through the crowded halls inches behind him, a shadow to his flame.

Our school had started a gay-straight alliance, which I joined as soon as I could. I knew that the club would be small, but at least it was somewhere that I could go to complain about the daily strife of high school teenage life. The teacher monitoring us really supported me and kept everything that we said in that room completely confidential. Finally I was surrounded by people like me, gay and hiding, afraid of our peers and teachers in high school.

CONSIDER THIS . . .

Many high schools are starting to **support** the formation of gay-straight alliances—student-led clubs that support gay, lesbian, bisexual and transsexual students. Today more than 2,000 high schools have gay-straight alliances.

Well, we weren't hiding for long. Kids ridiculed us and mocked our club, mocked our ideas, and further harassed our dying gay-student community (as tiny and fragile as it was). We were the lowest of the low at that point, and it left me no other choice than to finally come out of the closet, be proud and let everyone know they couldn't keep me in the dark anymore.

I stood up one day in front of my English class and read my persuasive essay, all about the discrimination and hate of gays that our school, city and country contained. I was nervous enough to be shaking, wondering if I would be murdered after school, my body never found. I knew it was a good essay, and even though it was about discrimination and hate and becoming tolerant, it was really my own secret revenge. On that day and in that class, I came out to each and every one of them. I let them know how proud I was without ever wearing a rainbow-colored ribbon, and I let them know that they couldn't force me back into the shadows without me ever firing a gun. I finished reading my essay with steel in my voice, staring into their eyes rather than hovering behind my paper. For a few seconds there was nothing, as if I had put them all in comas of shock. But then the clapping began. And one by one, students stood up. I had to catch my breath, my spine tingling. I was getting a standing ovation. I knew then that a new revolution had begun, one that I would single-handedly control.

HOW ABOUT YOU?

Do you place stereotypes on people who are **different** from you?

Over the course of the year, I grew to be like that senior who I had worshipped. I wore rainbow key chains on my lanyard and my buttons from Gay Pride 2004. When I had first come into the high school, I believed that the out and proud students were the ones who got bashed and harassed. Sure, it is hard some days, and there are a few cruel words here and there, but I have never been tied to the flagpole and burnt after a gay-straight alliance meeting.

The gay students who are most picked on are those who are still in the shadows, like I used to be. I think that my peers are afraid of me, afraid of how I stand up for my rights and how

I don't keep my mouth shut. But they have no reason to be afraid of the poor kids still in hiding, so the mute ones get the brute force of their attacks. I can only hope that someday teenagers will stop being so afraid to come out because it will definitely be the best thing they ever do for themselves.

Today I saw a small freshman hovering behind me in the crowded halls of Harold High School. I made sure that my flame burned bright and my spirits soared, so that someday I will light his match.

Aubrey Restifo, Age 15

For Real?

43% of students think that drugs and alcohol are a fairly serious to **very serious problem** at their school.

IT SEEMS THAT BEING A TEENAGER is all about experimentation. Experimenting with hairstyles, fashion, friendships, foods, classes, sports. In nearly everything we do as teens, we're doing it as a way to explore who we are and figure out what it is that drives us, makes us tick, inspires us. Not all of the teenage experimentation is positive though, as I'm sure you know all too well.

When I was in school it seemed like everyone was experimenting on some level, myself included. Luckily I had very involved parents and supportive friends, so I never got to the point of putting my life in danger. But I can see how easily it could happen. With enough pressure from others, you'd be surprised at the kinds of things you might find yourself experimenting with—everything from alcohol to drugs, even sex.

CONSIDER THIS . . .

Perhaps the best way to avoid being put in a bad spot is to have a plan, a plan for how you'll handle pressure, how you'll handle it when you're put in the hot seat at a party and don't know how to get out of it without feeling embarrassed. The less prepared we are in life, the more unexpected the results we'll get.

Parents consider teen **experimentation,** with everything from drinking to hair color, a **"rite of passage."** Because teens are more likely to experiment when there are no parents around, summer vacation is a particularly vulnerable time.

We Promised

Ever since kindergarten, I had attended a small, private school. My class consisted of only nineteen kids, and we grew up with each other. Our class had become as close as a family, so as middle school approached, we suddenly realized that come eighth grade the unthinkable would occur. We would all be separated, scattered to different public schools—forced to meet new people, form new friendships.

When we finally reached eighth grade, we waited for graduation with terrified anticipation, excited to finally experience the fabled life of a public school student, frightened about not fitting in and saddened at the thought of abandoning the close friendships we had created within our small, comfortable community.

On June 23, we donned our blue robes and caps and participated in a long, sentimental graduation ceremony.

Afterward we had a huge sleepover, filled with tears and promises of never forgetting each other or our wonderful years together.

Throughout the summer, we got together as much as possible. Discussions often turned to the dangers we would encounter at public high schools. Drugs. Drinking. Sex. Would we be pressured to submit to these temptations? "Probably not," we said. "We'd be too scared," we joked. But still the question hung in the air. *What if? What if fitting in was more important?*

For Real?

Only **7%** of teenagers say they feel **very** pressured to experiment with illegal drugs.

That summer something else happened. Tiffany Parks, a senior at the public high school and my next door neighbor, died from a drug overdose. Her body was found at a friend's house where a bunch of high school kids were having a party. My parents were horrified. I was stunned. I couldn't believe it.

When I was younger, Tiffany used to baby-sit for me. I remembered how we would sit on the floor and play spit or watch movies. Since my family didn't have a microwave, Tiffany used to make popcorn at her house and then bring over the steaming, buttery bag for us to share as we watched. I still associate the delicious smell of freshly popped popcorn with her, remembering how it filled the house upon her arrival. One time we got locked out of the house, so Tiffany pulled a bunch of brightly colored nail polish bottles from her bag and we painted our nails on the porch until my parents got home.

As I got older, Tiffany stopped baby-sitting for me, but every morning as I stood at the end of my driveway waiting for the bus, she'd walk past on her way to school, blonde curls bouncing. When she'd see me, her gloss-covered lips would form a genuine smile and she'd greet me by name.

The whole town mourned her.

When the summer ended, my girlfriends and I got together a couple of days before the first day of high school. As we sat on my friend's large bed, I told them Tiffany's story. We all sat in a circle, put our hands together and promised each other that we would never try drugs.

HOW ABOUT YOU?

Do you have a **plan** for how you'll handle it if you find yourself being pressured to try **drugs?**

High school has been hard to adjust to. But eventually we all adapted to our new environments and met new friends. However, I'm still very close with my classmates from private school and I'm happy to say none of us have tried drugs. I think it's because we promised.

Rachel A. Stern, Age 14

Spotlight On . . . DRUGS IN SCHOOL

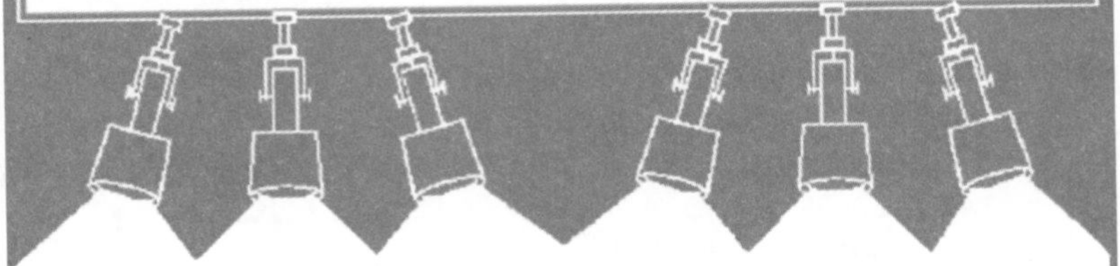

Drug use is up in schools, and more and more students use drugs as they get older and older. Check out these statistics:

- Marijuana is the most common drug used by students. Nearly 20% of eighth-graders and nearly 48% of twelfth-graders report smoking marijuana.
- Ecstasy is the next most common drug used by teenagers. More than 4% of eighth-graders and nearly 11% of twelfth-graders use it.
- Heroin is the least common drug used by teens. Fewer than 2% of students report ever trying it.

For Real?

Would it surprise you to know that nearly **one-third** of high school seniors **don't graduate** every year? More than **50%** of those who graduate go on to some sort of college or university.

I COULDN'T WAIT UNTIL THE DAY WHEN I GRADUATED and I'd be set free to pursue my goals, to get on with my life. So I found it pretty odd when the summer after senior year I found myself wishing time would slow down. What was I afraid of? Why had I stopped chomping at the bit?

One night in late August, just a few days before I was heading off to Penn State to start my freshman year of college, my BFF and I double dated with two guys from another school. It was a great evening . . . dinner and a play, followed by hanging out in a nearby park. The night had been going great, so I was surprised when my emotions crept up out of nowhere and I ended the evening in tears.

"Things are never going to be the same," I kept crying. As I hugged my friend, I thought of her moving to Boston and us being so far away from each other. Everything was going to change. I knew something significant was happening, a rite of passage that had to be conquered, yet I felt this incredible desire to go back, to stop all the clocks.

What a bizarre sensation, being so excited about what's to come while being terrified to let go of the past. The urge to freeze time, to change my plans and hold on to the way things were, was overwhelming. But there was no going back, and I knew it. So I did what I had to do. I moved forward. I shook off the fears, loaded up the old Plymouth Voyager, and drove with my parents down Route 83 to start chapter two of my life.

The emotions I felt that night in August have come to be familiar ones. Moving out, saying good-bye to friends, changing jobs, falling in and out of love . . . it's all part of life. Luckily, I've discovered that there is one great thing about good-byes. They're usually followed by a brand new "hello."

Seen It?

Ever wish you could just make time stand still? In the movie *Clockstoppers* (2002), Zac Gibbs is able to do just that with a special wristwatch his father invented.

Consider This . . .

Graduation can bring up all kinds of emotions, especially when it comes to saying good-bye to good friends. Here are some ways to get through the ups and downs:

- Make a plan with your friends for how you'll stay in touch.
- Have realistic expectations. Chances are your current relationships will change after school ends.
- Be open to making new friends.

REMINISCENCE

How the years fly by
When you're having fun,
Being with your friends,
On the beach, in the sun.

The work was hard
But I guess it paid off.
And just look at us now,
Ready to take off.

It's been four fun years,
Filled with many emotions.
But the love we hold for each other
Could span many oceans.

I remember back
To that very first year—
You took my hand,
And I no longer felt fear.

All through these years
You've been there for me,
And it scares me that you
I'll no longer see.

I'm off to something
Exciting and new,
But I'm afraid to
Be doing it without you.

You, my friend,
Who has always been there,
Where will you be?
The thought I cannot bear.

But you'll be starting
Your own adventure, too.
Who knows what that is
Other than something new.

And when we graduate,
And hug, and cry,
Know that I will miss you,
And that it hurts to say good-bye.

Krystle Nichols, Age 17

Take the Quiz: DO YOU KNOW HOW TO HANDLE TOUGH STUFF AT SCHOOL?

1. You couldn't be more psyched because you're the only freshman to have made the varsity football team this year. But early on in the season, you notice some of the other starters are popping steroids like they're Life Savers, and you are even more surprised when they offer some to you. What do you do?

___ A. Say "no way" to the steroids and anonymously tell the coach about what's going on. You don't want to be considered a narc, but you don't want to keep this secret either.

___ B. You nervously make up some excuse for why you can't take the steroids, but act like you would if you could.

___ C. You're caught completely off guard, and not wanting to come across like a dorky freshman, accept the offer and take a pill. You figure you can say "no" the next time.

2. You borrow a friend's notes to photocopy so you can get ready for the big test. In the middle of copying, you stumble across a poem your friend wrote in which she expresses that she wishes she had the guts to commit suicide. How do you handle it?

___ A. You don't want to infringe on your friend's privacy, but you know this is something that has to be taken seriously, so you go to your parent or another trusted adult and tell them what you found so you can get your friend help.

___ B. You're conflicted over what to do, but decide to wait until your friend brings up her poetry to say anything about what you found.

___ C. You pretend you never read the poem, figuring your friend is probably just venting, and that it's none of your business anyway.

3. As you're rifling through your locker to find a notebook, you glance at the open locker next to you. You can't be absolutely positive, but you're fairly sure you saw a handgun hidden beneath a sweatshirt. You know the student the locker belongs to has gotten in trouble for violent outbursts at school before. What do you do?

___ A. Even if you're wrong about what you saw, you know you can't afford to not say anything, and you immediately head to the main office to tell them of your suspicions.

___ B. You tell your friends about what you think you saw, but decide that you'll do some further investigating on your own before making any accusations.

___ C. You convince yourself that you must be mistaken about what you saw. Anyway, you're too intimidated by this guy to risk getting on his bad side by accusing him.

4. You're sitting in the cafeteria with a group of friends when someone pulls out a copy of last year's social studies midterm. You've heard that the teacher gives the same test every year. Your friend offers to give you a copy and you're caught off guard, especially since you think that cheating is wrong. How do you handle this one?

___ A. You don't accept the test, and let your friend know that cheating hurts everybody, since perfect scores by cheaters bust the curve for those students who actually studied hard.

___ B. You initially take the test, too surprised to say anything, but later return it, telling your friend that you don't need to cheat to get good grades.

___ C. You don't want to look like a goody-goody, so you take a copy of the test and stick it in your notebook. You might not use it, but your friends don't need to know.

5. You're psyched that a cool group of girls have included you in their slumber party plans, but after the host's parents go to bed, she whips out a bottle of gin from the liquor cabinet and starts pouring. You promised your parents you wouldn't drink at the party, and you want to keep your word but not look stupid at the same time. What do you do?

___ A. You confidently smile and say, "No thanks, I don't drink" and leave it at that. You know that if you're secure in your decision, the chances are better that your peers won't try to talk you into doing anything.

___ B. You accept the drink, but don't actually have any of it. The next chance you get to go to the bathroom, you pour it down the sink and replace the alcohol with water. Your friends never have to know.

___ C. You figure that your parents will never know what really happened at the party and take one little drink. It's worth it to save face with these girls.

How'd you do? Give yourself 10 points for every A, 20 points for every B and 30 points for every C. Look below to find out how confident you are:

50–70 points = You've got a good head on your shoulders, and you're ready for whatever tough stuff comes up at school. You know that the more confident and self-assured you are, the less likely you are to find yourself in a tricky situation.

80–120 points = You know in your gut how you feel about tough stuff, but you're not quite sure how to handle the trickier situations. It would be worth your while to spend some time giving some thought to how you want to handle yourself when faced with a difficult decision.

130–150 points = You're not very prepared to face the tough choices that are part of life as a teenager, and if you don't come up with a plan, before you know it you might find yourself doing things you don't really want to do.

CHAPTER 6

LIFE OUTSIDE THE CLASSROOM

For many students, school wouldn't be bearable without the stuff that surrounds school—sports, clubs, band, chorus and other extracurricular activities. That doesn't mean it's all smooth sailing. These activities come loaded with their own issues, like the nervousness that comes with competition, the anxiety about putting yourself out there when you run for student government and the possibility of competing against your best friend. In "Life Outside the Classroom," you'll hear from teens who capture these emotions through their compelling stories and poems.

For Real?

Approximately **15%** of all middle school and high school students participate in student government at some point.

WHEN I WAS IN SCHOOL, student government wasn't taken too seriously. It was basically the same group of kids every year who threw their hats in the ring, slapped a few posters up on the wall the day before ballots were cast, and with very little effort would find themselves victorious, being decreed new class president or student council treasurer or whatever position they had been running for.

Seen It?

Who can forget Reese Witherspoon's excellent portrayal of Tracy Flick, a classic overachiever who'll do just about anything to win the title of class president in the comedy *Election* (1999)?

Today, student politics are a much bigger deal. Campaigns are organized and run with the intensity of the U.S. presidential race. Well, maybe not *that* intense, but close. And it's hard work, too: Students who want to win know it's serious business. Making buttons, T-shirts, stickers and mugs, and coming up with a detailed political platform—you name it and wannabe school politicians are doing it to win.

I think it takes a lot of guts to put yourself out there and run for student government. As if it's not hard enough to blend in and feel accepted at school, those running for government are basically putting themselves out there and waving a big banner around saying, "Hi! This is who I am! What do you think of me?" Some students decide the risk is worth it, even if it is a little scary. And as you'll read in this next essay, the payoff is totally worth it.

Seen It?

The excellent documentary *Spellbound* (2002), which was nominated for an Academy Award, shows that the National Spelling Bee can be as full of **drama** as any good **thriller.**

Just Do It

When I started junior high, my only expectation for myself was to stay invisible. I was shy, sensitive and intimidated by the rest of the school. Everyone seemed so much older, more educated and experienced. Basically they were everything I wasn't but wanted to be. So it's strange how I aspired to run for sixth-grade secretary.

The announcement was broadcast on the intercom that anyone interested in running for student council should see the math teacher for qualification forms. Even though I'm normally a cautious person, I followed the massive crowd to the math classroom. Without even thinking twice, my mom and I filled out and turned in the forms, but I had no idea what I had gotten myself into.

HOW ABOUT YOU?

Would you ever **consider** running for a student political office? What would be **your** reason for running?

The only thing you could see in the sixth-grade hall were neon posters adorned with pictures of winning-obsessed pupils. Buttons, bookmarks and flyers littered the hallways and cafeteria. Most found a permanent home in the trash can.

Meanwhile, my printer lazily spit out what seemed like a million bookmarks. I cut them out, punched holes in them and finished them off with ribbons, finally bringing them in to school. That week my friends and I passed out the bookmarks. Everything was going as planned . . . until it was time for my speech.

Spotlight On . . . STUDENT GOVERNMENT

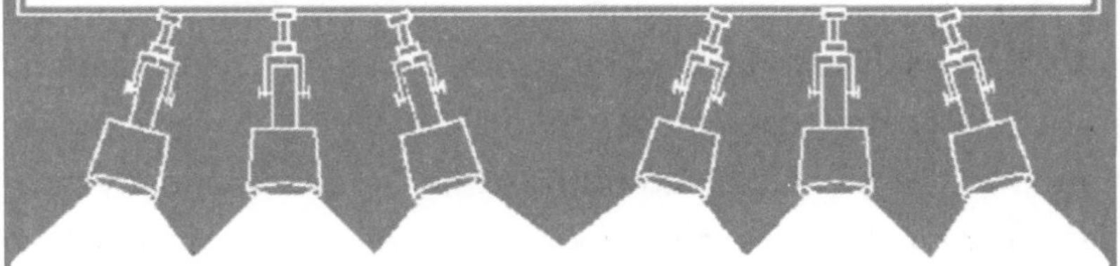

Participating in student government, including student council and class positions like president, VP and so on, can be a rewarding activity for many students. In a lot of schools, student government actually does have some power, and if there's an issue on the students' mind, the student government can get the administration's attention. Here are just some of the kinds of things those in student government are responsible for:

- participating in votes for change in school policies
- organizing and running school dances
- running the on-campus student store
- advising the school administration on key issues
- organizing class trips and other special events

If you've never considered participating in student government before, take a look at the list below. These are just some of the reasons it might be worth checking out:

- You can include it on your résumé.
- It looks great on college applications.
- You get special privileges, like getting out of class for meetings.
- You can have some influence to change things that you don't agree with at school.
- You may have the opportunity to go on special field trips.

I had never been afraid of being on television before. In fact, I had been on my school's morning news program for two years. But as I got ready to present my speech, my hands clammed up and my sweat glands went into overdrive as the camera fixed on my face. My short, page-long speech hadn't taken more than a minute to read, but I felt as if I had been on that musty old stage for an eternity. Anxious thoughts spun in my head like a tornado. *What did my hair look like? Did I look at the camera? And most of all, did I look as petrified as I felt?*

For Real?
Nike's famous **"Just Do It"** campaign shot Nike to the top of the athletic wear market.

Somewhere between handing out bookmarks and delivering my speech, I asked myself one question: *What the heck are you doing, Laura!?* I felt trapped. Enclosed. But in the midst of the fury and panic was something unexpected. I had learned some amazing things about who I was. Not only did I give a speech in front of 300 kids, but I'd introduced myself to people I'd never even met before while actively campaigning. In fact, I felt incredibly confident. I could do anything!

After that, things happened so fast that I can't remember every little detail about the election. But what I do remember so vividly is the one thing everyone now knows. *I won!* It wasn't that easy, though. I actually tied with another student, but in the end, my class picked me! Me! The shy and quiet girl! Destined to be invisible? NOT! Why be invisible when you can shine?

I'm already planning my reelection campaign. And I've learned the importance of taking a chance. Going out on a limb. Believing in yourself. And next time there's something I want to do but am a little intimidated, I'm going to *just do it!*

Laura M. Watkins, Age 11

OUTSIDE THE BOX

Do you want to run for student government but aren't sure where to start? Try some of these tips to get your campaign off the ground and running:

- Ask a friend to nominate you for the position you want if your school requires it.
- Figure out what the key issue or "platform" of your campaign will be, in other words, the "why" behind your running.
- Come up with a slogan to support your campaign. This can be as simple as "Paul for President" or "Improving school one classroom at a time."
- Make posters that include not only your name but also why people should vote for you.
- Remember that you want everyone's vote, so reach out to people beyond your inner circle of friends.
- Write a kick-butt campaign speech explaining why you're the right person for the job.

THINK ABOUT YOUR FAVORITE SPORTS MOVIES: *Bend It Like Beckham, Bring It On, Seabiscuit, Rocky*. What do they all have in common? Well, they follow a common theme in Hollywood movies: They all center on characters who overcome great hardship or adversity to achieve their goal, whether it's winning the race, speaking up for themselves or making the right decision. Let's face it: Everybody loves a good comeback story. Why? Because they're inspirational. They serve to remind us all that the human spirit prevails, and that when faced with difficult situations, we all have the ability to make our own comeback.

Read It?

For a great **true story** on an athlete defying incredible odds, check out *Touching the Void* (1989), by Joe Simpson, about a climber who is left for dead and **fights** his way off a mountain in Peru.

Oxygen Is a Crutch

I step onto the starting block—head down, hands down—and explode at the pistol's crack, body arcing up into the air and down. I slice through the water, pull hard, kick hard, strain, set my teeth and force more strength from loudly protesting muscles. I gulp in oxygen when I turn my head for a precious breath. But mostly I just keep my head down and swim like there's no tomorrow.

THE WORD

Asthma is a disease that affects the **respiratory system**. People who suffer from asthma sometimes have trouble breathing because the muscles surrounding their airways tighten, making it harder to get oxygen in and out.

By all rights, I shouldn't have even been there. By all rights,

Consider This . . .

Participating in **sports** as teenagers does a lot more than just keep you physically fit. Here are just a few of the other emotional and mental **benefits:**

- Athletes have more positive self-esteem and better body images.
- Athletes gain confidence in who they are, and that crosses over into other areas of their life.
- Female athletes are much less likely to get pregnant while in school.
- Athletes are less likely to be depressed and suicidal.
- Athletes in team sports learn the valuable skills of working together and problem solving.

I should have been on the sidelines at the Blossom Valley Athletic League Championships, watching my teammates fight to maintain Evergreen Valley High's 200-medley relay winning streak. I should have been cursing the bodily limits that kept me from doing what I wanted to do. I should have been sulking in a corner, spirits crushed, hopes asunder, dreams damned.

But instead, only months after a near-fatal asthma attack, here I was in the water again, anchoring the relay team.

Asthma has been my constant companion since I turned five years old. An inhaler has always sat in my back pocket, a medical bracelet on my left wrist, and medicines and breathing devices on my bedroom dresser. But none of that ever meant that I couldn't torpedo through the water as well as the kid in the next lane. None of that ever weighed on my mind much, because I knew that I (whoever that was, because I was still in the process of figuring that out) was surely much bigger and much stronger than some puny medical condition.

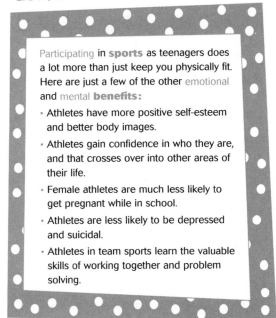

Swimming became my refuge, my passion, my reason for living strong. I didn't love it because of any natural talent or biological blessing. I think the challenges of being a severe asthmatic made me embrace athletics more because I have to push myself for each race, each game, each meet. Because competition is a constant challenge. Because when I lose and flail and fall, I get up and do it all over again. And so I do not fail, because I do not give up.

For Real?

More than **6 million** children under the age of 18 have **asthma** in the United States! That means that around 1 in 10 teens have the disease.

When an intense practice sent me spiraling into unconsciousness and a near comatose state last year, my doctor and parents were leery of ever letting me anywhere near sports again. But I wasn't about to be deterred. I wasn't about to turn my back on the love of my life. I wasn't about to quit—no way, no how.

Consider This . . .

Having asthma doesn't have to **stop you** from being **active.** In fact, here are a few of the superstar athletes who are asthmatic:

- Dennis Rodman (former NBA Player)
- Jackie Joyner-Kersee (gold medal Olympic runner)
- Nancy Hogshead (gold medal Olympic swimmer)
- Greg Louganis (gold medal Olympic diver)

I like to think this is akin to the sort of character that drives Olympic athletes, that if I can't yet equal my idols in speed or strength or stamina, I might look them eye to eye in terms of pure grit.

And so, with a pack of epinephrine syringes, a stethoscope and a whole army of inhalers in my duffel bag, I marched back toward the pool. Ready to get back into fighting trim, train until I puked, rebuild myself.

Ready to race and begin again.

Julia Lam, Age 17

CONSIDER THIS . . .

A recent study found that teenagers who have **asthma** are more prone to being depressed and nervous, mostly because they feel unhappy about having the condition or are uncomfortable about feeling "different" from their friends.

HAVE YOU EVER BEEN CHALLENGED TO DO SOMETHING you didn't think you had the courage to do? My earliest memory of being faced with such a challenge was when I was around ten years old. I went on this canoe trip on an island in the Susquehanna River with a group from my summer camp. The whole point was to "rough it" for a few days (if "roughing it" means s'mores and indoor bathrooms).

Anyway, on the last day, our activity was cliff jumping. And I mean *cliff*. This was a 60-foot rock face jutting out over the river, and one by one we were encouraged to put on a lifejacket and leap over the edge. Now, this wasn't one of those camps where they *force* you to participate to make you stronger, but I wasn't one to turn down an adventure, and so next thing I knew, I found myself staring over the edge.

CONSIDER THIS . . .

The **benefits** to teens of physically challenging themselves include **improved** self-esteem and confidence.

For Real?

You might think that school sports are limited to the biggies like football, baseball and soccer, but schools **across the country** are starting to dabble in more obscure sports. Does your school offer any of these new activities?

- surfing • archery • curling
- power-lifting • snowboarding

My friends at the bottom yelled up to me to go for it and assured me that it was awesome, that I could do it. I didn't believe them. I stared into the water, knees shaking, and felt fear holding me back. But I didn't want to back down. So I took a deep breath, convinced myself that if they could do it, so could I, and asked the rest of the kids to count to three. As the number "three" was shouted from below, I stopped thinking with my head and just jumped. That's when my stomach came up through my throat. But no matter—I had done it. Mind over matter.

That memory stays with me even today, because when I'm faced with that proverbial cliff of something I don't think I can do, I remind myself of what I'm capable of and I take the plunge.

Struggle of a Preteen Couch Potato

In fifth grade, I weighed, well, *a lot*. I was short and, as much as I hate to admit it, *fat*. As an inactive couch potato, I didn't fit in. My parents were constantly trying to limit what I ate, control what I did and send me out into the backyard to run around. In general, I was an unhealthy kid who ate junk food, and needed a growth spurt and *a lot* of exercise.

One summer, in a last-ditch effort to get me to lose weight, my parents cut out all snacks and made me run a mile each day around our backyard. (Twenty laps. It was like running around in a tiny circle.) The only things that gave me motivation were the fifty cents a day my parents promised me for running and a need to have more money than my little brother.

For Real?
"Overweight" means someone who weighs at least **20%** more than the expected weight for someone his or her weight and height.

Throughout that year, my parents continued to fuss about my weight. I had lost a few pounds, but I was far from the "ideal standard" set by most people. But the school year went by much better than the last, and so that spring I decided to try out for the varsity swim team the following year. I joined a local club team to train with over the summer and started out swimming with kids who were eight years old to my twelve. I felt slow, old and, in general, weak. But I grew hopeful as fall approached, until I saw the fitness test that middle-schoolers had to pass to make the team.

Read It?
If you want to **lose** weight safely, check out Jay McGraw's bestselling book *The Ultimate Weight Solution for Teens: The 7 Keys to Weight Freedom* (2004).

I couldn't do anything that was on the test.

Instead of giving up or waiting until I was a freshman, I spent my seventh-grade year swimming off-season, still working toward varsity. I quickly moved up to where I was swimming with kids who were mostly my age, although not very fast. Soon I was first in my lane, set after set. I worked with that same

For Real?
It will take an average person 2,000 steps to walk **one mile.**

CONSIDER THIS . . .

It's no secret that **losing weight** happens through a combination of diet and exercise. Exercise is so important to the **equation** because it burns calories, which offsets the food you're taking in. Exercising also raises your metabolism, which means that your body **burns** calories more efficiently, which contributes to weight loss.

group from September to Christmas, struggling as my unathletic body learned what working out actually meant.

When my coach, Katie, left, I switched to a group where I knew no one and everyone looked down on me. Some thought that I wasn't worthy of swimming with them, but that changed quickly as I worked my way up the lane. As people left the club, others moved up, and I got faster. Within a few months I was invited to advance into a highly competitive group that meets five days a week for two hours.

For Real?

Because of the gravitational pull of the moon, if you weigh yourself when the moon is **directly** overhead, you'll **weigh less** than usual.

The next summer I once again put my name on the sign-up list for the varsity team. By this point, I was truly in shape. My whole life had changed.

But I still had to pass the physical fitness test, and that was a challenge. I did the forty-four sit-ups in a minute on my first try—that was the easiest part for me. I ran my mile and a half in the allotted fifteen minutes my first time out. (Thank goodness! I don't think I would have wanted to do *that* twice!) I cleared my long jump with ease, leaving only one challenge to go: holding my chin above a bar for fifteen seconds. That day I tried it and missed by a second and a half. My heart was broken, but a week or two later, I came back to do better. Once again I failed. On my third try, I filled my mind with determination and made it with a second to spare! My hopes soared as I was cleared to be on the team.

Address Book

If you're looking for information on a **sport**, check out this Web site for links to just about every site having to do with teens and sports: *www.cbel.com/kids_and_teen_sports/*

I'll admit it: The first day I was scared to death. *Do they make cuts? Am I going to be the slowest one? Will I just be humiliating myself? What if I can't finish the practice?* The only thing that kept me sane was my friend Caitlin, who was a year older and helped me through the first few days.

After filling out some paperwork and talking, Bob, the coach, told us to get in the water, new people in lane one, returnees in the other lanes. Caitlin told me to come over to lane six with her, and I was skeptical. Although I protested, Caitlin finally convinced me. I began leading the lane, and then found myself moved up, lane after lane. I figured it was just because all these girls were out of shape, and soon I'd be back in lane six, going last and hopelessly behind everyone.

Surprisingly, I never got moved down. I stayed in one of the fastest lanes for a few days, and the coach told me that in the first meet I was going to swim distance—the dreaded 500-meter freestyle. I fought. Maybe he thought I could swim a seven-minute race, but my best time was eight minutes. He didn't care, and a few weeks later I found myself facing my first varsity event, the 500-meter freestyle, with a stomach full of butterflies.

WHERE DO YOU STAND?

How much do you know about extracurricular activities at school?

__ YES __ NO 1. Articles written for high school newspapers can be used to get jobs after graduation.

__ YES __ NO 2. Colleges only look to recruit high school athletes who are number one in their sport.

__ YES __ NO 3. Colleges and universities don't recruit marching band musicians, only athletes.

__ YES __ NO 4. Volunteering and regular community service can be included on your résumé.

__ YES __ NO 5. Filling up your free time with extracurricular activities usually makes your grades suffer.

1. **True.** The quality of writing at many high school papers is considered so high that professional editors take notice.

2. **False.** Smaller schools are always looking for athletes who have potential to fill out their roster. While you may not get a full ride, a supportive coach can help you get accepted.

3. **False.** Ever seen *Drumline*? Some college marching bands are their school's biggest draw.

4. **True.** Just because you're not getting paid for a job doesn't mean the experience isn't worth noting.

5. **False.** In fact, recent research shows that involvement in extracurricular activities can actually contribute to academic success.

I stepped up on the block, strapped on my goggles and took a deep breath. I sucked up my fear and got ready to race. I started out last, then caught up to one girl and passed her. With every breath, I could see my entire team lining the side, cheering me on. My adrenaline ran high as I raced against another girl close to me. I caught up to her, and although my sprinting has always been horrible, I edged her out in the end,

CONSIDER THIS . . .

Swimming is one sport where the superstars can be teens. Just look at 19-year-old Michael Phelps, who won six gold medals in the 2004 Athens Olympics! He first made the Olympic team when he was only 15 years old.

finishing fourth in my first varsity meet ever. I pulled myself out of the pool, exhausted, and my whole team congratulated me. I was on cloud nine when I found out I'd swum the race in a personal record: 6:52! Coach Bob was right. I was a distance person.

After the race, my coach told me something I'll never forget. "We never expected you to *beat* anyone! Good job!" he said. And in some ways, he was right. Who would have expected the overweight couch potato to beat varsity swimmers in the longest race known to high school swimmers? *No one,* that's who. I'm still amazed that I did it.

Sometimes I feel like I'm in a dream, and I picture myself back in lane six, in the very back, struggling to keep up. But then I wake up and remember how far I've come, and I know there's no going back.

Katelynn M. Wilton, Age 15

OUTSIDE THE BOX

If you have a tryout coming up for a sports team, make sure you're prepared. Here are some things you might want to consider:

- Find out what you will be expected to do at try-outs (fitness tests, sprints, drills, strategy).
- Practice drills and other skills.
- Wear sports-appropriate clothes to the tryout (don't wear a skirt to soccer tryouts!).
- Be dedicated to the task at hand. It will shine through.

For Real?

51% of middle school and high school students **play** after-school **sports.**

IF YOU'VE EVER BEEN PART OF A SPORTS TEAM, you've surely had the same victory fantasies as the rest of us: fantasies of scoring the winning goal, running the last leg of the relay and flying across the finish line, spiking the volleyball so hard that the other team runs for cover. We can picture it all so clearly in our minds: how it will feel, how loud the crowd's cheering will be, what the pats on the back from our teammates will feel like, what the slow-motion replay will look like. But where do we get these images from anyway? It's got to be from Hollywood, the masters of fantasy, complete with emotional soundtrack, slow-motion and extreme close-ups.

HOW ABOUT YOU?

What do you consider to be the best victory scene in a sports movie?

While some people do get to experience those powerful and victorious moments, many of us are on the other side. We're the goalie being scored against, the losing anchor on an opposing relay team, the volleyball player unable to dig the spike. Why aren't movies about these people, the losing team? Well, I think Hollywood is missing out on a great opportunity, an opportunity to tell the story of an athletes who get stronger through their experiences, even if they're not the best athlete around.

Seen It?

The comedy *Dodgeball* (2004) is about a bunch of former high school outcasts pitted against the super jocks in the Dodgeball World Championships.

SOFTBALL SORROWS

The hot sun burns a hole in my back
I play even though talent I lack.
I see Coach flick his hat
A giant of a girl steps up to bat.
The pitch is wound, I hope and pray
Please don't let that ball come my way.
But against my wishes
right field is where it's hit
I close my eyes
And hold up my mitt.
I stand there alone
As time slowly crawls by
I hear ball hit grass
And try not to cry.
The crowd goes wild
As I chase 'round the ball
But not before seeing
My coach's face fall.

For Real?

You might not have caught it on television, but the U.S. Women's Softball Team won the **gold medal** in the 2004 Athens Olympics.

Shawna McBroom, Age 16

WHERE DO YOU STAND?

They say that all's fair in love and war, but how fair do you play when it comes to after-school stuff? Would you . . .

accept a friend's offer to rig the school election so you win?

___ NO WAY! (0 points)
___ YOU NEVER KNOW. (1 point)
___ SURE, WHY NOT? (2 points)

use a writing sample you found online to get onto the school paper staff?

___ NO WAY! (0 points)
___ YOU NEVER KNOW. (1 point)
___ SURE, WHY NOT? (2 points)

not tell your coach that your relay handoff wasn't legal after you won the race?

___ NO WAY! (0 points)
___ YOU NEVER KNOW. (1 point)
___ SURE, WHY NOT? (2 points)

"forget" to tell your biggest rival for band auditions about the change of date?

___ NO WAY! (0 points)
___ YOU NEVER KNOW. (1 point)
___ SURE, WHY NOT? (2 points)

let your teammate take the blame for a scuffle in soccer so you can stay in the game?

___ NO WAY! (0 points)
___ YOU NEVER KNOW. (1 point)
___ SURE, WHY NOT? (2 points)

Add up your points:

0–3 = You play fair and square.
4–7 = It's a tough call.
8–10 = I want to win at any cost.

HOW ABOUT YOU?

Are there **any** sports you'd like to play?

PEOPLE WHO DON'T HAVE BROTHERS AND SISTERS tend to toss off the idea of sibling rivalry like it's no big thing. Well, as someone who grew up with a sister two years older than me, let me make it clear: It is.

I should have known I was in trouble when my older sister started bringing home report cards from high school with straight As or when she was on honor roll semester after semester. The big tip I was in trouble was when she graduated second in her class.

Then along came Debbie (that's me). After my sister graduated, straight As were never to be seen by my parents again. Honor roll was out of my reach. So was graduating in the top two.

I excelled at other things, though. I was more successful in sports than my sister was, and I played piano with the school chorus. And, might I add, my sister never did earn the prestigious title of "Best Excuse Maker" that I received senior year.

While my sister and I were in school, there was just no getting around the sibling rivalry that existed. Without even realizing it, we were always competing against each other, and it could get pretty intense. Luckily our parents didn't foster this competition; they saw what each of our strengths were and supported us in focusing on them. And today? My sister and I are able to do the same thing.

Seen It?

A Cinderella Story (2004), starring Hilary Duff, is a remake of the classic tale of sibling rivalry.

Seen It?

The small indie film *Bend It Like Beckham* (2002) was a hit because it is about sports and teen life.

Spotlight On . . . SIBLING RIVALRY

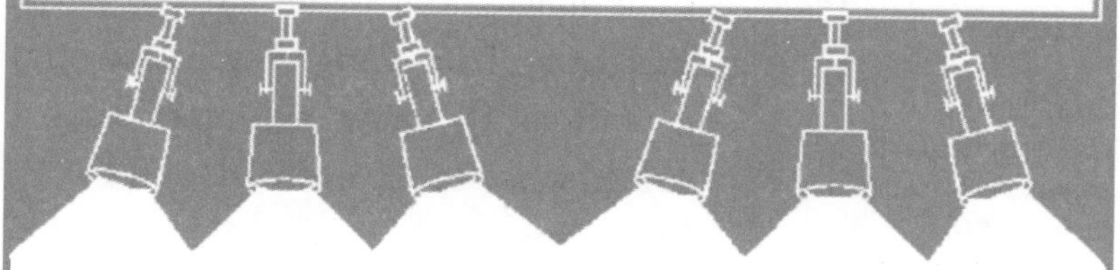

What is sibling rivalry anyway? While not all brothers and sisters experience it, sibling rivalry is a very common and very natural response some siblings have toward each other. Rivalry between two or more siblings can be the result of parents favoring one child over the other, one child (like the older) having more responsibility on his or her shoulders, one child (like the younger) being disciplined more leniently than another, one sibling excelling at a sport or hobby, and so on.

Believe it or not, sibling rivalry doesn't just happen with humans. Just about every animal on the planet who has more than one offspring experiences it in its own family.

My Sport

I'm the youngest of four children, so I often feel like I have to prove myself to my siblings. Cheerleading has become a tradition in our family. Both my sisters are cheerleaders, and my mom was a cheerleader as well. Therefore, I felt an unspoken expectation to continue in their footsteps.

CONSIDER THIS . . .

Those who **don't** take cheerleading seriously should think twice. Cheerleaders earn thousands of dollars worth of college **scholarship** money every year for their skills.

Whenever my mom and I went to watch my sisters cheer, I scrutinized their moves and made sure to point out every little thing they did wrong. I wanted to show my mom that I knew what to do even though I was younger.

When I was in sixth grade, my mother suggested that I take tumbling lessons. I was at the top of my gymnastics class because I learned to do round-offs and round-off back handsprings with superb grace. I even learned how to do a back handspring before any of my sisters did. My success in tumbling made me determined to be just as good, if not better, at cheerleading than my sisters were. When we were young we used to have competitions to see who was better at things. Of course, I got frustrated when they defeated me. I lost my share of backyard races because Jaclyn had longer legs. But cheerleading was different. I had excellent hand-eye coordination, and I could use this to my advantage. I was able to picture each move before I made it, so my performances were fluid and free of noticeable errors. I looked forward to proving my expertise to my sisters.

CONSIDER THIS . . .

Cheerleading isn't just about cartwheels anymore. Today, cheerleaders must be in **excellent physical shape** to do gymnastic stunts like back handsprings, back tucks and full layouts.

It was about eleven o'clock the night before cheerleading tryouts. I was so excited I couldn't sleep. I stayed up all night practicing and hoping I wouldn't make a fool out of myself the next day. In the morning, I raced around the house, doing my best to get ready. Feeling both nervous and excited, I couldn't stop myself from shaking. I just had to prove to my sisters and myself that I could make the team.

For Real?
More than one and a half million American teenagers are **cheerleaders.**

Finally it was time to try out. When my turn came, I got up, took a quick breath and spirited my way into the judges' hearts. I chanted, cheered, jumped and danced with no mistakes. I was so happy that I had actually done it! No one could ruin my euphoria. Or at least I *thought* no one could. My sister came out of the tryout room and told my mom how I didn't spirit enough and I'd made small errors that I hadn't even noticed. This was my first time trying out for cheerleading, and her harsh critique made me think I failed.

CONSIDER THIS . . .
Super-famous sister musicians Jessica and Ashlee Simpson couldn't be more different in their approach to fashion and fame, yet rumors of **sibling rivalries** abound.

I held my tears back until I went to the bathroom so my sister wouldn't know she'd beaten me. I wanted to be strong, but I couldn't. I began to cry even harder. I told myself that I had to face Jaclyn and show her that I still had confidence in my performance. I walked back to the library and waited for the results. My friends could tell something was wrong with me, so I told them what happened. They told me that as long as I did the best that I could, I was fine. I hadn't failed because trying out for something isn't only about getting on the team (although it's a big plus). It's about

CONSIDER THIS . . .

Twin brothers, Morgan and Paul Hamm, were both members of the 2004 Olympics men's gymnastic team, but each **excelled** on a different apparatus.

having fun and doing what you like. At that moment, I realized that even if I didn't make it, it was okay, because in life things don't always go your way. So I could either pout and whine about it, or I could accept it and go on to bigger and better things.

With my hands still shaking, I told myself it was okay, no matter what happened. Still, there was a battle inside me—in my heart I wanted to be on the squad so terribly. We all sped outside when the coach posted the results. I looked at the poster for the number two . . . I couldn't believe my eyes! Number two was the very first number! I looked away and looked back . . . it was still there! I had made it. I hadn't failed; I had accomplished what I wanted. I was overwhelmed with joy and couldn't wait for the year to start. I imagined the day when my coach would hand me my beautiful uniform so I could represent my school with pride and help others learn how to show school spirit. My sister nonchalantly congratulated me. But I didn't care. I was too happy to let anything bring me down.

That day I learned to stop worrying about what other people thought about me, especially my sister. The only thing that mattered was what I thought about myself. Sibling rivalry can get ugly, but in the end, who cares what others think of you? Just do what you want to do and believe in yourself, because you can get farther in life if you depend on yourself. Your siblings can only steal your spirit if you let them.

Julie Blackmer, Age 14

OUTSIDE THE BOX

Believe it or not, if you're feeling negative or down about yourself, your performance can be affected. Keeping a positive attitude can bring powerful results, so don't let others get you down by being negative or filling your mind with doubt. If you find yourself feeling down because of what others are saying, try these tips to pick yourself back up:

- Listen to music that puts you in a positive mood.
- Turn to friends who respect and admire you and tell them you need a pick-me-up.
- Close your eyes and visualize a time when you felt really confident and good about yourself.

WHEN I WAS NINE YEARS OLD, I announced to my parents that I wanted to volunteer at the local nursing home during my summer vacation. I had never even been inside the nursing home, so I'm not sure what the draw was. I must have seen some TV show or something with a girl my age volunteering.

Anyway, the nursing home was about a mile away from our house, and a few days a week I would walk down our hill in the humid heat of an East Coast summer and spend hours refilling water pitchers in patients' rooms or helping in arts and crafts. Even

For Real?

38% of teens think it's **important** to volunteer their time to help others.

though volunteering had been my idea, I have to admit, I was pretty nervous about the whole thing, and very uncomfortable at the beginning. Sometimes I felt like my presence wasn't even needed, that I was just getting in the way and that the staff had to scratch their brains to come up with jobs for me. Other times I'd get really uncomfortable at the thought of going into the room of a really old person who would glare at me while I poured water. Some days I just didn't want to go at all.

THE WORD

Volunteerism is another word for doing work without pay, usually for some sort of a cause.

But every now and then, something great would happen. It wasn't necessarily something big or exciting, but rather I'd have a conversation with a patient and see a smile on her face from the joy she got just by having such a "young person" hanging out with her. Or John, an elderly stroke patient, and I would sit on the balcony upstairs and watch a thunderstorm together. Or the cranky old lady in room 120 would give me a smile out of the blue. And then I knew it was all worth it.

My desire to volunteer has stuck with me well into adulthood, and it is still one of the most satisfying things I do. Most high schools encourage volunteerism and community service by rewarding students who take part with credits that can go toward their graduation. Some schools even make it mandatory. Whatever the reason, try to keep an open mind about volunteering. You may be making a difference in the lives of someone else, but you'll also improve the quality of yours.

Address Book

If you're looking for a volunteer opportunity near you, check out **Volunteer Match** and search by your zip code: *www.volunteermatch.org/*.

Gaeton

"I can't believe I'm doing this. I promised myself I wouldn't. This isn't me—I don't do stuff like this. I should be asleep for at least four more hours." I repeated that to myself over and over and over again as I walked past the parking lot, past the flowers and through the front doors of my lovely church. It was a beautiful June day, and I should have been sleeping through it, not watching over hundreds of kids between the ages of three and nine. I couldn't believe my mom had actually signed me up. I thought she was joking. I didn't need it. There was enough on my mind at the time as it was. I didn't need a couple of brats' squeaky voices crammed up there, too. I didn't need little things pulling at my pants to get my attention. I didn't need to be dealing with kids. That was the last thing I needed.

Read It?

Catch the Spirit: Teen Volunteers Tell How They Made a Difference (2000), by Susan Perry, tells the stories of teens who've had a **big impact** through **volunteerism.**

Or it was exactly what I needed.

Walking into that gymnasium was like stepping straight into another dimension—another time in life. All around me I could see toddlers crying, little boys playing a much more physical form of tag than I ever did when I was younger and little girls giving out cootie shots with such urgency you'd think they were curing smallpox. It was definitely something to behold. I sat there for at least two minutes with my jaw dropped, until I felt the first of many tugs on the side of my shorts.

CONSIDER THIS . . .

No matter what your **interests** are, chances are you can find an organization out there that would welcome your time as a volunteer. Have you ever considered any of these volunteer opportunities?

- local animal shelter
- soup kitchens and homeless shelters
- park and beach cleanups
- mentoring or tutoring
- Special Olympics
- political campaigns

"Hey, big kid! Big kid! You know you have an earring on? You've got an earring, in your ear, right there! Guys don't have earrings! Are you a guy?" So far, so good. I was about to play along and say I didn't know what he was talking about, but he was called back to join the group by his baby-sitter. And that's when I noticed. I should have figured it out before I even stepped out of the car. I was one of the only teenagers there who was male. Perfect. It was going to be a long week.

About an hour later, after singing the hippo song (which is quite a toe-tapper) and saying a morning prayer to God thanking him for everything ("except my kid sister," I heard one of them mumble), we spent some time doing arts and crafts.

You want to make a mess? You want a room that looks like a bomb went off in it? Okay. Gather up about twenty or so third-graders and give them some glue, scissors and rice. They go buck wild. The assignment was to make a design to show their love for the big man in the sky—with rice. Some kids designed crosses or made the symbol of that weird fish. "I luv u." There were an awful lot of "I luv u's." And the art teacher gave the same exact response to every single one. She tilted her head slightly to the left and let out a sweet "aww." You'd think her neck would get sore after enough *awws*. But it didn't—she kept them going all day.

I'll be honest with you. I'm not usually that great with kids. I can get along fine with one or two of them for a while, but too many for a long amount of time drives me insane. It might be because I'm stubborn. I met one kid who thought he had outsmarted me with his Ninja Turtle trivia. No way. *No way.*

Then I met Gaeton. During story time, when the kids were supposed to stand and play along, I noticed he was hopping up and down much more vigorously than all the others. He had to go pee pee. And it was an emergency, he assured me. So of course, we were quick to get into the hallway. On the way there, you'd think he'd be intimidated by me and keep quiet. But he made small talk, which I thought was really odd for a kid his age.

He looked like me when I was younger. Maybe that's why I was so open with him. He got my whole life story out of me. He was really good. Why I was in a bad mood; why I didn't want to be there. I told him it all. Turns out, he didn't want to be there, either. We both blamed our mothers. And when I was done spilling my guts to a five-year-old, he said something that I'll never forget. "It's okay. My dad told me that after rain there's always a rainbow."

God, I wish I were that age again. Here's to you, Gaeton. Wherever you are.

Michael Wassmer, Age 16

Spotlight On . . . CELEBRITY VOLUNTEERING

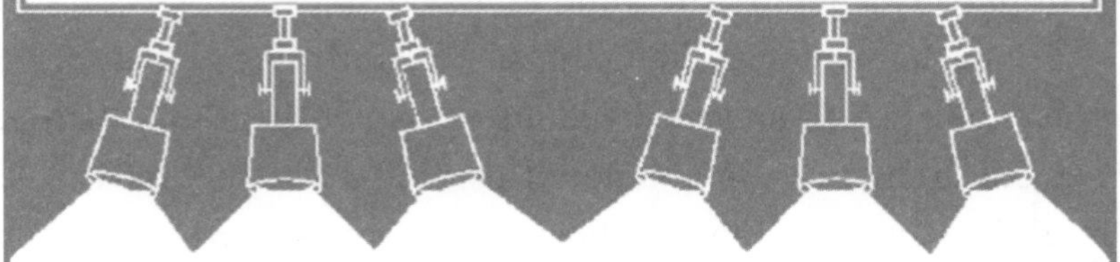

Many celebrities volunteer their time to promote causes they feel are important. Here's just a short list of celebrities who give their time to help others:

- Bono
- Angelina Jolie
- Oprah Winfrey
- P. Diddy
- Tiger Woods
- Lance Armstrong

THOMAS EDISON (you know, the guy who invented the light bulb) once said, "Opportunity is missed by most people because it is dressed in overalls and looks like work." I like that quote, in part because I believe the best opportunities are the ones you don't expect, and in part because, well, I like to wear overalls.

For Real?

Thomas Edison was actually **afraid** of the **dark,** which is why he invented the light bulb.

What Edison is really saying is that sometimes the things most worth doing are overlooked because people can't see what the purpose is. Here's an example. Say your English teacher encourages you to apply to be editor of your school newspaper. Maybe you're not really into being on the newspaper staff, but you feel pressured by the teacher, so you decide to give it a shot. As you write your audition essay, you realize it comes pretty naturally. Before you know it, your writing is winning awards, including getting you a full scholarship to a college that has a great creative writing program. By taking advantage of that initial opportunity presented by your teacher, you've changed the direction of your entire life in a way that could never have been predicted.

Granted, not every opportunity is easy to grab onto. And sometimes, taking advantage of all the possibilities might cause conflict among your friends, as you'll read in this next essay. But if you are true to yourself and stay open to the opportunities that come knocking at your door, you can't lose in the long run.

From Another Angle

"Clara, can you come over after school?" my best friend Olivia whispered to me. "I just got something really cool I want to show you! You're going to love it!" But I was stopped before I could reply.

"*Right,* Ms. Dell?" Mr. Davis, our teacher, was glaring at me from the front of the room. "By the way, I need to talk to you after class." I gulped. From the way he said it, I thought I was in big trouble. I slipped Olivia a note telling her I'd try to stop by her house after my little after-class ordeal—I really wanted to see what she was bouncing off the walls about.

At 3:30 the last bell rang and the rest of the class rushed out the door. I bit my lip and waited, but as it turned out, Mr.

Davis wasn't on the warpath after all. Instead, four of my peers streamed into the classroom, all looking as curious as me.

For Real?

David Hume Kennerly won the Pulitzer Prize for feature photography in 1972 for his photos of the **Vietnam War.** One of his most famous photos is of former U.S. President Richard Nixon waving good-bye right before resigning from office.

"I'm sure you're all wondering why you're here," Mr. Davis started off. "Well, because of your outstanding academic performance this year, you've been handpicked to participate in a national photojournalism competition."

Mr. Davis explained that over the next two months we would be photographing people who worked for the city and writing a short paragraph about each one. When we were done, the best photographs would compete against photos from other Chicago-area schools. The whole thing was being overseen by David Hume Kennerly, a Pulitzer Prize–winning photojournalist.

A giant smile spread across my face. I'd never done any photography except for the Instamatic-camera kind. But I loved a good challenge, and the project sounded totally cool. Suddenly I wanted to be the best. *What if a picture I took was the winner? How cool would that be?* When I left the meeting, my mind was racing so much that I totally forgot to stop by Olivia's.

The next day I still hadn't talked to Olivia and was dying to hear about what she'd gotten. But when I caught up with her at lunch, she turned her back to me. I asked what was wrong, but all she said was "nothing."

She turned to walk away and I broke into an apology. "I'm really sorry I didn't come over last night or call you." I explained how my mom had bawled me out for being late and how I'd totally forgotten.

"Okay," she said finally, with a smile, "you're forgiven. Did you get in trouble with Mr. Davis?"

"Oh!" I said. "No. In fact, the coolest thing happened!" I excitedly downloaded the whole photojournalism project to her.

For Real?

It was at the **1893** World Fair in Chicago that the **hamburger** was first introduced to the United States!

I expected Olivia to be thrilled, but instead she just stared at me. Obviously it didn't interest her at all, so I changed the subject. "So . . . what was that thing you were going to show me yesterday?" I asked.

"Oh, it's nothing," she answered. "Just forget it."

At home that evening I tried calling. Her mom answered, "Oh, hi, Clara! Olivia isn't here right now. Are you calling because she told you the news?"

"What news?"

"The camera! I'm so proud of her. Olivia has been into photography for as long as I can remember, but she's kept it so quiet! She didn't want to tell anyone until she had something to show for it."

"Really?" I said. I felt like someone had punched me in the stomach.

"She worked so hard to save up for this camera, and now I know she's going to blossom. She's beyond excited about it." I hung up feeling horrible. I knew Olivia liked to snap a

CONSIDER THIS . . .

Just like the invention of automatic cameras in the late 1900s changed how photographs captured the world, **digital** cameras are doing the same thing today. How do you think **new** inventions will change photography in the future?

picture here or there, but hadn't a clue that it went any further than that.

The next day after math class, I confessed to Olivia everything her mom told me. "Yes, now I've got a great camera and a book about how to be a photographer. But do I get to learn from a famous photojournalist? *No.* Obviously only people who've never even thought about photography get to do *that.*"

"Why are you angry at *me*?"

Olivia shrugged, staring at me.

"Olivia, you know it's not my fault," I said. "I didn't ask to be chosen over you. I didn't even know you were into photography. I'm sorry, but what am I supposed to do about it?"

She rolled her eyes. "Whatever. Let's just go eat."

The following week, my photography team got started. Taking pictures was amazing. But it wasn't just the photography that made it great. I was making friends with kids I probably wouldn't have gotten to know if it hadn't been for this project.

In fact, everything was going great, except for my relationship with Olivia. She had barely talked, and she never wanted to know a single detail about the photography project. She even

THE WORD

Photojournalists are just like journalists, but they tell **stories using pictures** instead of words. Photojournalists working for newspapers and magazines might also have to develop their own pictures, scan them into a computer and get them ready for print.

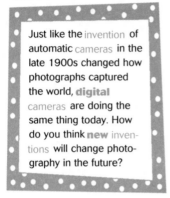

started avoiding me. I hated not having my best friend to talk with about everything.

But one thought kept returning—it wasn't my fault that I was part of this project and Olivia wasn't. So why was she taking it out on me?

Seen It?

If you've ever watched the Chicago-based drama *ER,* then you've probably seen the characters taking the "el," or "elevated train," to work.

Over the next two months, our photo team captured the city at work. Documenting people who worked for the city was eye-opening. One weekend, toward the end of the project, I got my best pictures. I crawled into a trench under an "el" train and shot half a roll of film as a train mechanic worked on the underbody of the car. In one of those shots, the mechanic's body was silhouetted by a splash of sunlight, her determined, intelligent face visible but almost in shadow.

HOW ABOUT YOU?

Have you ever had a friend get **mad at you** for something that **wasn't** your fault? How did you handle it?

Chicago came alive to me in a whole new way. People I'd never noticed before now seemed vital and real to me. It was like getting to see things from another angle—one I hadn't appreciated before.

The only thing I didn't appreciate was Olivia's ongoing hostility toward me. I tried everything. I'd suggest we eat lunch together, but she'd shake her head and say she had other plans. I'd invite her over but she wouldn't even pretend to be interested. I even tried to coax her to do our own photo shoot—just the two us. But she said no.

Every time Olivia rejected me, anger rumbled in my stomach. I was beginning to hate everything she did to try to guilt-trip me. I hated it even more that it was working. By the end of the project, Olivia and I weren't speaking at all. *Fine. Let her be that way. Let her be the victim, not me.*

Meanwhile, my team had pored over every photograph we'd taken and selected the fifteen best shots for the competition. Five of them were mine. It was a major vote of confidence in my work by the other kids on our team.

Finally the big night arrived. The judges had selected sixty-five photographs from all the schools to be displayed at the Chicago Historical Society. Two were my shots of the "el" train mechanics at work.

I was jazzed that night. Dozens of kids from the participating schools were there. My mom, grandparents and I had our picture taken in front of my winning photograph with David Hume Kennerly.

As I crossed the hall where the celebration was taking place, I glimpsed someone through the crowd. A wave of shock went through me. Standing there and looking in my direction was Olivia.

I quickly veered off in another direction. *What was she doing here? Showing up to spoil my night?* I couldn't believe it. Just seeing her sent me into a boil. I felt anger, sadness, even a feeling I hate to admit—pride with a cocky "too-bad-for-you" tinge to it.

I wanted to avoid any up-close contact with Olivia, but before I could get lost in the crowd, there she was. She stepped in front of me.

"Hey Clara," she said. Right away I noticed that her voice

didn't sound cold or mean. I just stood there warily, saying nothing.

Address Book

Are **you** into **photography?** Check out some of these Web sites for more information:

Exposure—A Beginner's Guide to Photography
(www.photonhead.com/exposure)

Kodak e-Magazine: The Online Photography Magazine
(www.kodak.com/US/en/corp/magazine/index.shtml)

Young Artists' Workshops
(www.theworkshops.com/high school/index.asp)

"Your picture is really good," Olivia said. She actually sounded sincere.

"Thanks," I replied begrudgingly. I took a step, wanting to get away from her as fast as I could. I didn't want to go into it with her, even if she was acting nicer than usual.

"Listen, I just . . ." Olivia stopped.

"What?" I said. For a moment neither of us said anything. It was one of the longest, most uncomfortable silences I'd ever experienced. Finally she spoke again.

"You know when you said we should do a photo shoot together?"

I nodded.

"Well, I've been thinking about it. I think we really *should* do that. I mean, I'd really like to . . . okay?"

Olivia looked a little bit sad, but also hopeful. Looking at her standing there, every hard thing I'd felt against her for the past few months left me. I blinked, hardly believing it.

"Really?" I said.

"Really," Olivia confirmed. "I've been a total jerk and I'm really sorry. Just looking at your work proves you deserved getting picked for the project. Maybe you could even show me some things you learned."

"Wow," I said. "But maybe we could *both* show each other some stuff."

"That would be great." A hint of a smile showed on Olivia's face. Suddenly it seemed like maybe things really had changed with her. A huge feeling of relief and freedom came over me. Over the past few months I'd done the best I could. I'd seen a lot of things in my world from a different angle. I'd tried hard to see things from Olivia's point of view, too. I'd learned a lot. And now it looked like I might even have my friend again.

More than 1,000 photographs were submitted to the photojournalism competition. Eventually, twenty were chosen to compete at the national level. As it turned out, I had one more thing to be grateful for—mine was one of those twenty. Ultimately, my photograph wasn't one of the three national winners, but I didn't mind. I'd come a long way, and I'd still won a lot.

Most important, I'd won my best friend back.

Clara Dell, Age 13

HAVE YOU EVER HAD AN *"AH HA* MOMENT"? You know, when you realize something isn't as it appears, or you make a discovery about yourself that really blows your mind, and a big light bulb goes off inside your head as if to say, "Oh, *now* I get it!"

Ah ha moments give us a chance to see things from a different perspective and can truly be life-changing events. Once our eyes open up to a new way of looking at things, the world is never quite the same. Read on to discover what made this next author sit back and have her own *ah ha* moment and gain perspective on the kinds of things we're all guilty of taking advantage of.

OUTSIDE THE BOX

Are you in need of an AH HA moment? Do you want to put your life in perspective? Here are some ideas for getting out of your usual rut and opening up to a whole new point of view:

- Volunteer at a homeless shelter or soup kitchen for an afternoon.
- Rent a movie about another culture.
- Pass an evening without speaking to anyone at all.
- Go through your wardrobe and see how many things you own that you haven't worn in at least one year.
- Don't look in the mirror for one full day.
- Participate in Take Your Child to Work Day with one of your parents.

I Could Be Hauling Water

Like many schools in the United States, mine offered a variety of after-school activities. It didn't matter if you were athletic, studious or dramatic—a club or program existed for just about every interest. Yet I wasn't satisfied.

My school offered girls' soccer, but I wanted to play *lacrosse*. The drama department was doing a serious play, but I wanted to perform in *musical* theater. I could sign up for the chess club. Instead I complained because there was no debate club. For each after-school activity, teachers gave their time to help students. Clean classrooms and supplies were always available. Buses took students to other schools for competitions or enrichment programs. I took all of this for granted until I got a different perspective on after-school activities.

For Real?

Lacrosse, which is becoming more and more popular around the world, was actually invented by Native Americans. Explorers in the United States saw them playing it in the 1600s.

In the winter of 2001, I had the opportunity to go to Kenya and Uganda. My family and I visited a school where the students studied on hard wooden benches, walked over dirt floors in bare feet and had no after-school activities at all. Who had time for fun and enrichment? Many kids walked five miles just to get to and from school. The students living in orphanages went to their group home to do chores, like walking three miles to fill buckets of water. Without running water or electricity, teachers were challenged just to teach lessons, let alone plan arts and crafts or sports activities. If the students were lucky enough to have a few free minutes after school, they jumped rope or played the

Consider This . . .

Kenya and Uganda are in East Africa, and in both countries the average age a person can expect to live to is 45 years old. Compare that with the United States, where people live an average of **77 years.**

bongo drum—sharing *two* jump ropes and *one* drum between 230 students.

The schools in Kenya and Uganda were so poor that students shared pencils and paper. They didn't have white boards, so teachers used big slabs of slate as blackboards. The rough texture of the rock made it hard to write with their precious pieces of chalk. These students had few books, no computers, no colorful posters and definitely no creative after-school programs.

CONSIDER THIS . . .

Although many people think **bongo drums** come from Africa, their origin can be traced to Cuba in the 1800s.

One day after school my family and I ran an after-school craft program to teach the kids how to make paper bag puppets. We passed out glue and markers and told the kids they could start working. They just sat there and looked at us with big eyes. They understood English, so I couldn't figure out why they hadn't started decorating their paper bags. We suddenly realized they had never seen markers and didn't know how to remove the caps. I demonstrated pulling the cap off. The kids laughed and got excited when they saw how the markers made colorful designs on their bags. They had never seen glue either, so they figured you pulled the cap off the glue, just like the markers. It got a little messy, especially when the kids pulled the orange caps off the glue bottles!

For Real?

Elmer's glue is undeniably the most popular brand, maybe because it's been around so long. It was invented in 1947, and back then it was sold in glass bottles with Popsicle sticks attached to spread the glue.

It struck me that these kids, many my own age, had never

watched television or worn uniforms on a sports team. Uniforms? They didn't even own a basketball! Throughout my visit, I never heard any students complain. They didn't moan and groan about walking over hot dirt to carry heavy water containers. They gladly shared the markers we gave them and treasured their simple paper bag puppets. And they never complained about being bored.

Read It?

The No. 1 Ladies' Detective Agency book series, by Alexander McCall Smith, is hugely popular and tells the story of the only detective agency for women in the African country of Botswana.

Looking back on the lives of the students I met in Africa, I returned to school with a new outlook on activities. I stopped complaining about after-school programs and joined the soccer team without another complaint about the lack of a lacrosse team.

Address Book

Interested in working or studying abroad? Check out **Transitions Abroad** Web site at *www.transitionsabroad.com/* for info on what's out there for teens.

Sondra Clark, Age 15

Take the Quiz:

DO YOU HAVE THE RIGHT ATTITUDE TO EXCEL IN AFTER-SCHOOL ACTIVITIES?

Now that you know participating in extracurricular activities—sports, clubs, politics—can have many benefits, do you have what it takes to be a star after school?

1. Your older brother is the most talented athlete in school, so when it comes time to go out for the track team, you're conflicted over what to do. You know that you're a much slower runner than he is, and you're afraid that everyone will think you're a big loser for not being as good as him. What do you do?

___ A. You decide the humiliation isn't worth it and skip the tryouts. You know you're not one of the fastest runners there, so what's the point?

___ B. You figure you might as well try out, but even though you want to be a runner like your brother, you decide to focus your tryout on the long jump and javelin.

___ C. Running is what you want to do, so you go for it anyway. Besides, since your brother got faster as each year went by, maybe by the time you're a senior you'll be the best athlete in school, too!

2. The junior class play this year is one of your favorites, and you're planning to audition but are concerned that your best friend is after the same role as you. You've gotten into fights over competition before, so you want to tread carefully. How do you handle this sticky situation?

___ A. You've almost lost your friend over an audition once before, and you decide it's not worth it to go through that all over again. If she wants the role, she can have it.

___ B. You don't want to ruffle any feathers before you have to, so you don't tell your friend you're going for the same role until she sees you at auditions.

___ C. You are upfront to your friend and tell her what role you're auditioning for, but that you'll be happy for whoever gets it in the end. You suggest that the two of you help each other prepare for the big audition.

3. You've been the class president freshman year, sophomore year and junior year, so you figure the election's in the bag for senior year. You couldn't be more shocked when you find out your BFF wants to be senior class president. What do you do?

___ A. You get really annoyed that your friend would want to run against you. She should know that you deserve the role and ask her why she doesn't try for something else.

___ B. You respect your friend's decision to run, but can't help but be a little annoyed. You decide that it's best if you both take time off from your friendship until after the election.

___ C. You understand that this might be as important to your friend as it is to you, and you wish her the best of luck on her campaign. May the best person win!

4. You and your group of friends decide to try out for the cheerleading squad together, imagining the fun you'll all have when traveling to away games together on the bus. But when all of your friends make varsity but you, you're totally bummed out and don't know what to do. How do you handle your disappointment?

___ A. You get really annoyed and decide that it's varsity or nothing, so you quit. Anyway, it's not fair—your friends aren't any better than you are!

___ B. You can't help but be slightly mad at your friends who made varsity, and you tell them that you don't think it's fair. As far as JV goes, you're not sure you're going to stick around.

___ C. You still want to cheer and decide to set your sights on making varsity next year. As a JV cheerleader, you'll still get to participate in all of the home games.

5. You've been in the yearbook club for three years and are expecting to be handed the plum position of yearbook editor senior year by the club advisor, but you are surprised when he decides that you should share responsibility with a hotshot junior. What do you do?

___ A. You ask for a one-on-one meeting with the club advisor and tell him that if he doesn't give you sole editorship, then you're not interested.

___ B. You begrudgingly agree to the arrangement, but make sure that the junior editor knows who's really in charge.

___ C. You decide to work with the junior editor. Obviously the advisor thinks he's talented and together the two of you can make the best yearbook ever.

Well, how'd you do? Give yourself 10 points for every A, 20 points for every B and 30 points for every C. Look below to find out how prepared you are to excel in extracurricular activities:

50–70 points = You could take a few lessons on playing fair and winning and losing gracefully. If you continue to be a poor sport, the only one who's going to miss out is yourself.

80–120 points = You want to have the right attitude, but sometimes your emotions get in the way. Whenever you're feeling conflicted about how to handle a tough after-school situation, take a deep breath and remember what's really important.

130–150 points = Great job! You know the value of participating in school activities, and you've got a great attitude to boot. With your approach to conflict you're going to be very successful in your career someday!

CHAPTER 7

LOVE

Would biology class be even remotely interesting without your crush sitting two seats in front of you? Have you ever envied the couple who makes out in front of their lockers every day before school? Or maybe you've been half of that couple yourself? What happens when the love of your life, who just happens to be a senior, graduates and leaves you behind? This chapter explores the intense emotions that go along with dating and crushing, falling in love and breaking up.

THERE IS NOTHING QUITE LIKE THE WAY WE FEEL when we realize we're in love for the first time. It is a sensation unmatched by any other. Flushed faces are the result of a simple smile. The sound of a voice can be the most beautiful music you've ever heard. A wink can send you into cardiac arrest.

The thing about first loves that makes them so memorable and powerful is the intensity of the feelings. I remember the boy I first said "I love you" to. We were both fifteen. It was a warm Friday night and we were having soft ice cream after playing a round of miniature golf. He said it first. It was so unexpected, caught me so off guard. I blurted out the words in response, "I love you, too."

CONSIDER THIS . . .

One of the most famous **romantic couples** of all times, Shakespeare's Romeo and Juliet, were just teenagers.

It probably wouldn't surprise you to find out that that boy and I are no longer together, and in fact, we broke up about six months later, even though we did remain friends and even went to the senior prom together. Yet today, when I hear the song "Crazy for You" by Madonna, I'm instantly transported back to that breezy night and remember the sparkle in my boyfriend's eyes when he confessed his true feelings. They say you never forget your first love, and you know what? It's true.

Spotlight On . . . BEING IN LOVE

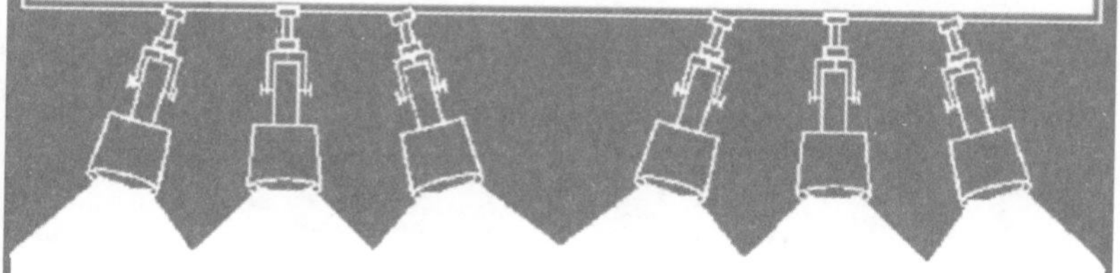

Sure, love feels great, but believe it or not, there are actually physiological and tangible benefits to being in love! Here are just a few of things you might experience while in love:

- be healthier
- live a longer life
- feel encouraged
- have a stronger heart (literally)

FIRST LOVE

His early '90s Buick pulls up to my house
The gray-blue exterior gleaming.
A smile consumes my face
And the muscles in my cheeks begin to tighten.
This boy doesn't pull at my heartstrings
He rips them apart.
He tells me he loves me
And I believe him.
His floppy brown hair falls in my face,
I welcome its scent.
His arms hold me tight.

Nothing moves when he is near,
The world stops cold.
Everything matters,
Nothing matters.
The buttons on his jacket reflect the sun,
And the light from his eyes feels warm
But there is sweat on his palm.
He is scared to leave.
Scared to move on.
I am scared of the chilled, dark air.
I sit and count the days before he's gone.

Maggie Reyland, Age 17

Seen It?

One of the most memorable "I love you's" in sitcom history was when Chandler first told Monica how he felt on **Friends.**

WHERE DO YOU STAND?

It's been two months since you and your significant other decided to "take a break" from your relationship. You don't want to believe that the relationship is really over, but as time goes by, you're starting to give up hope. Go through each question below and figure out how you would handle these scenarios.

1. It's the one-year anniversary of your first date, and you don't even get a phone call. You . . .

   a. reread every "I love you" note you've ever received and sit by the phone.
   b. decide to get your mind off things and catch a movie with a friend.

2. You're on vacation with your family and you don't have access to your computer. You . . .

   a. spend your whole vacation at the Internet cafe checking your e-mail just in case.
   b. enjoy the vacation—your e-mail inbox will be waiting for you when you get home.

3. You're doing laundry and you find an old T-shirt from your significant other shoved behind the hamper. You . . .

   a. refuse to wash the shirt and keep it under your pillow so you can smell it.
   b. wash it, fold it and put it away.

4. Your parents surprise you with a dinner out on your birthday, but they don't realize the restaurant they picked is the site of your first date. You . . .

   a. burst into tears when you pull up and insist you go somewhere else.
   b. decide to create a new memory for this restaurant. The food is really good!

5. A friend calls you to say they ran into your significant other at a party and he or she was flirting with someone else. You . . .

   a. call up your significant other and demand an explanation.
   b. decide to wait for the phone to ring. The ball's in his or her court.

WHEN IT COMES TO DATING AND SCHOOL, it's all about who's done what with whom . . . and where . . . and when . . . and *why*? But while it sometimes seems like everyone's dating and has a ton of experience, the thought of even kissing someone else can turn some teens into nervous bundles of anxiety. I was one of them.

It's not that I was a "prude" exactly. It's just that when I was in middle school, I was really "inexperienced." My idea of dating was passing notes back and forth in class and having someone to walk me to the bus-loading zone. I'd never had a real kiss, at least not the kind that counted: a French kiss.

All my friends had done it. They even seemed to like it. I definitely wanted to do it, but didn't have a likely candidate. Until my church group went away for a winter weekend retreat. My scope at the time was a cute guy my age who was into football and Def Leppard. We definitely liked each other, but since we went to separate schools, our "relationship" consisted of saved seats in Sunday school and swapped class photos, signed with lines like, *Deb—to a cute girl I met in church. RMA*. The retreat was the perfect opportunity for the two of us to hang out outside of our church environment, and I couldn't wait.

For Real?

Did you know that the average high-school teen relationship lasts for a year and a half?

The weekend was fun, and my crush and I got to spend enough time together to know that I really did like him. All of that changed on our last day. I had gone back with him to his cabin to get something (a bag of nacho-flavored Doritos comes to mind, but I can't be sure), and as soon as we closed the door,

THE WORD

The term French kiss was coined in the early 1920s, when the adjective "French" was commonly being used as a word for "spicy."

he made his move, leaning in toward me and kissing me. The French way. If even one of us had known what we were doing, this might not have been as disastrous as it was. But since we were both clueless, the kiss left me wanting to gag with horror. In fact, I think I did. I clearly remember pushing him away and saying, and I quote, "That's enough of that."

As soon as I said it, I was horribly embarrassed, both from my lame reaction and how gross the kiss had been. But it turns out that it *was* the "end of that." Our "relationship" fizzled. I'm sure he thought I was pretty uncool, and I, well, I just didn't want to ever have to kiss that boy again.

I remained scared of the French kiss for another year or two after that, a fact that my high school friends found quite amusing. But I wasn't alone in my fear and anticipation . . . it turns out that my predicament then is still just as real for teenagers today.

Consider This . . .

Kissing and making out is one area where it's easy to feel **pressured** to do something just because everyone else is doing it. Remember, the only one who knows what you're ready to handle is you. If something doesn't **feel right,** then it's okay to say **no way.**

Never Been Kissed

It was at a recent sleepover with my high school cross-country team that I truly realized how bad things had gotten. I was feeling pretty mature and sophisticated as I looked around at the shy, innocent faces of the incoming freshmen. Had it really been only two years since I was one of them? It seemed like ages.

That is, until we played our annual "get to know each other" game. Here's how it works: Everyone takes a turn sharing an interesting fact about herself, and then those who have had the same experience raise their hands, so we can see what we all have in common and bond as a team. It's sort of like "truth or dare," except a lot less exciting because, well, there are no crazy or embarrassing dares.

Everything was fine as we went through the standard boring statements ("I have run cross-country before," "I am an only child," "I have a pet goldfish named Stan"). Then some daredevil decided to spice things up by casually voicing the statement that has plagued my teenage years: "I have had my first kiss."

For Real?

Every year on the MTV Movie Awards, MTV gives an award to the movie couple with the **"Best Kiss."**

I watched with red-faced embarrassment as all around me arms began to go up. Only three of us kept our hands in our laps: me, a sixteen-year-old junior, and two other freshmen who looked so young that waitresses undoubtedly still offered them the twelve-and-under kids' menu and movie theaters still gave them the child's ticket price.

Yes, indeed, I'm part of a species that is slowly growing extinct. I'm sweet sixteen and I've never been kissed.

I never imagined it would be like this. When I was younger, I pictured high school as something straight out of television shows like *Saved by the Bell* or *Boy Meets World.* A bright, clean indoor campus where everyone

Seen It?

Saved by the Bell has been a hugely popular television show in two incarnations: first from 1989 to 1993 and then from 1993 through 2000. The show was known for its **comedic approach** to sharing the lives of a group of high school friends.

wears letterman jackets, has his or her own shiny locker, and students wave pom-poms at football games. There was no doubt in my mind that by the time I was an oh-so-old, oh-so-cool teenager I would have experienced my unforgettably magical first kiss. I mean, *duh,* I would have a *boyfriend*. Every girl has a boyfriend in high school, right?

HOW ABOUT YOU?

Do you and your friends talk about **who's done** what **with whom?** Who do you go to for questions about sex?

It came as a big shock when I entered my freshman year and discovered that the high school campus was littered with trash, math class was just as boring as it had been in middle school and our football team was horrible. As for having a boyfriend, well, a great majority of the guys in my classes were those I had known since elementary school. You know who I'm talking about. The ones who used to eat paste and make farting noises with their armpits. (And even though they're now in high school, most of them are still so immature it wouldn't surprise me to find they still do those things.)

Seen It?

In *Never Been Kissed* (1999), Drew Barrymore stars as a journalist who goes undercover to report on what it's like to be in high school. While she's at it, she gets to rewrite her old reputation, from **geek** to **chic.**

As freshmen, my fellow "kissing virgin" friends and I made a pact that whoever was the first to touch lips with a boy would tell the others what it was like. You know, so we'd have a clue of what to expect. The thought of kissing was scary. *What if we don't do it right? What if we were horrible? What if our braces got stuck together? Can that really even happen?*

Weeks turned to months, months to years, and eventually most of my friends found that Nosepicker Nick wasn't nearly as gross as he used to be, and Dorky Dan the Stamp Collector really was a nice guy. One by one my friends jumped off the never-been-kissed diving board into the mysterious yet exciting waters of high school dating. But when I asked them about it, they suddenly became shy and didn't elaborate much besides, "It was really great."

Even my best friend backed out of our pact. When I asked her how she knew what to do when she kissed, she replied, "Oh, Dallas, it's something you just know. It's like in that movie *When Harry Met Sally.* Remember at the beginning, when they interview all those old couples, and that one lady says, 'I knew he was the one. I knew the same way you know a good melon?' It's like that. You just know."

For Real?

If you **like** watermelon and cantaloupe, you might want to give other melons a try. There are over 25 different varieties of melons, including the horned melon, musk melon and Santa Claus melon.

So that, sadly, is the most helpful advice I've received on the subject. *Some things you just know, the same way you know a good melon.*

But what if I'm not very good at choosing fruit? What if I take the time and energy to pick out a melon only to later discover it's bruised inside, or even rotten?

My mom tells me not to worry: Boys are just stupid. My

dad tells me I'm too young to have a boyfriend anyway. (Funny, he wasn't too young to have a girlfriend when he was my age!)

I like to think it just hasn't been the right time yet. I mean, I'm not a total loser. I've been to a few school dances and even out on a date or two. But at the end of the night, when my date and I were standing on my front stoop under the fluorescent porch light my dad is always sure to turn on, it was actually me who initiated the hug first in order to preempt the goodnight kiss. For some reason it just didn't feel right—I really don't know why. And it turns out that the only guy I wouldn't have minded receiving my first kiss from ended up liking me just as a friend. Go figure. But that's another story altogether.

WHERE DO YOU STAND?

What's your view on love: Are you a hopeless romantic or a realist?

Your favorite romantic comedy is . . .

- ___ SCREAM (0 points)
- ___ LORD OF THE RINGS (1 point)
- ___ SWEET HOME ALABAMA (2 points)

Your ideal first date is . . .

- ___ WATCHING SPORTS HIGHLIGHTS (0 points)
- ___ GOING FOR A HIKE (1 point)
- ___ A CANDLELIGHT DINNER (2 points)

Your favorite television couple is . . .

- ___ SEINFELD AND KRAMER (0 points)
- ___ WILL AND GRACE (1 point)
- ___ ROSS AND RACHEL (2 points)

For Valentine's Day you expect . . .

- ___ A PHONE CALL (0 points)
- ___ A CARD (1 point)
- ___ A LOVE POEM (2 points)

If your date showed up without flowers you would . . .

- ___ NOT EVEN NOTICE (0 points)
- ___ BE DISAPPOINTED (1 point)
- ___ KICK HIM OUT (2 points)

Add up your points:
0–3 = 100% realist
4–7 = somewhere in the middle
8–10 = 100% hopeless romantic!

So, as for now, the closest thing I have to a boyfriend is my boxer puppy, Gar. He gives me lots of slobbery dog kisses and is actually a very good dance partner when I hold onto his two front paws. If only I could take him to the prom.

I'm trying to stop worrying so much about getting my first kiss and just let life take me where it will. In the meantime, I'm working on new facts about myself to share at next year's cross-country sleepover. How many hands will raise when I ask who else has climbed Mt. Whitney? Or learned how to speak sign language? Or published a story in *Chicken Soup*? I bet not too many.

I've learned I don't need a boyfriend to make my life fun. As for my first kiss? I'll get it eventually. There are some things you just know—the same way you know a good melon.

Dallas Woodburn, Age 17

Spotlight On . . . DATING

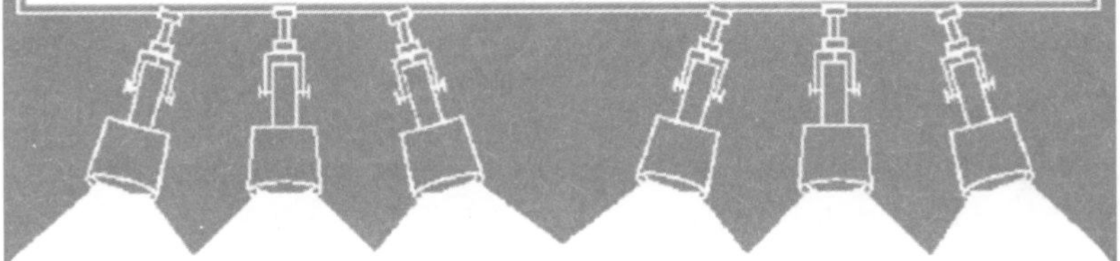

When are you old enough to date? What is too young? What should a date consist of? Parents often find themselves wondering when they should allow their kids to "date." The truth is, "dating" means different things depending on age. In seventh grade, dating might consist of hanging out at school or simply making it known that two people are together. In high school a date might be going to the movies or a party together. There's a lot of discussion over how young is too young, and many parents find themselves allowing sons to date at younger ages than daughters, which just doesn't make any sense. The truth is, every teen is different, as is their relationship with their parents. As teens mature differently, and levels of trust between teens and their parents vary, figuring out what dating means for you is something that will have to be decided in your family.

I STILL REMEMBER A CRUSH OF MINE WHO BROKE MY HEART. We were both eighteen years old, and we became friends after getting to know each other in a film class at school. It was one of those "like at first sight" kind of things for both of us, and we soon began hanging out a lot together, studying for tests, grabbing a bite to eat, catching a movie. We discovered we had so much in common, and I was convinced this guy was "the" guy. He was everything I wanted in a boyfriend. He was cute, nice, sensitive, funny. Just the sound of his voice gave me goose bumps.

For Real?
Have you ever **fallen** hard for a friend? How did you **handle it?**

Things felt so right that I thought my feelings were mutual. While nothing had happened to indicate we were more than friends,

I felt very clearly that's where we were going, so when I confessed to him how I felt one rainy night while sharing an umbrella and he didn't respond the way I'd hoped, I was crushed.

My friend explained that while he did like me, he had just gotten out of a relationship and didn't want to go there again. In the same breath, he told me that he still liked me a lot and wanted to continue spending time together. Well, I couldn't do it. I knew I'd never be able to just "hang out" as friends, knowing I felt something more for him than he did for me.

Sometimes I wonder if I made a mistake, confessing my true feelings to my crush. Maybe if I hadn't said anything, things might have turned out differently. It's a common dilemma when friends crush on other friends. To speak up or not to speak up . . . *that* is the question. It's one that the author of this next essay, "Friends . . . Forever" ponders as well.

Seen It?

Mandy Moore plays the daughter of the president who falls hard for a guy who insists he just wants to be her friend in the romantic comedy *Chasing Liberty* **(2004).**

OUTSIDE THE BOX

Looking for an original way to tell someone you like him or her? Here are some subtle and not-so-subtle ways to get your point across:

- Grab your friend's hand at the movies during a scary part.
- Write a personal note explaining how you feel.
- Drop subtle hints to see if he or she picks up on them.
- Invite your friend to a group thing, but when you get there, it's just the two of you.

Friends . . . Forever?

A story about falling for your best friend and not knowing what to do

Those ever-so-famous words, *"If only she knew."* I've been saying them ever since I lost her. But she doesn't know about me losing anything. She doesn't even know that I've felt this way ever since that first day she smiled and said "goodbye" as she flipped back her hair. It keeps me up at night, staring at the ceiling, thinking about everything.

Once I realize that just pondering won't change anything, I pull out my pen and paper and lay out my heart with ink. I stare at the even, blue lines, wondering what shapes and characters could fill up those lines and explain everything to her. But none of them will.

All I know is that she's what I've been searching for. She's my golden ticket to the gates of happiness. Yet these gates remain locked. I'm left in that lonely field of "friendship." Sure, a friendship is an outstanding occurrence. But I want to take it one step further. I want to take her to a place she's never been. A place only my heart can describe.

Consider This . . .

Dating someone who started out as a close friend can have great benefits. After all, chances are this person has seen you at your best and worst before, so you don't have to waste time pretending to be someone you're not. If he or she **really** likes you, you can be sure it will be for **who you are.**

One Saturday afternoon, my mind wandered as she sat there talking about "Mr. Perfect." Before I knew it, I saw myself as that person. A smile came over me. She asked what the smile was for. I wanted to tell her it was from the way the wind blows her long, shiny hair. I wanted to tell her it was from the way her nose scrunches up when she laughs. Yet I told her nothing.

Then a month later I got a phone call. I was anticipating it. Every time the phone rang, my stomach dropped as if I just went down the first dip of a roller coaster, hoping it was her. This time, it was. And she needed to talk. She wanted me to stop by. Her boyfriend had dumped her.

As I made that eight-and-a-half minute drive (not that I've ever timed it or anything), I thought of ways to make her feel better. My ideas were endless; I'd obviously been thinking about this for quite some time. I knew I would treat her like a queen. She smiled at my concern and told me what a true friend I was. "Friend." The word hit me like a hurricane's wave on a beach.

My frustration returned, just as the tide finds its way back to the ocean. Maybe "friends" is all we were ever meant to be? So I just sat there, silent. I kept my real feelings hidden deep inside, behind that little plastic smile I gave her.

Maybe one of these days I will tell her. I will spill everything out to her in a flood of emotion. That day is coming. I've written it out fifty times, what I would tell her, yet I can't remember a darn thing. When the time does come, and I speak from my heart instead of some little paper I wrote and memorized, I'll realize that this could possibly be the best thing I have ever done. But I'll never know that feeling, I'll never feel that love, and I'll never love like I did that one night, sitting outside with her, under the porch light, where I began to open the door to my heart.

Chris S. Lewis, Age 17

Spotlight On . . . FALLING IN LOVE WITH A FRIEND

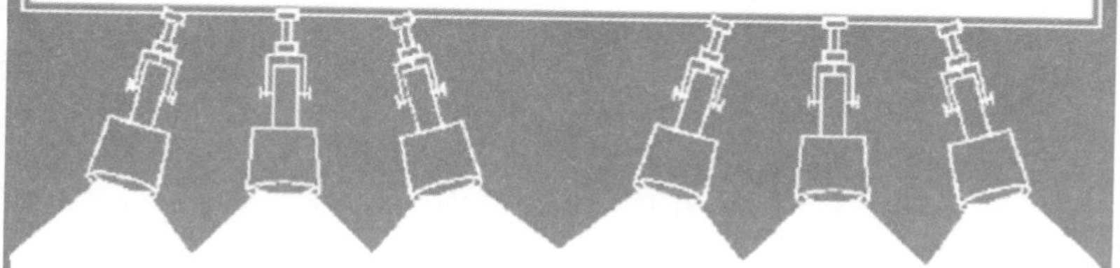

You spend time together. You share secrets. You're practically inseparable. It's only natural that one of you might develop feelings for the other. But that just leaves you with a big ol' dilemma: What to do? The way I see it, here are your options, along with some pros and cons:

- You do nothing and keep your feelings a secret. This might seem like the easy choice, and you might keep your friendship intact initially, but down the road you might find you're unable to bottle up your feelings any longer and burst.
- You tell your friend how you feel. If your friend feels the same way about you, the results of this option could be awesome! On the other hand, if he or she doesn't, there's a chance that your friendship might suffer, as one or both of you might feel awkward once the beans are spilled.

At the end of the day, you have to make a decision you can live with. If your friend is a close one, hopefully your relationship will stand the test of time no matter which option you choose.

TO SAY I WAS BOY CRAZY when I was in high school would be an understatement. And I know I wasn't alone. As a teen, the hormones are flowing, and it's all we can do to keep our eyes focused on the blackboard instead of on the back of our scope's head, admiring his new haircut or counting the freckles on her neck.

I had it down to a system. By the end of the first week of school, I would have picked out a scope in every class, someone I would look forward to seeing, find out what he was wearing, see if I could get him to make eye contact, maybe even find an excuse to talk to him. Even though these distractions sometimes made listening to the teacher more challenging, I looked at the flip side of the equation. Having scopes in every class was excellent motivation to never miss a class. Russian history can be a whole lot more exciting when your scope forgets his textbook and is forced to share with you. This next essay, "The 10:15 Vixen," tells with drop-dead accuracy just how the very glimpse of a crush can turn you to jelly.

THE WORD

A vixen is another word for a **female fox** (the animal kind of fox), but it has come to be used as another word for a woman who likes to cause trouble.

The 10:15 Vixen

To tell you the truth, I've had my share of girlfriends. I know how to pick them, too. Every girl I've ever been with is nothing short of a genius, and good looking to boot. And I'd imagine there are quite a few more girls out there who will eventually have the misfortune of thinking I'm the kind of guy they want to spend their time with. But as of right now, any kind of relationship that requires any schedule whatsoever—including calls every night, dates every weekend and/or the occasional use of the phrase "I love you"—is completely out of the question. Words cannot explain how sick and tired I am of regularity. It's predictable. It's boring. It's something that I really don't want to deal with right now.

Seen It?

In *A Cinderella Story* (2004), Hilary Duff plays a geeky high-schooler who meets the love of her life **online,** who just happens to be the most popular boy in school.

But I'll let you in on a little secret. There's this girl at my school I see immediately after third period who simply drives me up the wall. Every day, at about 10:15—you can practically set your watch by it—this girl comes striding down the hallway wearing an outfit that would make an old man double over with excitement. And it's not just her outfit. Her hair is amazing. She has enough hair to give Rapunzel a run for her money. I've got a thing for girls with a ton of hair. And if I didn't before, she made me have one. I'm not even going to talk about the days when she wears pigtails and go-go boots.

I don't even know this girl's name. I don't know what grade she's in. I have no idea what her interests are, or if she plays any sports, or if she has a boyfriend who wouldn't even think twice before breaking my neck if he knew how much I studied his girl. I don't know if she's the worst person to ever grace this Earth, or if she's the much sexier form of

Read It?

The **Grimm Brothers** wrote many famous fairy tales, including the tale of **Rapunzel,** who had incredibly long, beautiful, blonde hair.

Mother Teresa. The only thing I know about this girl is that her smile almost makes it worth rolling out of bed at five in the morning, and when I miss our daily 10:15 "date"—a quick glance and an attempted suave walk from me—my day is considerably worse. The funny thing is, I doubt she even acknowledges my existence.

Not that I do much to change that fact. I have to pretend I don't notice her either, because that's the cool thing to do. And I've discovered that it's much more difficult to be cool when you're actually trying to be cool. The other day I glanced over at her for two seconds and I ran straight into the back of an assistant principal who informed me, in not exactly the softest voice possible, that I need to watch where I'm going and get my head out of the clouds. I'm pretty sure she heard him. I'm also pretty sure the color of my face matched perfectly with the red tie worn by the man I collided with.

Seen It?

In *Bridget Jones's Diary* (2001), Bridget Jones has an incredible **crush** on her boss, Daniel Cleaver. But when she finally gets the guy, she realizes he's nothing like what she'd hoped for.

I know I could find out more about her. Word travels fast in high school, with rumors flying up and down the hallways like crazy. Surely a lot of people other than me find that girl intriguing. But honestly, I don't want to know. I don't want to know anything about that girl because I'm afraid it

HOW ABOUT YOU?

What would **you** tell people who say that teenagers **can't** really know the **meaning** of **love?**

might ruin our "relationship" completely. I mean, what are the odds that she's the kind of person I'd imagine her to be? What if she only dates older boys, or treats everyone like crap or is one of those girls who leads you on only to have the nerve to want to stay friends after she beats your heart in with a bat? I don't think I could handle any information like that.

I think I've fallen in and out of love with this girl quite a few times. You're probably thinking that's stupid, that fifteen-year-olds can't fall in love with anyone. And you might be right to some extent. Teenagers don't fall in love with reality. They fall in love with false hopes and dreams that usually lead to heartache and digestive problems. That's where I am right now. And I don't think I mind all that much. Because as I write this on Monday night I know that tomorrow is Tuesday, and she often wears pigtails on Tuesday. Tuesday's a good day.

Michael Wassmer, Age 16

Consider This . . .

Do you get distracted by members of the opposite sex at your school? Well, keep your eye out for single-sex classes. Today, more and more public schools are offering classes marked "girls only" or "boys only." The theory is, boys and girls have different learning styles; girls do better in quiet classrooms, and boys tend to thrive on fast-paced drills. Plus, single-sex classes take the pressure off students who want to look good for students of the opposite sex. What do **you** think?

GRADUATION IS A TIME OF MIXED EMOTIONS. There's the happiness and excitement of moving on, blended with the sadness of saying good-bye to the past. But if you're not the one graduating, these May ceremonies can be especially difficult.

When someone you care about, maybe even love, passes this milestone and sets off for the whatever comes next—college, a new job, moving away—it can leave you feeling empty. You might think that life for the other person is full of big changes, and he or she will probably be too caught up in the new world to remember about you, the one left behind.

Saying good-bye to someone you love can be one of the most difficult things you do in your life. I've found that no matter how many times we do it, it never gets any easier. But big changes like good-byes don't have to mean "the end." They can also mean "the beginning"—the beginning of a new chapter of your life.

CONSIDER THIS . . .

Many high school **couples** decide the **fate** of their relationship by the time one or both of them graduates. Some decide to break up right away, rather than risk a more painful breakup down the road, and others choose to stick it out and see if they can make the long distance thing work.

MISS YOU

I know that as the years go by
I'll miss you more and more,
But I have to stand here watching you
walking out the door.

Your robe has been donned,
Your tassel turned,
You've passed all your tests,
the lessons you've learned.

I've only known you
for one short year,
But I've grown to love you,
And now I'll shed a tear,

For as the many years go by
I'll miss you more and more,
But I must stand here watching you
Walking out the door.

Jessi Panico, Age 14

For Real?

In 2002, a couple from Detroit who were high school sweethearts got married 64 years after they graduated. When they broke up after graduating in the 1930s, they went their separate ways. But 64 years later, the two were both widowed and found each other, falling in love all over again!

WHY IS IT THAT PEOPLE SEEM TO BE SO OBSESSED WITH LOVE? Think about it. There are whole industries that exist just because of this little four-letter word—dating services, magazines, television shows, romance novels. In fact, more plays, movies, books and songs have been written about love than any other subject.

Perhaps people keep writing about love because they want to find some way to make sense of it. But when the complicated emotions inspired by love are involved, logic and reason tend to fly out the window. This next writer captures the elusive nature of love in her heartfelt poem.

Seen It?

The 1989 cult film *Say Anything,* starring John Cusack, is about two high school sweethearts who must figure out what their pending graduation will do to their relationship.

ADVENTURE

There's this funny little thing called love
It can come and go like a gust of wind
It can trade off from one person to the next
Unpredictable and unexplainable are what it's about

You never know when it's coming or how you'll receive it
But once you have it, you'll never want to let go
Though it often does go, shattering your heart along the way
Makes you never want it again out of fear and sadness

Only, slowly you heal and smile once again
And suddenly there's a new face that makes your heart flutter
So you forget your old sadness with your new excitement
On and off it goes throughout your young life

As sad as it may seem, most of us will go through
People as we do clothes
Yet some have long, loving relationships
That blossom into marriage

Some wonder why people put up with it
It can hurt you, stab you in the back,
and sadly
Even make you want to take your life

Yet the reward seems to be the catch
The ability to share with someone
The secrets you thought you'd carry
to your grave

HOW ABOUT YOU?

What word comes to mind when **you** think about **love?**

To trust someone with all you have
And know that it's returned
Receiving unbelievable happiness and joy
From just the sight of someone

Ultimately,
It's a wonderful feeling,
Shared between two,
That can turn into the adventure of a lifetime.

Linda Gonzales, Age 18

For Real?
One out of every ten teens is in a **relationship** that has lasted more than **one year.**

For Real?
Most teens (**73%** of boys and **83%** of girls) say they want to get married someday.

MEMORIES OF FIRST CRUSHES LAST FOREVER. Whether your story had a happy ending or a sad one, there's something unforgettable about the first time the very sight of someone, maybe even someone you didn't know, made your heart race and your face turn bright red.

My very first crush was a guy on the stage crew for a high school musical I was in. Because the production of *South Pacific* required younger kids, I was only in sixth grade at the time, while he was a freshman.

Talk about puppy love . . . I followed this boy around with a grin from ear to ear, spazzing out when he was near and loving the attention he gave me. To him, I was a cute little kid, like a sister. For me? At the time I guess I thought anything was possible, especially when we were still friends a few years later.

The year I was a freshman and he was a senior, the musical was *The King and I,* and he was still on the stage crew. I cherished the note he wrote in my playbill opening night:

Debbie, You're a really cute, funny girl who can always make me laugh. Remember the fun we've had in the other plays we've been in and at the lunch table. Have fun once our great class has graduated and keep in touch. It's been real.

For Real?

The soda pop **Orange Crush** was invented in 1906, and today people buy and sell Orange Crush vintage bottle caps and signs on Ebay for up to fifty bucks.

Can you guess what I fixated on? That's right—the opening line. *You're a really cute, funny girl.* I wondered what he meant. Did he like me? Did we have a future after all? I reread that note over and over, looking for some sort of hidden meaning between the lines. And now, years later, I realize there was no hidden meaning. He just thought I was really cute and funny. And you know what? It turns out that was enough.

Seen It?

For a **hilarious** take on a small-town musical, check out the movie *Waiting for Guffman* (1996), in which an untalented group of locals in Missouri put on a production no one will ever forget.

You Always Remember the First

I cried the night I realized I liked him—as in *liked* him. Since I'd already had bad luck in the "love department," I didn't want to like anyone that way.

He worked his way into my heart by being the perfect gentleman in summer band practice. As a freshman carrying the largest bass drum the marching band owned, I tired easily. But I was too proud to let any volunteers carry my drum. Noah didn't volunteer—he'd take my drum before I could even say anything. (Not that I protested much beyond rolling my eyes.) Sometimes I'd get frustrated with him for skipping practices, but when he'd hold up a cymbal to block the sun from my face, all was forgiven.

For Real?

The bass drum is the **biggest** drum of any orchestra or band and was first introduced to bands in the 1700s.

It was about two weeks into school when I realized that my feelings had crossed that big line. Soon it was obvious to the entire school that I was head over heels in puppy love. What wasn't obvious was how Noah felt about me.

That year our band took a trip to the state capital to play at a college football game. As innocently as I could, I managed to ride on the same bus as Noah and sit across from him on the way home. It was about 3 A.M. and I thought it would be the perfect time to figure out how he felt. Yet every time I tried to get close or say something, he would push me away. Eventually I got discouraged and stopped trying.

On another band trip, things came to a head. It began when I made a sarcastic comment as Noah and his friend were talking. After about ten minutes, I was making jokes just as quickly as they were. My hope was renewed until he crushed whatever enthusiasm I'd had by not looking my way the entire day.

Read It?

The Marching Band Handbook, by Kim Holston, is packed with information on everything from **drum corps** to color guard to competitions.

When we got back on the bus to go home, I decided I just didn't care anymore. I was joking around with my friends and without thinking I turned to him in the seat behind mine and said, "You know you love me."

He said only one word. "Yes."

I turned away, still laughing until I realized what he'd said. I spent the rest of the night in shock, trying to get him to say it again. He never said the exact words but he said it in every other way. I was so excited I could barely stop talking, even though I pretended to sleep against his shoulder for a little while.

Consider This . . .

Sometimes having **"the talk"** with someone you like can be paralyzing. What makes it worse is that it always seems to happen at the oddest of places and times. Have **you** ever had "the talk" in any of these awkward ways?

- over e-mail or IM
- on your cell phone in the middle of a movie
- in the back seat of a crowded school bus
- right before the midterm you've studied a week for
- through notes passed in class

Noah didn't speak to me for the next few days. I was so upset that I became a zombie, dreading the class we had together. I knew he was pushing me away, and it hurt. He tried to speak to me, asking me to sit by him in class, but we'd sit in silence. He began doing all kinds of little things, like taking my assignments up to the front of the room, but I was still hurt and confused.

Then, on the night of homecoming, we were the only ones in the band room and he said, "Wait."

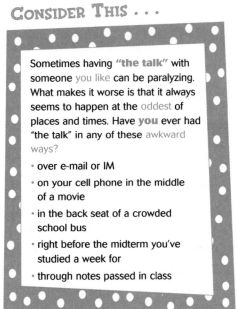

I didn't want to, but I could hear something in his voice that made me stop. I shivered and waited for him to speak. There in the band room, we had "the talk." He knew that I liked him and it was obvious that he liked me too. He went on that, though we may feel the same, he was a junior and I was a freshman. I pleaded with him, telling him that I didn't want dates or presents or . . . I stopped when I realized that I wasn't quite sure *what* I wanted. He seemed to know what I was thinking.

We looked at each other for a while.

He said he had to hurry to catch a ride and asked if I wanted to come along. We both knew that he was asking if we could still be friends. I nodded and followed him.

Things were different after that, but he continued to help me when I needed it and comfort me when I cried. My warm feelings for him soon grew into cold loneliness, but he always tried to make me smile. My friends also tried, knowing that all I'd gotten was a friend when what I really wanted was a boyfriend.

When Noah graduated, I said good-bye for the last time. I gave him a kiss on the cheek, not caring if it bothered him or not. I went home, feeling empty. My mom, knowing how I felt about him, said, "You don't always get what you want, but sometimes you get what you need." Her words didn't help, even though I knew they were right. Noah had gotten me through some tough times.

I went to band practice that summer, now the age he was when we first met, and found the memories painful. I looked at the new freshman bass drummers and didn't even want to care about their struggles. Then I remembered the way Noah had helped me when I was a freshman and how great it made me feel. I started helping the freshmen with a smile and soon after became the section leader.

I once read that *you always remember your first love.* Noah broke my heart and taped it back together more times than I can remember. Yet as time goes by, it's the taped-together times that shine through more than the broken times. Even though I've loved again, a joke or clumsy move of mine seems to remind me of him. I guess whoever wrote that saying was right.

Jaime Rubusch, Age 18

Take the Quiz: HOW DO YOU HANDLE LOVE AND CRUSHES AT SCHOOL?

1. You stay after school for volleyball practice, and right before you're about to go into the locker room to change, your boyfriend of four months dumps you. If this wasn't bad enough, you see him hanging out with another girl after practice. What do you do?

___ A. You're shell-shocked, but realize if he doesn't have the class to wait a few days before going after other girls, who needs him!

___ B. You can't believe he's flaunting his flirting and decide to do the same with another boy to get him back.

___ C. You're devastated and spend much of the practice holding back tears. When you see him talking to another girl, you lose it and make a scene.

2. It's a Wednesday night after dinner when the phone rings. Your heart jumps when you hear the voice on the other end is that of your crush. Then your heart stops when he asks to talk to your younger sister so he can ask her out on a date. What do you do?

___ A. You hand the phone over to your sis. Your crush doesn't know how you feel about him, and you can't make him like you.

___ B. You pass the phone over to your sister, but spend the rest of the night making her feel guilty for talking to your crush.

___ C. You tell him your sis isn't home and then "forget" to give her the message.

3. You and your friends are at the spring fling dance, and you've all decided to go without dates. You're standing along the side when a slow song comes on and this shy girl from study hall comes up and asks you to dance. You're caught completely off guard, but know that you're not really interested in dating her. How do you handle it?

___ A. You respect that this girl had the guts to ask you to dance, so you say yes. What's the harm of one little dance?

___ B. You don't want to dance, but don't want to make her feel bad either, so you tell her you're allergic to dancing and offer her a glass of punch instead.

___ C. You tell her, "Sorry, I was just leaving," and then ditch out for a while. You don't want an ugly scene, but you don't want to be seen dancing with her either.

4. You fall hard for the new kid, especially when you're matched up as lab partners in chemistry. When hanging out with your best friend after school, you tell her about your new crush, but aren't prepared for her response: She's got a crush on him, too! How do you respond?

___ A. It's a bummer that your best friend likes the same guy as you but a crush is a crush, and until the situation changes, there's no need to worry over it.

___ B. You roll your eyes and say, "It figures," then decide to try and tell her why this guy is perfect for you and not quite right for her.

___ C. You decide to go into combat mode and keep your interaction with this guy a secret from now on. You're gonna get your man!

5. You're finally on a date with the guy you've been scoping for all of sophomore year, but as he's dropping you off at your house afterward, he leans over and wants to make out. You might have been up for a little peck on the cheek, but anything more doesn't feel right. What do you do?

___ A. You shake his hand good-bye, thank him for a wonderful time and hightail it out of there. Maybe he's not the guy you thought he was.

___ B. You start to make out with him, but then get nervous and push him away, telling him you're past your curfew and you've gotta run.

___ C. You feel uncomfortable, but don't want to blow it with this guy either, so you make out with him.

Well, how ready are you for the drama of love and stuff? Give yourself 10 points for every A, 20 points for every B and 30 points for every C:

50–70 points = You're confident in who you are and know how to handle yourself when it comes to love and relationships. While you are ready to date and fall in love, you know that it's not the only thing in life.

80–120 points = You're a little rocky when it comes to handling tough situations about relationships, especially when things don't go your way. Listen to the voice inside your head and let it lead you toward good decisions.

130–150 points = You want to be in a relationship, but tend to follow your emotions instead of your head. If you want to make smart choices about love, you might want to wait a little longer before getting in the game.

CHAPTER 8

GET REAL

If you've ever felt like nobody quite understands where you're coming from, you're not alone. Add that to the already overwhelming pressure to conform every time you walk through the front doors of your school, and it's enough to make you want to shout "GET REAL!" at the top of your lungs. Through the words on the pages, this last chapter does just that. In thoughtful poems and essays, you'll read from teens who celebrate who they really are, without the masks and façades that so many of us hide behind.

CONSIDER THIS . . .

Not all celebrities wear Prada and Armani. Some choose to keep their own sense of style, whether it's in or not. Check out some of these non-conforming celebs:

- Björk
- Kelly Osbourne
- Diane Keaton
- Sarah Jessica Parker

THERE'S A GREAT NONFICTION BOOK out there called *The Tipping Point,* by Malcolm Gladwell. It talks all about how trends and phenomena are started. For example, did you know that Hush Puppies, those comfy and kind of dorky shoes, were about to disappear because of slow sales when a couple of hip trendsetters in Manhattan's East Village decided they were cool and started wearing them around town? In no time, Hush Puppies were back in style, smattered all over the pages of *Vogue* and *GQ,* all because a couple of kids decided to be nonconformists and blaze their own trail.

For Real?

24% of teenagers say they would feel better about **themselves** if they wore cooler clothes.

So, what do Hush Puppies have to do with school? I'm glad you asked. *Everything.* When it comes to issues of fashion and popularity, sometimes school seems to be a big game of follow the leaders: follow the way certain people act, look, dress, wear their hair. But where did these leaders get their inspiration? By copying Paris Hilton and Nicole Ritchie's looks from glossy pin-ups in *Teen People,* that's where. But if you look around, you're sure to find students who defy all the fashion do's and don'ts, the ones who wear tweed when

For Real?

Research shows that teens are more concerned with wearing **brand names** clothes than ever. Teenage **girls** spend more on clothes than boys do.

velour is all the rage and plaid when stripes are in vogue. And a year later, those velour-wearers will be scouring the pages of the latest magazines in search of another trend to grab onto, while the tweed-wearing crowd will still be in tweed, still be styling in their own way. And most important, they'll still be themselves.

But don't take my word for it. Check out the next story, "Blizzards and Sweater Vests."

For Real?

Hush puppies, those comfy, casual shoes, were first put on the market in 1958.

Blizzards and Sweater Vests

While in middle school, students seem to have one goal: to be *popular*. More than anything, most of the students fervently hope to not be accused of going against the grain. These young teenagers would much rather conform and be accepted by the "in" crowd than focus on finding their own identity, style or path. Like most thirteen-year-olds, I succumbed to this need to fit in. One afternoon, however, I had a conversation with my father that made me think twice about following the rest of the lemmings over the proverbial cliff.

Read It?

Jerry Spinelli's popular novel *Stargirl* (2000) won praise for its tale of the ultimate nonconformist.

My dad and I were sitting in the dining area of the local Dairy Queen eating Blizzards on a dreary winter afternoon. We had run the gambit of usual conversation topics: school, orchestra, my plans for the weekend. Then, and I'm not quite sure how the discussion began, we started talking about popularity. I told him that I wanted to be popular, or at least accepted favorably by those who were. He looked at me and asked me why I felt that way. I shrugged my shoulders and looked back into my drink. I had never stopped to think about why I felt the need to fit in . . . I simply did. I had been told by my friends that I should want to be popular, and since I had always trusted them, I was inclined to believe them.

THE WORD

Blizzards are yummy treats from Dairy Queen made up of soft ice cream blended with candy, cookies or fruit. DQ sold more than 175 million the first year they were on the market in 1985.

My father proceeded to tell me a story from his college days. His mother, my grandmother Lorraine, had made him several sweater vests to wear at school. These sweater vests were practical and comfortable, but hardly "in style." Nevertheless, they became a staple of my father's wardrobe. He didn't care that he wasn't sporting the latest fashion. In fact, he didn't care what everyone thought of him, either. I was shocked. What was even more surprising was that after a few weeks, other students at my dad's school began wearing sweater vests. By deviating from the norm, my father had started a trend. What he wore became fashionable because the other students saw the confidence with which he dressed.

HOW ABOUT YOU?

How confident are **you** in making your own personal fashion statement?

This information was a lot for a thirteen-year-old girl to process, especially one who had been carefully taught about what was "cool" and what was most certainly not cool. I found it hard to believe that going against the grain could have benefits for me, so I continued to wear the same clothes, listen to the same music and go to the same places that my peers did. Surely my father was mistaken. This is also, of course, the stage in which children think they know infinitely more than their parents. I had not yet seen the light, and I continued on my quest for popularity. However, our conversation that bleak winter day replayed over and over in my mind.

CONSIDER THIS . . .

Take a close look at advertisements for clothing and fashion accessories. How many of the ads appeal to **your** sense of wanting to stand out in a crowd? Don't **you** think it's kind of strange that in our quest to be unique, many of us are drawn to wear the same things as everybody else?

As the days passed and I mulled it over, I realized that my father's words might have some validity after all. I began to evaluate my wardrobe to find which items I had bought because they were cool and which items I'd bought because I truly liked them. I also looked back at my actions, attempting to determine how many of them I performed to please the crowd and how many of them I performed because I actually enjoyed them. I found myself caring less and less what people thought about

CONSIDER THIS . . .

If you've got a pair of pants that you just **love,** but they've sadly gone out of style, you might want to hold on to them. Fashion tends to be cyclical, and in another twenty years those pants might be all the rage again.

WHERE DO YOU STAND?

Are you a conformist or a nonconformist when it comes to life at school? Would you . . .

wear something just because it's in, even if you don't like the style?

___ NO WAY! (0 points)
___ I MIGHT (1 point)
___ I'VE DONE IT BEFORE (2 points)

go for a salad at lunch instead of the pizza because all of your friends are eating salads?

___ NO WAY! (0 points)
___ I MIGHT (1 point)
___ I'VE DONE IT BEFORE (2 points)

keep your violin case hidden away in a bag so no one will know you play the instrument?

___ NO WAY! (0 points)
___ I MIGHT (1 point)
___ I'VE DONE IT BEFORE (2 points)

stop skateboarding to school because your new friends think the fad is totally over?

___ NO WAY! (0 points)
___ I MIGHT (1 point)
___ I'VE DONE IT BEFORE (2 points)

take your glasses off in between classes because you think you look dorky in them?

___ NO WAY! (0 points)
___ I MIGHT (1 point)
___ I'VE DONE IT BEFORE (2 points)

Add up your points:
0–3 = Nonconformist all the way
4–7 = Depends on the situation
8–10 = You don't like to stand out.

me. It was wonderfully liberating.

I have come a long way since middle school. It no longer bothers me that those who still feel compelled to follow the herd do not accept me as one of their own. I do not strive to dress in the latest fashions; if anything, I attempt to create my own. The conversation I had with my father about wearing sweater vests and feeling the need to fit in sparked in me the desire to deviate from the beaten path and form one of my own. I have learned a valuable lesson in the process: Swimming against the current can only make me stronger.

Esther Sooter, Age 16

Spotlight On . . . FASHION TRENDS

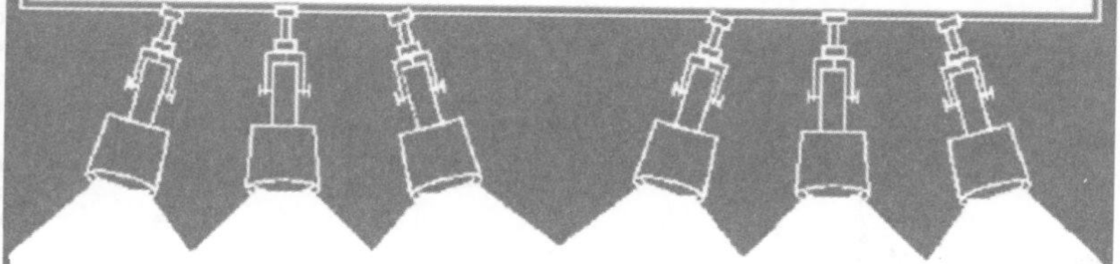

So how do fashion trends start anyway? You might be surprised to find that a small group of people have already determined what's going to be "in" six months from now. Most fashion trends start on the fashion runways in Europe, where top designers from all over the world show off their new creations. After photographs from the runways end up in the top magazines, like *Vogue* and *Cosmopolitan,* the fashion wheel is in motion.

IF YOU HAD HUNG OUT AT MY HOUSE for a week back when I was in middle school, you would surely notice a recurring argument between my parents and me. I wanted to wear makeup; they said "no way." I don't know what your parents

For Real?

Many girls want to wear **makeup** before their parents think they're ready, but studies show that parents who prohibit their teens from wearing makeup may be in for **big** surprises. These teens are more likely to go to **drastic** measures, like getting piercings or tattoos!

are like, but when my parents said "no" to something, that was it. End of story. *Finito.* No discussion, no nothing.

It didn't stop there. No earrings, nose rings or piercings of any kind were to be tolerated ("Not while you're living under my roof"), and designer jeans were a waste of money ("the Lee Jeans' Outlet has everything we need"). Suffice it to say that this state of affairs left me feeling down and out. And very unglamorous.

But what was my hurry, anyway? I knew I didn't want to look really done up or anything. I was striving more for that fresh-faced, Noxema, girl-next-door look. The natural beauty. An ideal. But it wasn't to be.

A few years later, I was allowed to wear makeup, and my dad finally consented to me getting my ears pierced (only after my friend and I had pierced one of them in my bedroom armed with an ice cube and a little gold stud). I wore hand-me-down designer jeans from my girlfriend. And surprise of all surprises, I still didn't feel glamorous. Still didn't have that "natural beauty" thing going on. It's taken me a long time to finally get comfortable in my own skin, to accept the way I look and not compare myself to other girls who I admire for their beauty, shape and sense of style. It's a lesson I learned later in life, but I could have saved myself a lot of heartache if I'd just gotten more comfortable with the girl in the mirror.

Consider This . . .

Some people **think** before-and-after transformations, which are regular features of most teen magazines like *Teen People, ElleGirl* and *TeenVogue*, place too much emphasis on the way girls look.

For Real?

The average age that girls begin wearing **makeup** is between 12 and 13 years old.

GIRLS WITH NO NAMES

No one ever taught me to properly apply
Eyeliner or lipstick like
The girls at school who
Spend lunch in the bathroom with
The dirty floors and
The stubborn doors

Prodding their eyes with ink tips
And lips looking like shallow ponds
beneath
colored-in cheeks
Handmade lashes and penciled-in brows
that won't survive the sun and
that must be
why they spend lunch in

In the bathroom is where they practice
Hip swinging struts and they
Never neglect to remove
Peach fuzz frizz bruise or blemish

Split ends hanging on heads
Hiding behind
Makeshift faces
Opening up
Cleansing
Cleaning
Clogging
Closing
Pores on faces
Of girls with no names

Perla Melendez, Age 18

Read It?

The popular *Gossip Girl* series, by Cecily von Ziegesar, follows a group of wealthy and popular NYC teens in high school.

CONSIDER THIS . . .

If you're wearing makeup to get the **attention** of boys, think again. Surveys show that most boys **aren't** big fans of makeup, especially when it looks like it's "painted on."

HOW ABOUT YOU?

Do **you** think that most teens are too concerned with their **appearance?**

THERE'S NOTHING I HATE MORE THAN BEING JUDGED BY SOMEONE ELSE. You know what I mean—when people make up their minds about who you are and what you're like just by the way you look, the clothes you wear, who your parents or siblings are, or what religion you are. Yet for someone who hates to be judged, I used to do a lot of it myself.

Why do we judge others, anyway? What is it inside of us that feels the need to decide what other people are like before we really even know them? Some would say it's all based on our own insecurities, and maybe they're right. Maybe if I cared less about what other people thought of me, I would be more accepting of others. And the sad fact is, those who are quick to judge are often dead wrong, and they miss out on incredible friendships, or more. How much of a bummer is that?

Consider This . . .

Author Gary Zukav says that **judging** others is something people do because they feel inferior themselves. Instead of working on their own lives, some people lash out at others.

As I look around at my circle of friends, there are a few who surprise me. I mean, when I first met some of them, I leapt to conclusions about the kind of people they were, and immediately discounted them as possible friends. Maybe they had a weird sense of humor or had really bizarre hair or seemed more interested in material things than I was. Whatever the reason, I'm so thankful that I took a step back and let these friends show me who they really were and gave myself the chance to let them into my life. I couldn't imagine it without them.

Seen It?

In *A Walk to Remember* (2002), Mandy Moore and Shane West totally misjudge each other until they end up studying together and fall in love, realizing that their first impressions couldn't have been more wrong.

OUTSIDE THE BOX

Sometimes judging others happens so quickly after meeting someone, we may not even realize we're doing it. The next time you meet someone new, keep these things in mind to prevent yourself from jumping to conclusions:

- Some people are shy or act differently around new people, so don't assume you're seeing everything there is.
- Clothes and fashion sense ultimately don't have anything to do with personality.
- Try to disregard what you've heard about someone from a friend . . . keep an open mind.

Perfection Is Just an Illusion

I didn't mean to stare, but I couldn't help it. She was just so perfect. There, across the room, sat Stephanie, the most popular girl at school. History class was just about over and my notes thus far consisted of my name and the date. I had spent the entire class admiring the qualities that made her the crush of all the boys and the envy of all the girls. She had everything I ever

HOW ABOUT YOU?

Look around at your circle of **friends.** Is there someone there who you judged in the beginning only to find out that you were totally **wrong?**

wanted—beautiful blonde hair, a twenty-four-inch waist and the most extensive wardrobe of anyone I knew. Most important, though, she had Craig, a guy I had had a crush on for the past three years. He was the most popular guy at school, so it was only natural that he and Stephanie would be dating. Stephanie led the most perfect life imaginable for a sixteen-year-old girl, or so I thought.

One rainy Monday afternoon, I sat in the locker hallway catching up on some biology homework. Stephanie suddenly walked in, sobbing uncontrollably. Her best friend, Alyssa, was desperately trying to console her. I wondered what could have possibly gone wrong in Stephanie's "perfect" life. *Maybe the rain made her hair a*

WHERE DO YOU STAND?

Are you a judgmental person?

To find out, see how many of the following statements you say yes to:

1. An overweight student is in line for lunch in front of you. You can't help but wonder why he's got two desserts on his tray instead of a salad.
2. You know from a very reliable source that the redhead in your Spanish class has had sex with more than one senior. You're not really interested in being her friend because she must be sleazy.
3. You've got to do a team project in English with a guy who wears the same clothes day after day. When you forget a pencil, you're reluctant to borrow one of his, figuring it probably has germs all over it.
4. The teacher introduces a new girl in class, and when she stands up to say hello, she speaks in a super high voice that occasionally squeaks. When she joins your reading group, you have a hard time taking her seriously.
5. Your dad invites his boss's family over for dinner, and you're floored when a girl from your school walks in the front door. You only know her as a chorus geek, and you don't want to be too friendly in case people at school find out that you've hung out together.

If you answered yes to even one of these questions, then you might be making judgments about other people that aren't fair.

little frizzy, I thought. As I listened to Stephanie and Alyssa's conversation, I discovered that Stephanie's life was not nearly as perfect as I thought.

She explained that her mother had been diagnosed with breast cancer over the weekend. She also said that she turned down the opportunity to go away to her dream college because she refused to leave her mother's side during this difficult time.

For Real?

Breast cancer is the most common form of cancer among women, with nearly **250,000** new cases being diagnosed every year. If caught early, chances of survival are excellent—more than **85%** will live at least five years after treatment.

I had been jealous of popular girls like Stephanie all throughout high school. After all, they had everything they wanted and absolutely nothing to worry about. That Monday afternoon in the locker hallway, I came to realize that I couldn't have been more wrong. It's easy to assume that popular people lead perfect lives, but in reality, they have problems just like everyone else.

Valentina Cucuzza, Age 19

DO YOU WEAR A MASK? I'm not talking about a Halloween mask of the killer from *Scream* or anything. I'm talking about going out of your way to look different on the outside than how you feel on the inside. These masks can be made up of many different things: the way you dress (designer clothes, goth garb, prim and preppy), the way you act, the people you hang out with.

Seen It?

Comic actress Amanda Bynes stars in *What a Girl Wants* (2003) and finds herself putting on a mask of her own to **try** and fit in with her prim and proper father and his royal family.

We received many essays from teens about feeling pressure to wear masks and be someone on the outside that doesn't match who they are on the inside. So why do so many teenagers wear masks? Is it because they're not comfortable with who they are? Or because they have it in their heads that there is a standard way to be and look, and anything different is unacceptable?

I wore many masks as a teen. I decided early on how I wanted to be perceived, and then did what I needed to do to get that image across, whether it was wearing certain clothes, or laughing at things that weren't even funny, or hanging around with a certain group of people even if they weren't the ones I felt I had the most in common with. But at the end of the day, I couldn't change who I was. And wearing these masks just left me feeling more frustrated than ever that I wasn't the person I thought I should be. That's because the person I thought I should be didn't exist.

I've finally stopped wearing masks, and let me tell you, it's heck of a lot easier to breathe without doing it through a piece of plastic. The best part is, no one treats me any differently now. People actually do like me for who I am, even when I let my true colors show.

Consider This . . .

Pretending to be someone you're not, or being a **"fake,"** can be habit forming. If you fake it long enough, you might be afraid to let people see the real you.

ILLUSION OF PERFECTION

This perfect little princess
No one sees her pain
The way she bottles it up inside
She'll most likely go insane.

She has everything she could want
There is nothing else she needs
How could she feel so unhappy
In this perfect life she leads?

She has all the material things
She can even get the guys
But she's searching for internal happiness
In this perfected life of lies.

If people only knew
The thoughts that go through her head
Maybe they'd reach out to this princess
Before she ends up dead.

Luckily she's afraid of death
The thought of never awaking again
Hopefully this fear stays with her
So her life does not come to an end.

Everyone sees the small things
They don't make the connection
If they were to look at the big picture
They'd see it's all an illusion of perfection.

Alicia A. Vasquez, Age 19

Take the Quiz:
DO YOU KNOW HOW TO GET REAL?

1. You find out that your school is hosting its first student talent show at the end of the month. You love to tap dance and are really great at it, too. You've always dreamed of having the perfect opportunity to show off your talent, but you're afraid that tapping might come across as totally lame. What do you do?

___ A. You keep quiet about your talent and decide not to sign up. It's safer to sit in the auditorium and watch everyone else put themselves out there on a limb.

___ B. You're not up for a solo performance, but decide to take part in a group song that your friends are doing. There's safety in numbers.

___ C. You decide you'll always regret it if you don't take this chance to strut your stuff. Besides, how many other students can do a shuffle ball change?

2. You're one of the only female pole-vaulters in the county, and you usually feel great about standing out. But you're thrown off when this guy you've got a huge crush on shows up at one of your track meets. You're suddenly feeling very self-conscious about your muscular thighs. What do you do?

___ A. You keep your sweatpants on for your jumps so this guy doesn't get a good glimpse of your legs, even if the baggy material makes it harder for you to clear the bar.

___ B. You try to ignore his presence, but slip your sweats on as soon as you're done jumping.

___ C. You zone out the fact that he's there and continue on with your meet as usual. If he's going to like you, it might as well be for who you are . . . strong legs and all.

3. This girl that you like at school tells you how much she admires you for sticking up for a kid who was being teased at school. In reality, it was your friend who was doing the teasing, and you just stood there and watched, but you don't want to burst this girl's bubble. How do you handle this one?

___ A. You see this as an opportunity to land the girl, so you go along with it and explain to her that you always feel a need to stick up for the underdog.

___ B. You don't dissuade her from thinking what she thinks, but you quickly change the subject and talk with her about something else.

___ C. You tell her the truth, but say that if you had it to do all over again, you would have stuck up for this kid. You know that if you want to get the girl, you need to start out on the right foot.

4. Your dream is to be a fashion designer, and you are thrilled when your mom gets you a sewing machine for Christmas. You've spent all of break working on your original designs, but the night before school starts again you're feeling timid about wearing your homemade outfits to school. What do you do?

___ A. You decide that maybe your high school isn't ready for your fashion genius and leave the original stuff at home. Besides, you can still wear it on the weekends around the house.

___ B. You introduce your homemade clothes one item at a time and try to disguise them with trendy accessories.

___ C. You have so much confidence in your designs that you wear your clothes with pride. Who knows? You might even start a new trend!

5. You sit down at the lunch table to find your group of friends talking about the assembly on suicide and depression and how stupid the whole thing was. You couldn't disagree more—you were really moved by the guest speaker.

___ A. You join in and reiterate what everyone else is saying. Clearly, no one else feels the same way, and you don't want your friends to think you're weird.

___ B. You decide to sit this one out and keep your opinions to yourself. Sometimes neither agreeing nor disagreeing is the way to go.

___ C. You speak up and tell your friends how you feel. Who knows, maybe some of your other friends feel the same way too, but were too shy to say so.

Well, do you know how to get real? Give yourself 10 points for every A, 20 points for every B and 30 points for every C:

50–70 points = You're not so confident in who you are, and that comes through in how you act. If you don't let the real you shine through, you might not be fulfilled in your relationships or how you spend your time.

80–120 points = You struggle with being yourself, because at the back of your mind there's a fear of not being accepted. You'll find that if you work at getting real, your confidence will continue to grow.

130–150 points = Absolutely! You feel good in your shoes and speak your mind, even if it goes against the general consensus. If you continue "getting real" you can be sure that the people in your life are there because they like you for who you are.

EPILOGUE

SO THERE YOU HAVE IT. I know that we've only just scratched the surface of your complicated lives when it comes to surviving school. But we hope you were touched and inspired by these stories, and that you realize that with a little support and guidance, you can stay afloat no matter how high the waves go or how many leaks your lifeboat might spring. Maybe you've even earmarked a couple of stories, found some favorites and learned a few interesting things along the way. Most of all, we hope that you use this book like you would a friend, and that you turn to it when you're feeling down or are trying to make sense of something you're going through. Best of luck as you continue your journey onward in school. May this book be the armor that protects and guides you!

SUPPORTING OTHERS

IN THE SPIRIT OF INSPIRING TEENS to achieve their dreams, a portion of proceeds from *Chicken Soup for the Teenage Soul's The Real Deal: School* will support the nonprofit group WriteGirl.

WriteGirl, a project of Community Partners, pairs professional women writers with teen girls for creative writing workshops and mentoring. WriteGirl mentors are accomplished journalists, novelists, poets, editors, TV and film writers, songwriters, marketing executives, and more. Mentors meet with each teen girl one-on-one to develop communication and critical thinking skills. All members gather for monthly group workshops, focusing on specific themes such as identity, family, community, culture and self-empowerment.

WriteGirl provides girls with role models to teach them communication skills for a lifetime of increased opportunities. By catching girls at a critical stage in their lives, WriteGirl provides a positive counterbalance to the challenges girls face at home, at school and in their communities.

WriteGirl's anthologies *Bold Ink* (2003) and *Pieces of Me* (2004) are available through Amazon.com. For more information on WriteGirl, contact:

WriteGirl
4003 Sunset Drive, Suite 9
Los Angeles, CA 90027
phone: 323-327-2555
www.writegirl.org

Who Is JACK CANFIELD?

Jack Canfield is one of America's leading experts in the development of human potential and personal effectiveness. He is both a dynamic, entertaining speaker and a highly sought-after trainer. Jack has a wonderful ability to inform and inspire audiences toward increased levels of self-esteem and peak performance. Jack most recently released a book for success entitled *The Success Principles: How to Get from Where You Are to Where You Want to Be.*

He is the author and narrator of several bestselling audio- and videocassette programs, including *Self-Esteem and Peak Performance, How to Build High Self-Esteem, Self-Esteem in the Classroom* and *Chicken Soup for the Soul—Live.* He is regularly seen on television shows such as *Good Morning America, 20/20* and *NBC Nightly News.* Jack has coauthored numerous books, including the *Chicken Soup for the Soul* series, *Dare to Win* and *The Aladdin Factor* (all with Mark Victor Hansen), *100 Ways to Build Self-Concept in the Classroom* (with Harold C. Wells), *Heart at Work* (with Jacqueline Miller) and *The Power of Focus* (with Les Hewitt and Mark Victor Hansen).

Jack is a regularly featured speaker for professional associations, school districts, government agencies, churches, hospitals, sales organizations and corporations. His clients have included the American Dental Association, the American Management Association, AT&T, Campbell's Soup, Clairol, Domino's Pizza, GE, Hartford Insurance, ITT, Johnson & Johnson, the Million Dollar Roundtable, NCR, New England Telephone, Re/Max, Scott Paper, TRW and Virgin Records. Jack has taught on the faculty of Income Builders International, a school for entrepreneurs.

Jack conducts an annual seven-day training called Breakthrough to Success. It attracts entrepreneurs, educators, counselors, parenting trainers, corporate trainers, professional speakers, ministers and others interested in improving their lives and lives of others.

For free gifts from Jack and information on all his material and availability go to:

www.jackcanfield.com
Self-Esteem Seminars
P.O. Box 30880
Santa Barbara, CA 93130
phone: 805-563-2935 • fax: 805-563-2945

Who Is MARK VICTOR HANSEN?

In the area of human potential, no one is more respected than Mark Victor Hansen. For more than thirty years, Mark has focused solely on helping people from all walks of life reshape their personal vision of what's possible. His powerful messages of possibility, opportunity and action have created powerful change in thousands of organizations and millions of individuals worldwide.

He is a sought-after keynote speaker, bestselling author and marketing maven. Mark's credentials include a lifetime of entrepreneurial success and an extensive academic background. He is a prolific writer with many bestselling books, such as *The One Minute Millionaire, The Power of Focus, The Aladdin Factor* and *Dare to Win,* in addition to the *Chicken Soup for the Soul* series. Mark has made a profound influence through his library of audios, videos and articles in the areas of big thinking, sales achievement, wealth building, publishing success, and personal and professional development.

Mark is the founder of the MEGA Seminar Series. MEGA Book Marketing University and Building Your MEGA Speaking Empire are annual conferences where Mark coaches and teaches new and aspiring authors, speakers and experts on building lucrative publishing and speaking careers. Other MEGA events include MEGA Marketing Magic and My MEGA Life.

He has appeared on television (*Oprah,* CNN and *The Today Show*), in print (*Time, U.S. News & World Report, USA Today, New York Times* and *Entrepreneur*) and on countless radio interviews, assuring our planet's people that, "You can easily create the life you deserve."

As a philanthropist and humanitarian, Mark works tirelessly for organizations such as Habitat for Humanity, American Red Cross, March of Dimes, Childhelp USA and many others. He is the recipient of numerous awards that honor his entrepreneurial spirit, philanthropic heart and business acumen. He is a lifetime member of the Horatio Alger Association of Distinguished Americans, an organization that honored Mark with the prestigious Horatio Alger Award for his extraordinary life achievements.

Mark Victor Hansen is an enthusiastic crusader of what's possible and is driven to make the world a better place.

Mark Victor Hansen & Associates, Inc.
P.O. Box 7665
Newport Beach, CA 92658
phone: 949-764-2640
fax: 949-722-6912
Visit Mark online at: *www.markvictorhansen.com*

Who Is DEBORAH REBER?

Deborah Reber is a former children's television executive who most recently wrote *It's My Life's Guide to Friendship,* the first book in a nonfiction series being launched by PBS's teen website, *It's My Life,* as well as the tween fiction novel *EverGirl,* based on the new property being launched by Nickelodeon. Deborah is also the coeditor and copublisher of *Bold Ink: Collected Voices of Women and Girls,* an anthology by WriteGirl, a nonprofit creative writing organization that matches women writers with teen girls for one-on-one mentoring. She is one of WriteGirl's founding board members. Deborah's first nonfiction book, *Run for Your Life: A Book for Beginning Women Runners,* is a self-help book with the goal of making the sport of running accessible to women of all abilities.

As the ancillary business manager for Nickelodeon's hit preschool show, *Blue's Clues,* Deborah edited and creatively approved seven Simon & Schuster *Blue's Clues* book lists, wrote more than a dozen *Blue's Clues* books, including two *New York Times* bestsellers, and coauthored a line of educational workbooks for Landoll.

Deborah is from Reading, Pennsylvania, and currently resides in Seattle with her husband Derin, son Asher and their dog, Baxter. She holds a master's degree in media studies from the New School for Social Research and a bachelor's degree in broadcast journalism from the Pennsylvania State University.

To contact Deborah, write or email her at:

The Real Deal
4509 Interlake Ave. N., #281
Seattle, WA 98103
email: *submissions@deborahreber.com*
www.deborahreber.com

CONTRIBUTORS

Cristina Bautista is a fifteen-year-old aspiring writer from Union City, California. Most of her inspiration is derived from friends, anime and hippos. She is proud to be out as a gay teenager in a Catholic high school and hopes to make students more aware of homosexuality.

Rachel Berman is a native of Northern California and moved with her family to New Jersey. She now studies in Jerusalem, Israel, where she enjoys meeting friendly strangers on the street, touring the ancient and holy sites, and sitting in cafes.

Julie Blackmer is currently a cheerleader at Alief Taylor High School, she is also in the speech and debate program. She hopes to one day be a cheerleader at the University of Texas, Austin.

Christopher Boire is a high school senior who wishes to major in English and minor in journalism in college. Chris likes to read and write. He hopes to write novels and short stories, becoming a professional author.

Sarah Brook is a senior at Carl Sandburg High School. She plans to attend the University of Illinois and graduate with a major in English. Sarah enjoys writing, singing, and playing the piano, guitar, and violin. She aspires to write poetry and short stories.

Demi Chang is a sophomore currently attending the High School of Fashion Industries. She is majoring in fashion design and is attending the Art Student's League. Please e-mail her at *swtdee86@yahoo.com*.

Diana Chang is a freshman at New York University. She is majoring in journalism and mass communications. She enjoys working as a certified makeup artist on the side. Please e-mail her at *swtdee86@yahoo.com*.

Sondra Clark has published five books, including *You Can Change Your World!*, which gives 150 ways teens can volunteer. She's a spokesperson for Childcare International, a Christian relief agency, and has visited Africa, Mexico and Peru to raise money to help educate children in developing countries. Sondra loves drama, writing and singing and is currently a student at Annie Wright School in Tacoma, Washington.

Valentina Cucuzza is currently pursuing an MBA in marketing and public relations from Baruch College in New York City. She enjoys traveling and music. She plans to be a marketing executive for a fashion company.

Clara Marie Dell was born in San Francisco and has been living in Chicago since she was four years old. Her interest in photography remains strong. She is in the eighth grade. In her spare time, she enjoys reading and writing.

Rhea Liezl C. Florendo is working towards her AA in liberal studies and then plans to transfer to CSU Hayward to major in political science and pursue a career in teaching. In high school, Rhea joined the school's literary club and has published poems on the Internet. She loves poetry, books, music and spending time with friends and family.

Stephanie Fraser is a normal teenager who loves to laugh and lives in the moment. She plays badminton, field hockey and soccer and enjoys them all. Writing is her main passion, and she hopes someday to write anything and everything possible, just as long as her voice is heard. Good times in English.

Araz Garakanian is currently attending Taylor High School as a freshman. She enjoys sports, listening to music, dancing, singing and shopping. She is very proud of her Armenian heritage and hopes that people will learn from her story.

Linda Gonzales is nineteen years old and has been writing poems and short stories since she was a freshman in high school. Linda loves to read and write and enjoys hanging out with her friends and her boyfriend. She recently graduated from Adult School and is looking forward to starting college. Linda is honored to be included in this book. She can be reached by e-mail at *Pinkangel852005@yahoo.com*.

Jean Huang is a junior at Technical High School in St. Cloud, Minnesota. Jean enjoys reading, writing and watching vapid television shows. Her ultimate goal in life is to be an alpaca farmer. She also dreams of writing a novel someday.

Alicia Jaynes received her bachelor of science in sociology from Brigham Young University of Idaho in 2004. She started to write poetry at age sixteen and has written more than 100 poems since then. Alicia enjoys writing, reading, playing tennis and hiking.

Allison Kueffner is a senior at Fairfield Warde High School in Connecticut. She is taking AP English literature at school and took AP language and composition last year. In her free time, she loves to play field hockey and hang out with her friends.

Julia Lam is a high school senior in the South Bay, California. Her passions include swimming, water polo, writing, U.S. history and piano. She hopes to become a writer.

Maryanne Lee is a ninth grader at Alief Taylor High School in Houston, Texas. She participates in JV cheerleading, jump rope, advanced courses and student council. She enjoys scrapbooking and hanging out with friends. In the future she plans to attend college.

Chris S. Lewis is a senior at Archbishop Spalding High School. He participates in many activities and sports at his school, including varsity soccer. In his free time, Chris enjoys hanging out with friends, drumming in his band and snowboarding. Chris plans to attend college in the fall.

Coral Marie Lozada is a freshman at Alief Taylor High School in Houston, Texas. She is a pre-AP student who loves writing poetry, fantasy and personal narratives. She also enjoys traveling with educational groups, swimming and reading. Her book, *Quentos Para Carmen Lynn* (a bilingual collection of poems and stories), is in progress.

Shawna McBroom loves to write poetry in her free time and is looking into writing stories in the future and wants to get a publisher. At sixteen years old, Shawna enjoys reading, sleeping, writing and just having fun. You can reach Shawna at *MmmGooood16@aol.com*.

Jessica M. McCann is an eighteen-year-old senior in Wallingford, Pennsylvania, who believes in the strength of the human soul, the healing power of love and the possibilities the future holds. She dreams of becoming a professional writer and traveling the world. Contact her at *CAgirlSOUL@hotmail.com*.

Perla Melendez has just started her freshman year at University of California, Santa Barbara, in the College of Creative Studies as a literature major. She'd like to think she was a little part of the Echo Park, Silverlake, Los Angeles writer's scene. She's going to continue loving good books, dancing, writing, getting published, hula hooping, making chapbooks, reading, playing tennis and smiling. P.S. She loves mail! *cantwalkinheelz@yahoo.com*.

Kimberly Menaster is currently enrolled at University of California, Los Angeles, in the College of Letters and Science. She is enjoying college.

Krystle Nichols attends Pymatuning Valley High School in northeast Ohio. She is currently a senior and is looking forward to attending college at Bowling Green State University to major in middle childhood education. Krystle lovers her friends and family more than anything else in life.

Chelsea Oakes is thirteen years old and in the eighth grade. She enjoys performing arts and is a member of a local performing group in her city. She writes for the school newspaper and is involved with other school activities. Chelsea also plays the French horn. She plans on attending New York University for prelaw.

Rosie Ojeda is a student at California State University, Channel Islands. Her major is English, and her goal is to publish many fiction novels. Rosie enjoys writing, surfing, spending time with friends and family, and shopping. Rosie loves animals and is a vegetarian and a member of the Church of Jesus Christ of Latter-Day Saints. Feel free to e-mail her at *ldsrosie@hotmail.com*.

Corina Oprescu is a sophomore in high school. She is involved with her school math club, community service club, youth in government club and tennis team.

Jessi Panico is in the ninth grade at Onteora High School in Boiceville, New York. She enjoys music and plays three instruments. She is a member of the Onteora marching band and the science olympiads team. She also enjoys reading, writing, traveling and talking with her friends.

Nicole Poppino attends high school as a freshman in Washington state, where she was born. Her hobbies include writing, playing the piano and taking photographs. She currently lives with her mother and youngest sister. Nicole plans to attend college after graduating.

Sara J. Reeves is currently in ninth grade and hopes to work in criminal justice. Sara lives in Ohio with her mom, sister and many pets. She enjoys writing, designing clothes and meeting new people. You can contact her at *siera_amanda@yahoo.com*.

Aubrey Restifo lives in Ohio. She is the president of her high school's G.S.A. and, besides writing, loves political debate and her violin. This is her first national publication, and she dedicates it to her friends, family and Angela, for hanging on when it was hardest to breathe.

Maggie Reyland is a graduate of St. Cecilia Academy in Nashville, Tennessee. She was the editor of her school newspaper. Maggie has been writing since she was little and plans to keep it up until she can no longer hold a pen properly or see the keys on her keyboard!

Jaime Rubusch has been passionate about writing since middle school. She now attends University of Wisconsin, Stout, as a technical communications major. When not writing, she enjoys working for other writers, editing their work.

Jody Schechter is a high school sophomore. She enjoys photography, music, Disney movies and travel. She hopes one day to circumnavigate the globe.

Karina E. Seto is a ninth-grade student in Sault Ste. Marie, Canada, where she lives with her dad, mom, grandma, little brother, Matt, and dog. She loves taking martial arts classes with her mom and playing violin in youth orchestra. She wants to become an author and a black belt.

Esther Sooter is a senior at Maryville High School. She has been writing since middle school and plans to major in vocal performance in college. Esther enjoys reading, singing and playing the cello.

Rachel A. Stern is a high school freshman in New Jersey. She enjoys reading, writing and dancing. In the future, she hopes to become a writer and neuroscientist.

Tracy Tanner is planning to attend college in the fall. She is undecided about her major, but it will definitely be in the arts field. To contact Tracy, e-mail *whsper2ascream@yahoo.com*.

Lovely Umayam is a sixteen-year-old sophomore in John Marshall High School. She is a member of WriteGirl, a mentor/mentee writing program, in which she has been published seven times in three WriteGirl anthologies. Lovely enjoys speech/debate, playing the guitar and simply not worrying about homework.

Alicia Aurora Vasquez is currently in her second year at Cal Poly, Pomona. She plans on getting her bachelor's degree in either psychology or sociology. Alicia enjoys running and spending time with her friends. She would like to become a social worker in the future.

Michael Wassmer began writing personal essays when he was eleven years old and hasn't stopped since. He currently attends high school and plans to graduate in 2008. What comes after that is anyone's guess, he says. Please e-mail him at *MJWassmer@hotmail.com*.

Laura M. Watkins is twelve years old and in seventh grade. She enjoys swimming, writing, reading, crafts and shopping. She plans on studying journalism and becoming a journalist when she grows up. This is her first published story.

Katelynn M. Wilton is a tenth-grade student who lives with her mother, father, brother and two dogs. Her past honors include a national award from National Geographic and the U.S. Mint, along with some smaller awards. Her obsession with swimming continues to play a huge part in her life.

Dallas Nicole Woodburn is a senior at Ventura High (California). Her writing credits include the magazines *Writer's Digest, Girls Life, CosmoGIRL, Justine, Listen, Encounter, Writing* and the nationally released book *So, You Wanna Be a Writer?* She also self-published a book of short stories and poems and wrote the play her high school produced. Check out her website at *www.zest.net/writeon*.

Joseph Workman is in the eighth grade and wrote his poem for those who are treated as nothing. He is an obsessed *Lord of the Rings* and King Arthur fan and loves to write, read, play chess, go for walks, hike, fence and ice skate.

Ashley Mie Yang is a sophomore in high school. Her favorite subject is history, and she participates in yearbook and Model United Nations. She has met many inspirational teachers and hopes to someday teach history. In her free time, she enjoys reading, shopping and being with her friends.

PERMISSIONS

Behind the Scenes of Two Teen Queens. Reprinted by permission of Jessica M. McCann. ©2004 Jessica M. McCann.

Being New Is Tough. Reprinted by permission of Corina Oprescu and Florinela G. Oprescu. ©2004 Corina Oprescu.

Popular. Reprinted by permission of Demi Chang and Vivien Chang. ©2004 Demi Chang.

Lonely. Reprinted by permission of Kimberly Ann Menaster. ©2004 Kimberly Ann Menaster.

We're Different, That's Enough. Reprinted by permission of Christopher Michael Boire and Linda Ann Boire. ©2004 Christopher Michael Boire.

One Wish. Reprinted by permission of Rhea Liezl C. Florendo. ©2004 Rhea Liezl C. Florendo.

Bad Day. Reprinted by permission of Monique Ayub and Lori Ayub. ©2004 Monique Ayub.

People Always Tell Me, "It's Just High School!" Reprinted by permission of Allison Davis Kueffner and Paul Stephen Kueffner. ©2004 Allison Davis Kueffner.

The Teenage Years. Reprinted by permission of Sara Jeanette Reeves and Lisa Hilliard. ©2004 Sara Jeanette Reeves.

The Real World. Reprinted by permission of Stephanie Fraser and Norm Fraser. ©2004 Stephanie Fraser.

Prison. Reprinted by permission of Jody Hannah Schechter and Lori D. Schechter. ©2004 Jody Hannah Schechter.

Like Water. Reprinted by permission of Jean Huang and Danrun Huang. ©2004 Jean Huang.

Imagine. Reprinted by permission of Ashley Mie Yang and Jean Pauk. ©2003 Ashley Mie Yang.

On Language. Reprinted by permission of Maria Lovely L. Umayam and Mario Umayam. ©2004 Maria Lovely L. Umayam.

The Hallway. Reprinted by permission of Cristina Bautista and Corazon Bautista. ©2004 Cristina Bautista.

Lyrical Ponderings. Reprinted by permission of Coral Marie Lozado and Ramon A. Lozado Jr. ©2004 Coral Marie Lozado.

Outcast. Reprinted by permission of Joseph Burke Workman and Mary B. Workman. ©2004 Joseph Burke Workman.

One of the Team. Reprinted by permission of Rachel S. Berman and Catherine S. Berman. ©2004 Rachel S. Berman.

The Ugly Duckling. Reprinted by permission of Diana Chang and Vivien Chang. ©2004 Diana Chang.

Excuses, Excuses. Reprinted by permission of Alicia Jaynes. ©2004 Alicia Jaynes.

The Seal to a Letter Unmailed. Reprinted by permission of Sarah Marie Brook and Gary Brook. ©2004 Sarah Marie Brook.

English Teaching Wonder. Reprinted by permission of Nicole Lee Poppino and Cheryl Poppino. ©2004 Nicole Lee Poppino.

Inside Out. Reprinted by permission of Maryanne Lee and Mary Chee. ©2004 Maryanne Lee.

Write for Life. Reprinted by permission of Tracy Marie Tanner. ©2004 Tracy Marie Tanner.

Girl Power. Reprinted by permission of Araz Nicole Garakanian and Shushan Garakanian. ©2004 Araz Nicole Garakanian.

Dangerous Depression. Reprinted by permission of Rosa Lea Vanessa Ojeda. ©2004 Rosa Lea Vanessa Ojeda.

Derek. Reprinted by permission of Karina Elizabeth Seto and Kan Seto. ©2004 Karina Elizabeth Seto.

Slice the Way to Happiness. Reprinted by permission of Chelsea Elizabeth Oakes and Laurie S. Oakes. ©2004 Chelsea Elizabeth Oakes.

Small Girl Learns a Big Lesson. Reprinted by permission of Dallas Nicole Woodburn and Woody Woodburn. ©2004 Dallas Nicole Woodburn.

Out. Reprinted by permission of Aubrey Diana Restifo and Leslie Restifo. ©2004 Aubrey Diana Restifo.

We Promised. Reprinted by permission of Rachel A. Stern and Tamar Stern. ©2004 Rachel A. Stern.

Reminiscence. Reprinted by permission of Krystle Lynn Nichols. ©2004 Krystle Lynn Nichols.

Just Do It. Reprinted by permission of Laura M. Watkins and Russell F. Watkins Jr. ©2003 Laura M. Watkins.

Oxygen Is a Crutch. Reprinted by permission of Julia Y. Lam and Peifen Lam. ©2004 Julia Y. Lam.

Struggle of a Preteen Couch Potato. Reprinted by permission of Katelynn Marie Wilton and Cindy Wilton. ©2004 Katelynn Marie Wilton.

Softball Sorrows. Reprinted by permission of Shawna Kay Anderson and Reacy James. ©2004 Shawna Kay Anderson.

My Sport. Reprinted by permission of Julie Ann Blackmer and Janie Marie Blackmer. ©2005 Julie Ann Blackmer.

Gaeton. Reprinted by permission of Michael Joseph Wassmer and William Wassmer. ©2003 Michael Joseph Wassmer.

From Another Angle. Reprinted by permission of Clara Marie Dell and Paula Dell. ©2004 Clara Marie Dell.

I Could Be Hauling Water. Reprinted by permission of Sondra Marie Clark and Silvana Clark. ©2004 Sondra Marie Clark.

First Love. Reprinted by permission of Margaret Rose Reyland and Debbie Reyland. ©2004 Margaret Rose Reyland.

Never Been Kissed. Reprinted by permission of Dallas Nicole Woodburn and Woody Woodburn. ©2004 Dallas Nicole Woodburn.

Friends . . . Forever? Reprinted by permission of Christopher Sean Lewis and Pam Lewis. ©2004 Christopher Sean Lewis.

The 10:15 Vixen. Reprinted by permission of Michael Joseph Wassmer and William Wassmer. ©2003 Michael Joseph Wassmer.

Miss You. Reprinted by permission of Jessica M. Panico and Robin T. Panico. ©2004 Jessica M. Panico.

Adventure. Reprinted by permission of Linda Marie Gonzales. ©2004 Linda Marie Gonzales.

You Always Remember the First. Reprinted by permission of Jaime Louise Rubusch and Bethany Rubusch. ©2004 Jaime Louise Rubusch.

Blizzards and Sweater Vests. Reprinted by permission of Esther Sooter and Edward Sooter. ©2003 Esther Sooter.

Girls with No Names. Reprinted by permission of Perla Yasmeen Melendez and Guillermina Taylor. ©2004 Perla Yasmeen Melendez.

Perfection Is Just an Illusion. Reprinted by permission of Valentina Cucuzza. ©2004 Valentina Cucuzza.

Illusion of Perfection. Reprinted by permission of Alicia Aurora Vasquez. ©2004 Alicia Aurora Vasquez.

MORE IN THE SERIES

Code #317X • $14.95

Code #4079 • $14.95

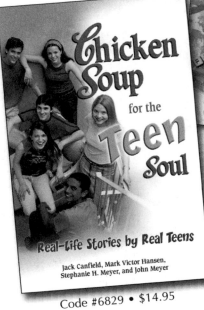

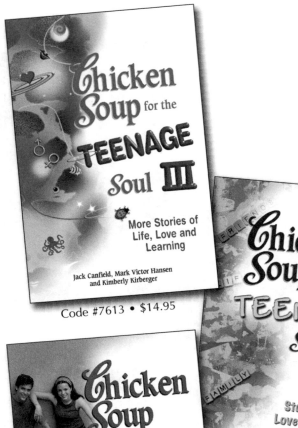

Chicken Soup African American Soul
Chicken Soup African American Woman's Soul
Chicken Soup Breast Cancer Survivor's Soul
Chicken Soup Bride's Soul
Chicken Soup Caregiver's Soul
Chicken Soup Cat Lover's Soul
Chicken Soup Christian Family Soul
Chicken Soup College Soul
Chicken Soup Couple's Soul
Chicken Soup Dieter's Soul
Chicken Soup Dog Lover's Soul
Chicken Soup Entrepreneur's Soul
Chicken Soup Expectant Mother's Soul
Chicken Soup Father's Soul
Chicken Soup Fisherman's Soul
Chicken Soup Girlfriend's Soul
Chicken Soup Golden Soul
Chicken Soup Golfer's Soul, Vol. I, II
Chicken Soup Horse Lover's Soul, Vol. I, II
Chicken Soup Inspire a Woman's Soul
Chicken Soup Kid's Soul, Vol. I, II
Chicken Soup Mother's Soul, Vol. I, II
Chicken Soup Parent's Soul
Chicken Soup Pet Lover's Soul
Chicken Soup Preteen Soul, Vol. I, II
Chicken Soup Scrapbooker's Soul
Chicken Soup Sister's Soul, Vol. I, II
Chicken Soup Shopper's
Chicken Soup Soul, Vol. I-VI
Chicken Soup at Work
Chicken Soup Sports Fan's Soul
Chicken Soup Teenage Soul, Vol. I-IV
Chicken Soup Woman's Soul, Vol. I, II

MK 6/10